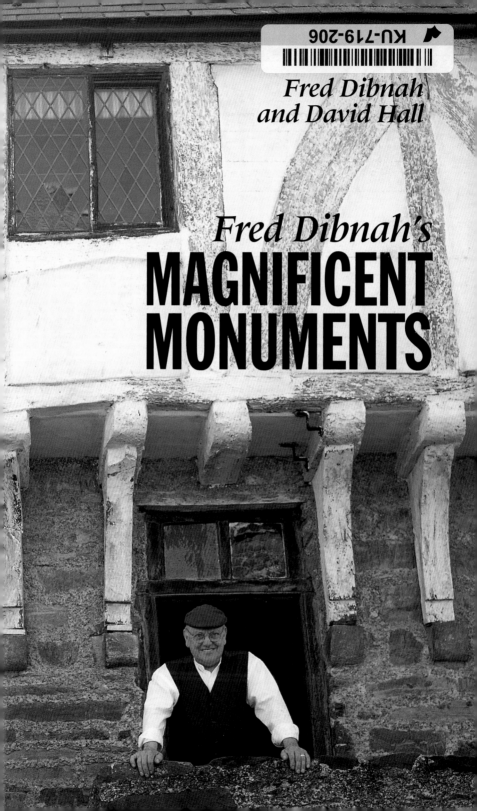

Fred Dibnah
and David Hall

Fred Dibnah's
MAGNIFICENT
MONUMENTS

ACKNOWLEDGEMENTS

With thanks to Kathryn Hall, Terri Langan and Bob Sandy
for researching and compiling the Gazetteer and to
Janet Smith for typing up the manuscript.

PICTURE CREDITS

Peter Ashley 182, 190; Howard Blakemore 62, 70, 75, 91, 92, 124, 133, 160;
David Hall 13, 17, 59, 120, 171, 173; John Jefford title page, 38, 54;
Bob Sandy 7, 34, 57, 111, 116, 120, 127, 136, 139, 140, 143, 145, 146,
159, 169, 185, 194, 197, 200, 203
We would like to thank the following for contributing their photographs:
Hever Castle Ltd 10; Leeds Castle Foundation 27; Warwick Castle 31; Historic Scotland
47, 51 108, 135; Woburn Abbey 78; Eastnor Castle 19; Harewood House Trust Ltd 100;
The Mellerstain Trust 104; Belfast City Council 106; The World Naval Base, Chatham 152;
Ironbridge Gorge Museum 155; The City of Edinburgh Council 162; Blackpool Tourism
Dept 178; The Environment Agency 188; Blackpool Pleasure Beach 199;
David Lee Photography Ltd 201

This book is published to accompany the television series
Fred Dibnah's Magnificent Monuments, which was first broadcast in 2000.
The series was produced by BBC Manchester in association
with The View From the North Limited.
Executive Producers: Mike Greenwood and Claire Powell. Producer: David Hall

Published by BBC Worldwide Limited,
Woodlands, 80 Wood Lane, London W12 0TT

First published 2000
Copyright © Fred Dibnah and David Hall 2000
The moral right of the authors has been asserted.

Title page photograph specially taken at Aberconwy House, Conwy, by John Jefford
Maps by Angela Wilson of All Terrain Mapping
Copyright © Maps in Minutes 1998

ISBN 0 563 55173 9

Commissioning Editor and Project Editor: Khadija Manjlai
Copy-editor: Hugh Morgan
Designer: Linda Blakemore

Set in Meridien by BBC Worldwide Limited
Printed and bound in Great Britain by Butler & Tanner Limited,
Frome and London
Cover printed by Belmont Press Limited, Northampton

CONTENTS

INTRODUCTION

Britain is full of magnificent examples of the architectural and engineering genius that we have had throughout the ages, and of the construction skills of armies of workers who have turned the visions of the architects and engineers into reality. For a number of people one of the first questions they ask when they visit a great castle or cathedral is: 'How the heck did they build something like that all that time ago? How did they manage to lift all that stone and wood up to such a great height?' And it's not just ancient buildings that we ask those sorts of questions about. What about a great marvel of twentieth-century engineering like a huge suspension bridge? How on earth do they get the first of those cables suspended between the towers?

For the television series *Magnificent Monuments* we went to see some of the country's most famous and historical monuments. We visited ancient castles, cathedrals, abbeys and great houses as well as more modern things like bridges and tunnels and other great engineering marvels. All of them are very different in style, in purpose and in what they look like, but what they all have in common for me is the great range of craft skills that went into designing, building and decorating them. From the remains of Housesteads, the Roman fortress we visited on Hadrian's Wall, right up to a shiny, futuristic, silver and glass structure like the Lloyd's Building in London – the skills of the architects and builders are there to be seen.

I first got interested in buildings when, at the age of fifteen, I was apprenticed to a joiner. At the time I lived in a small terraced house next to Burnden Park, Bolton Wanderers' football ground. My mum and dad wanted me to be an undertaker, but I didn't really fancy that, so I went to the Youth Employment Bureau, as it was called in the late 1950s. I had a bicycle and the other participants in this race for work had nothing other than the bus to get to see this man who owned a small joinery business, so I got there before all the others and I got the job.

I served all my time with him from being fifteen years old until I got called up and went in the army when I was twenty-two and I must say that I owe that man a debt, because he taught me a lot about joinery. My work started to take me into some of the Victorian

The craftsmanship of the past is being kept alive by talented stonemasons, carpenters, woodcarvers. This young lady is helping restore the stonework in York Minster

mansions that cotton-mill owners had built, much grander houses than I had ever been used to. When I began to see the quality of the workmanship in them, with their stone masonry, architraves around the windows and the doors, beautiful ornate skirting boards and all the rest of the splendid Victorian ornamentation in these houses, it intrigued me as to how they did it. What great lengths the Victorians went to just for something to look at. Whether it was structural engineering or architectural work, a lot of it served no other purpose than just to please the eye. It was all done for people to stand and look at, and the quality of their work wasn't just reserved for their houses.

About the time of my apprenticeship I also went to art school for a short period, and I'm glad that I did that as well. It didn't do me any harm because we used to have forced summer outings with a drawing board and paper and pencil to look at things that were of note in the building line. Learning about perspective and being able to draw a building so that it doesn't look as though it's going to fall down is very difficult for lots of people, but I find it quite easy, and I have no problem in drawing great big tall factory chimneys that look like great big tall factory chimneys. Not ones like Mr Lowry painted like a black line with a thing across the top and some squiggly lines coming out representing smoke.

I did my National Service in Germany and spent most of my time in Düsseldorf. Some of the buildings there impressed me immensely, but by this time I had already decided that I wanted to be a steeplejack and some of the chimneys that I saw in Germany fascinated me. They all seemed a lot taller and thinner than the ones back home in Lancashire, and they certainly had a lot more iron bands around them.

When I returned from Germany, I managed to get my foot on the first rung of steeplejacking so I had to know a bit about buildings and how they were constructed. I had to learn all about things like Gothic arches, flying buttresses, beautiful window frames, rose windows and all sorts of things that you see on cathedrals and churches that help to hold them together. I had to start finding out about things like why the top doesn't blow off a church steeple and what stops it squeezing itself apart. These are the sorts of things that I wanted to look at in the programmes that this book accompanies.

The book itself is essentially a guidebook, and we've listed over 400 places that we think are worth going to see. It is, of course, impossible to list every great house, every majestic castle and every monumental piece of engineering in the land, so the list is inevitably selective. The entries are listed alphabetically and contain the full address and contact telephone number, directions from a main road to the site and a description of what there is to see once there. The entry numbers in the Gazetteer correspond to the numbers on the maps, so you can see where each site is in relation to the others. The maps give approximate locations of all the entries in the Gazetteer, and are meant as a guide only. When planning a trip, use a good road atlas that shows more local detail than it is possible to show here. The maps are also useful as they show other sites that might be local to you.

The entries state opening times, too, where it's been possible to list them but, as many of the sites are staffed by volunteers, they often have irregular opening hours or ones that might change from year to year. Do bear in mind that some sites are in open spaces near houses and villages and, while there are no strict opening hours, readers are asked to visit during daylight hours ('any reasonable time'). While the details are correct at the time of going to press, it is always best to phone before visiting any site in order to avoid disappointment. For current admission fees (some places offer concessions for OAPs, children or parties), contact the sites.

The book covers a very wide range of architectural styles and different types of construction and, if it inspires you to visit any of them, we hope it will also encourage you to look at them afresh, with an eye for the skills and techniques of architects, civil engineers, builders and construction workers throughout our history, and of the craftsmanship of the carpenters, woodcarvers, stonemasons, blacksmiths and glass-makers whose work adorns their buildings.

For me the great thing is that there are still people around who have got these skills you see, so if you're going around and looking at some of these marvellous examples of craftsmanship from the past, don't take any notice of those people who say: 'They can't do work like that nowadays'. I've heard this myself so many times as we've been going around, and it's a bit annoying. It's an insult to the many craftsmen and craftswomen who are still able to do work of the quality of the best workers of the past. The big enemy now is time and, of course, money, because people's time costs money. Some of the cathedrals we've seen on our travels took hundreds and hundreds of years to build, and one stone-mason might have spent most of his working life on one part of it. Today, when the time for constructing modern buildings is measured in months rather than in years, it doesn't leave a great deal of time for any nice ornamentation. In the olden days, life was a lot slower, people didn't have computers and they didn't have big motor cars. When they got out of bed in the morning the only thing they knew really was a hammer and chisel and a big block of rock. But the skills that those workers had haven't disappeared completely, and on our little trips we've seen many examples of clever people, including young ladies with hammers and chisels making beautiful finials and fancy gargoyles and bits for window tracery in church windows and the like. I've been getting about a bit more in my old age than I used to do, and some of the buildings that I've seen on my travels have impressed me immensely. I hope you get as much pleasure out of visiting some of them as I did.

CHAPTER

1

CASTLES AND FORTS

Some years ago I met a gentleman who lives in a castle. It's never been under attack or under siege or anything like that because, as castles go, it is all rather new. It was built only in 1812, and it's actually a great country house that was built to look like a castle. Eastnor Castle is a magnificent Georgian mansion in a fairy-tale setting with towers and turrets and a lake in front. It all looks rather splendid, just like the sort of thing you would get if you asked a child to draw a picture of a castle.

Its owner is James Hervey-Bathurst, who took a bit of a shine to me because of my interest in steam engines. He's a collector of traction engines himself, a great railway enthusiast and an admirer of things of that nature in general. We've got quite chummy, and I ended up helping him repair and restore one of his best engines – Atlas. This lovely old engine once lived in the North of England but it now resides on the forecourt of his castle in Herefordshire. That's really how we became friends. He invites me down in the summer, when he has his steam engine day, and puts me up in the bridal suite, which has a great big four-poster bed. It's all very nice indeed. In the castle are great piles of staircases wherever you go and, as a stranger, it's easy to get lost. I would imagine living in a castle like this would have been a bit lonely at night. It's so far away from any street lighting that it's very dark, a bit like being down a coal mine.

When Eastnor Castle was built by the second Baron Summers between 1810 and 1824, the size and splendour of a country house were the most obvious indications of the standing and fortune of the family who lived there. The style that was proposed by the baron's architect was Norman revival. From a distance, Eastnor was intended to create the impression of an Edward I-style fortress guarding the Welsh Borders. The castle was designed to impress and

Hever Castle in Kent dates from 1270, but much that can be seen today was added to by the American millionaire, William Waldorf Astor, who bought it in 1903

was not intended for any serious military or defensive purposes. All true castles, though, were built for military purposes. Britain is full of forts, castles and fortified houses, probably more than anywhere else in the world. We must have been a very war-like lot. Many of the most impressive castles and military installations date back to the Middle Ages, but some of the earliest remains of fortifications that we have go back as far as Roman times.

Hadrian's Wall is the biggest and most important monument built by the Romans in Britain, and for 300 years it was the north-west frontier of their empire. It was in the year AD122 that the Emperor Hadrian came to visit Britain, and during this visit he ordered the construction of the wall. The work was carried out by soldiers from the three legions stationed in Britain at the time. Within their ranks they had architects, engineers, surveyors, masons, carpenters, glaziers and everybody they needed for such a huge engineering project. It took them six years to build it; it ran from Bowness on the Solway Firth to Wallsend on the Tyne, and its purpose was to keep out the marauding Scotsmen or, as Hadrian himself put it, separate the Romans from the barbarians.

By around the year AD400 the Roman Empire had declined in Britain and the wall and its forts were abandoned. It was left to become derelict, and during the centuries that followed it was plundered frequently. Most of the top two-thirds of it were removed or stolen for other building activity, such as abbeys, churches, farmhouses and dry-stone walls. This use of the wall as a convenient quarry carried on into the late nineteenth century, when people began to realise its importance and started to take steps to ensure that what was left was preserved.

Some sections are much better preserved than others and, as you travel along the various parts of the wall today, you can see how the workmanship varies tremendously. All along the wall's length are the remains of forts, turrets and watchtowers. One of the best preserved is the fort at Housesteads. The remains of the commander's house, the very interesting drainage system, barracks, granary, hospital and the toilets or latrines can all be seen on the site. At the various gates of the fort you can see where the iron gudgeons or the hinges of the wooden gates have been, and also the grooves worn in the paving stones by the wheels of wagons. The commander's house was the biggest building, consisting of a range of rooms around an open courtyard. The actual headquarters building wasn't quite as big; and you can see here how there was an assembly hall in the

Inspecting the latrines at Housesteads Roman Fort on Hadrian's Wall

centre, flanked by a courtyard and by rooms for the administrative staff. Food was stored in the granaries on a raised floor supported by stone pillars which can still be seen; ventilation slots in the wall helped the air to circulate below the floor and keep it fresh.

One of the most interesting and best preserved of the remains that you can see today are the communal latrines in the south-east corner of the fort. In here are the remains of the complex arrangements of tanks and channels that maintained the supply of water to the building, and you can see how a main drain carried all the sewage downhill out of the fort. The small channel you can see was used for washing the sponges that were used instead of toilet paper. You can also see how the stonework in the bathtubs was made watertight by grooves cut in the end of the stones then filled in with molten lead. The latrine and the water supply system, and the remains of the hospital, emphasise the Roman army's care for hygiene and for health. The whole thing shows that, as well as being a very ingenious race of people, the Romans were also very hygienic.

Over 600 years after the Romans, Britain was invaded and conquered again, this time by the Normans. The Tower of London has stood for over 900 years as the enduring symbol of that conquest. It was built by William the Conqueror to overawe London and to put off anybody who might be thinking about attacking the city. Since then it has been a fortress, a royal residence, a prison, a place of execution and a home for the Crown Jewels. Its history goes back to 1066, just after William had conquered the country, when he ordered the building of a wooden castle as part of the fortifications to help to secure the chief city of his new kingdom. Ten years later he began the transformation of the fort into a great stone palace with walls 15 feet (4.5 metres) thick. It became known as the White Tower because in its early days the whole building was painted white, and it is William's great tower that is right at the centre of the Tower of London as we see it today.

The White Tower was large by the standards of the day because it had to house a strong Norman garrison and occasionally the king and his court. The ground floor was taken up by storerooms, while the king and his court lived on the upper floors when they were in London. Although there have been repairs and alterations to the exterior of the building over the centuries, its shape remains as it was when it was first built. When you look at it you can see that the building materials they used were like an early form of concrete. It is only the mortar that holds the thing together because, although there are corners and things where they have used nicely cut blocks of stone, a heck of a lot of it is just rubble. Some people say that the mortar was tempered with ox's blood. Whether there is any truth in that I don't know, but they were damned good at making mortar. When I look at the way that it was built and the length of time that it has stood there, it gives me hope for my building work.

The White Tower remained unchanged for over a century. Then between 1190 and 1285 it was encircled by two towered curtain walls and a great moat. It was Henry III and his son Edward I who carried out these extensions, and by the beginning of the fourteenth century they had built a series of gateways, ramparts and towers around the original Norman keep. This turned it into one of the largest strongholds in Europe. The expansion of the tower included the construction of a new outer wall all the way round, with main entrances from the land by way of a series of gatehouses and drawbridges. The building of this towered curtain wall transformed the defences of the tower. Archers and missile-throwing machines along the walls and within the towers, which projected from them, had a good command of the land around the castle and could concentrate projectiles on an attack at any point. If an enemy did manage to get on to the wall or over it, they were still exposed to missiles from adjoining towers, as well as from the White Tower.

The Tower of London intrigued me a lot. It must have been a pretty impregnable place in the Middle Ages, and even in this modern age you would have a job to get in there with ordinary firearms and machine guns if there was a siege. I wouldn't like to have to try unless there was some really big artillery. But in the Middle Ages they didn't have anything that could do any real damage, other than great slow-moving things that must have weighed at least seven tonnes and needed a hundred men to drag them up the road.

Edward I, who was responsible for so many of the extensions to the Tower, was our greatest castle-builder. His best memorial, however, is not the Tower but the chain of castles he built in Wales. The Normans had defeated the English almost overnight, but Wales managed to hold on to its independence until Edward I's invasion in 1282. Within a year his armies had completed the conquest of Snowdonia, and he ordered a chain of castles to be built to subdue the Welsh. Within the space of twenty-five years he built eight massive stone strongholds – one of the greatest feats of royal building in British history. To carry out the work Edward employed a Frenchman, James of St George d'Esperance, the greatest military architect of his age, and it was in these outposts of English power, on the North Wales coast, that the medieval art of castle-building reached its peak. They were built to withstand any siege weapon that had yet been devised, and the whole structure was designed to make any attack difficult and dangerous.

Conwy Castle was built between 1283 and 1287 and when you look at it today one of its most striking features is the symmetry of its design and the compactness of such a great mass of building. It has eight almost identical towers – four of them on the north and four of them on the south. When you look closer, though, you can see that the four towers at the eastern end of the castle have an additional turret on the top of them. This is because the castle had two quite separate halves, each one with its own ward or courtyard, and each with its own independent way of entry from the outside. The inner ward was the most secure part of the castle; it could be approached only by water, and it was here that the king had his accommodation. It is around this ward that the four turreted towers are grouped; designed to provide lookout points for watchmen guarding the four corners of the royal residence. The larger outer ward, which could be approached directly from the town, provided accommodation for the castle's permanent garrison.

The structure is a piece of monumental engineering on a grand scale, a massive achievement for its time, and when you look closely at the walls and the towers from the outside you can get some clues as to how the place was built. On them there are lines of small round holes that are spaced six to ten inches (fifteen to twenty-five centimetres) apart, and set on a slant. The builders followed what was a common French practice at the time, which involved using inclined rather than horizontal scaffolds to wheel or drag the heavy loads of stone to the top as the building gradually rose higher. The holes in the walls that can be seen today were the points where the ramps were fixed to them.

Wales is full of interesting castles like Conwy, but Scotland must have more castles per square mile than anywhere else in the world. Scotland's most famous castle, Edinburgh, has a building history that is every bit as complex as the Tower of London's, and having watched the military tattoo many times on TV it has never failed to impress me. The whole thing stands on the sheer crag of Castle Rock, the core of an extinct volcano, which rises 435 feet (133 metres) above sea-level, and it is a pretty formidable natural defence. Building work started off at the top and the castle kept getting a bit bigger as they kept cutting another ledge out of the mountain and building another bit. The whole thing is one continuous corkscrew which reminds me of one of those chocolate swirling sweets.

The oldest building within the castle grounds is St Margaret's Chapel on the rock's summit, but most of the present castle evolved later during its stormy history of sieges and wars. Building work continued throughout the Victorian age and well into the twentieth century, with new buildings carefully designed to blend in with the existing structure. One of the most impressive buildings in the castle is one of the most recent: the Scottish National War Memorial. This was designed and built near the top of the castle rock after the First World War. Now, I've seen a number of war memorials in my time, but this one is something else. It is a magnificent piece of work-manship. Inside, there is a huge bronze relief which depicts every branch of the fighting forces in 1914. It's magical; it has everything on it from early aviators and machine-gunners to tanks, guns, foot-

On location outside Edinburgh Castle

soldiers, horses, nurses and even carrier pigeons; every possible bit of the 1914–18 war has been depicted and executed in realistic detail in bronze. There is also some fine woodwork and marblework in the memorial. The oak woodwork is so fine and beautiful that it brings tears to your eyes looking at it, it is so well done. People say that you don't get craftsmanship like that these days, but all the work was done in the 1920s – not that long ago.

Throughout its long history, Edinburgh Castle has had a variety of roles. As well as being a royal palace, it has been a fortress and a garrison, and, like Edinburgh, all our early castles had these dual roles. It was only in the time of Henry VIII that the twin roles of the castle, as stronghold and residence, began to split and go their separate ways. From Tudor times onwards, houses didn't have to be built with defence as the prime consideration. Houses and palaces no longer had to be fortified, so castles started to be built purely for military reasons, not as places for people to live in.

Hurst Castle in Hampshire is a good example of this. It belongs to a chain built by Henry VIII along the South Coast between 1539 and

1545 to protect important anchorages from attack by enemy fleets. Like the others in the chain, Hurst is really an artillery fort. A true medieval castle was a fortified residence for its lordly owner, a symbol of his position in society. The castles that Henry built were simply utilitarian buildings whose sole purpose was to provide a safe and effective mounting for artillery. Within them they had only very basic accommodation for the gunners. Henry didn't seem to have made any distinction, though, because, right from the start, all his forts were referred to as castles. At Hurst, the original Tudor castle was extensively modernised during the Napoleonic Wars, and then it was added to again in the 1860s, with the addition of two massive wings. Today it serves as a very good example of a castle that has seen active service from the time it was built in Tudor times right up until the Second World War, when it was garrisoned.

From Tudor times onwards, the traditional medieval castles that had been built as strongholds and residences continued to be used as residences, and many were added to and altered to make them more comfortable to live in. A good example of this is Hever Castle in Kent, the childhood home of Anne Boleyn. There have been three main periods in the construction of this little castle. The oldest part was built in about 1270 and consisted of the massive gatehouse – still there today – and a walled bailey (an enclosed court). All of this was surrounded by a moat and approached by a wooden draw-bridge. In about 1500, the Boleyn family built a comfortable Tudor house inside the protective walls of the castle. Finally, in 1903 the castle was bought by William Waldorf Astor, a rich American, who lavished millions of dollars on restoring it.

Within the castle itself some internal alterations were made to the layout of the rooms and the exterior was restored right down to the finest detail. Mr Astor then introduced the best craftsmen he could find to create panelling screens, stone fireplaces, plasterwork, marquetry, copperwork and leadwork, and stained and painted glass. It is all a little bit of a fake, but the quality of the Edwardian craftsmanship and the attention to detail is superb. The plastered ceilings throughout the castle were formed, as far as possible, from the same materials that a Tudor craftsman would have used. The twentieth-century workmen who made it were forbidden to use any form of straightedge; everything had to be done by eye. It all shows that this level of craftsmanship did not disappear in medieval or Tudor times; it is still around today. All that it involves is time and, more important, the sort of money that Lord Astor had.

PLACES TO VISIT

■1■ **CORFE CASTLE** ☎ 01929 481294
The Square, Corfe Castle, Wareham, Dorset BH20 5EZ
On A351 Wareham–Swanage road
Open early–late Mar: daily 10.30–4.30; late Mar–late Oct: 10–5.30; late Oct–early Mar:
11–3.30
Impressive ruins. The entire castle is separated from the town by a deep ditch across a narrow, natural tongue of land. Corfe Castle was a royal castle from the time of William the Conqueror until the reign of Queen Elizabeth I. The earliest surviving parts are the curtain wall around the inner ward and the Old Hall in the West Bailey. According to legend the hill on which the castle was built was the scene of the assassination of the Saxon King Edward in the year 978, and traces of Saxon building have been revealed by excavation under the Old Hall.

■2■ **DARTMOUTH CASTLE** ☎ 01803 833588
Castle Road, Dartmouth, Devon TQ6 0JN
1 mile SE of B3205; narrow approach road
Open Apr–Sept: daily 10–6; Oct: daily 10–5; Nov–March: Wed–Sun 10–1 and 2–4
Medieval castle in a superb waterside location guarding the entrance to the Dart Estuary. Built in the fifteenth century to protect homes and warehouses of the Dartmouth merchants. One of the most advanced fortifications of medieval times, this is the first castle to have been designed and specially constructed with artillery in mind. For 500 years the castle was kept in constant preparation for war, and was still in active service during both world wars. Visitors can explore the castle and see the completely re-created Victorian gun battery and climb to the battlements for spectacular views.

■3■ **FARLEIGH HUNGERFORD CASTLE** ☎ 01225 754026
Farleigh Hungerford, Bath, Nr Somerset BA3 6RS
3 miles west of Trowbridge on A366
Open Apr–Oct: daily 10–6 (5 in Oct); Nov–Mar: Wed–Sun 10–4
Sir Thomas Hungerford, first speaker of the House of Commons, fortified his manor house between 1370 and 1380, and Hungerfords lived there for some 300 years. The castle fell into ruins in the eighteenth century, but there are extensive remains of the towers and curtain walls. The chapel stands intact and contains some medieval wall-paintings, including a unique image of St George and the Dragon, and also a collection of tombs. In the crypt is probably the best collection of anthropomorphic coffins in England.

■4■ **LAUNCESTON CASTLE** ☎ 01566 772365
Castle Lodge, Guildhall Square, Launceston, Cornwall PL15 7DR
Take A30 to Launceston, head towards town centre
Open Apr–Oct: daily 10–6; Nov–Mar: Fri–Sun 10–4
Dating from the early years of the Norman Conquest, little survives of the castle now, other than its defences: the mound with its stone keep and high tower, the ruined gatehouses and curtain walls, together with the impressive earthworks. Excavation has revealed more, including the Great Hall which was

built by William the Conqueror's half-brother, Count Robert of Mortain. The castle was extensively remodelled by Richard, Earl of Cornwall, in the mid-thirteenth century.

■5■ **PENDENNIS CASTLE**   ☎ 01326 316594
Falmouth, Cornwall TR11 4LP
1 mile SE of Falmouth on Pendennis Head, signposted
Open Apr–Oct: daily 10–6 (5 in Oct); mid-Nov–Mar: daily 10–4
Four hundred and fifty years of history can be traced from the castle's origins as one of Henry VIII's coastal strongholds to its last military role as secret Second World War base. Today, the sixteenth-century keep, which is at the heart of the castle, is surrounded by later fortifications. Pendennis Castle now houses an exhibition of coastal defences from the Tudor period to the mid-twentieth century. There is public access to the restored underground Victorian and Second World War defences, complete with sounds and smells! The everyday movements of the garrison are brought to life in the war shelter.

■6■ **PORTLAND CASTLE**   ☎ 01305 820539
Castelton, Portland, Dorset DT5 1BD
Overlooking Portland Harbour adjacent to the air and sea rescue base
Open Apr–Oct: daily 10–6
Portland is one of the best preserved of the castles that Henry VIII built along the South Coast, and in it can be seen many characteristics of their general design. Built to defend Britain against the threat of French and Spanish invasions, its low, squat form and rounded profiles make it a good example of early-sixteenth-century military engineering, designed principally to withstand enemy artillery fire. The castle has a central keep with two wings which are connected by a gun-room, giving the whole building the shape of a letter D. Although the whole castle is very well preserved, castles like Portland, which were built during the first stages of Henry's building programme, soon became obsolete, when it was found that their design embodied areas of dead ground where besieging forces could attack the walls of the forts while remaining out of the firing line of the garrison.

■7■ **POWDERHAM CASTLE**   ☎ 01626 890243
Kenton, Exeter, Devon EX6 8JQ
Signposted off A379 Exeter–Dawlish
Open Apr–Oct: Mon–Fri and Sun 10–5.30 (last admission 5)
The present building was begun in about 1390 by Sir Philip Courtney, but the main entrance was moved during Queen Victoria's reign and it is the additions that were made at this time that are seen first on the approach to the castle. These include rearrangements to the courtyard, the building of two new gate-houses, renewing the west front and building on a new dining-room to the left of the entrance tower. From the courtyard the tall rectangular block of the original medieval castle, which contained the Great Hall, withdrawing-room and kitchens, can still be seen behind the more recent additions. The north tower at the northern end of the west front is original and is one of the six towers that Sir Philip built. The clock tower on the east side and the entrance tower were both rebuilt in brick in the eighteenth century. Prior to the Victorian alterations much work was done internally and externally throughout the eighteenth century. This all makes it hard to visualise what the medieval castle was like.

■8■ THE ROYAL CITADEL ☎ 01179 750700
The Hoe, Plymouth, Devon PL1 2PD
Eastern end of Plymouth Hoe
Pre-booked guided tours only. Open May–Sept: daily 2 and 3.30.
Tickets from Plymouth Dome
England's largest seventeenth-century fortress with walls up to 69 feet (21 metres) high. It was built to defend the coastline from the Dutch and is still in use today as a military installation. Massive ramparts overlook the Hoe, the sound and the entrance to Plymouth's ancient harbour. There is a spacious parade ground surrounded by imposing buildings and a peaceful royal chapel.

■9■ ST MAWES CASTLE ☎ 01326 270526
St Mawes, Nr Truro, Cornwall TR2 5AA
In St Mawes on A3078. Ferry from Falmouth, then signposted
Open Apr–Oct: daily 10–6 (5 or dusk in Oct); Nov–Mar: Fri–Tue 10–1 and 2–4
Magnificent military architecture and breathtaking waterside setting make St Mawes Castle the most picturesque of the chain of coastal fortresses built by Henry VIII. It is also the most complete. It was finished circa 1545 at about the same time as Pendennis Castle (see entry), which stands opposite it in Falmouth. Together they were designed to guard the mouth of the Fal Estuary. Like Pendennis,the castle's present-day state of excellent preservation is due largely to its comparatively trouble-free history. Its design, with its three huge, circular bastions, resembles a cloverleaf, and it is a particularly fine example of sixteenth-century coastal defences. Its importance rests in the lack of alteration to the Tudor castle and dungeons, barrack-rooms, and cannon-lined walls, which can all still be seen.

■10■ ST MICHAELS MOUNT ☎ 01736 710507
The Manor Office, Marazion, Cornwall TR17 0EF
1½ mile S of A394
Open Apr–Oct: Mon–Fri 10.30–5.30 (last admission 4.45); Nov–Mar: Mon, Wed, Fri –
guided tours only, phone to arrange
Small granite island rising from the waters at the edge of Mount's Bay, crowned by an imposing-looking castle that can be reached on foot by a causeway at low tide or by ferry at high tide in the summer. It has been a church, priory, fortress and private home in its time, and it is now owned by the National Trust. The different parts of the castle buildings vary in date from the twelfth to the nineteenth century, but they are all constructed of the same massive granite so that they all blend together without any architectural contradiction.

■11■ TOTNES CASTLE ☎ 01803 864406
Castle Street, Totnes, Devon TQ9 5NU
On the hill overlooking town
Open Apr–Oct: daily 10–6; Nov–Mar: Wed–Sun 10–1 and 2–4
A classic example of the Norman motte-and-bailey castle, Totnes dates from the eleventh century. A curtain wall erected in the thirteenth century and reconstructed in the fourteenth protects the circular shell keep. Built at the very heart of a Saxon town, it has commanding views of Totnes, the River Dart and the surrounding area. The once great ditch that surrounded the keep is today filled with cottages and gardens. The castle was a vital prize for the Normans, being an important trading town with access to the sea and with a large population.

⛪ SOUTH-EAST — MAP 2

■12■ ARUNDEL CASTLE ☎ 01903 882173
Arundel, West Sussex BN18 9AB
Signposted off A27
Open Apr–Oct: Sun–Fri 12–5 (last admission 4). Closed Good Fri
Great castle overlooking the River Arun in West Sussex built at the end of the
eleventh century by Roger de Montgomery, Earl of Arundel. Seat of the Dukes
of Norfolk and Earls of Arundel for over 700 years. The original castle was very
badly damaged during the Civil War and was restored during the eighteenth and
nineteenth centuries. The castle is approached over a wooden drawbridge and
through the barbican which dates from 1295. The eleventh-century inner gateway is one of the earliest parts of the castle to survive. The ranges that surround
the quadrangle date from the late twelfth century, although they were heavily
reconstructed and restored in the eighteenth and nineteenth centuries. The original Norman keep is in the centre of the castle. Magnificent late-Victorian reconstruction of the Baron's Hall with a hammerbeam roof on the site of the original
medieval hall. Grand staircase, dining-room and library are also very impressive.

■13■ BODIAM CASTLE ☎ 01580 830436
Bodiam, Nr Robertsbridge, East Sussex TN32 5UA
3 miles S of Hawkhurst, 2 miles E of A21 at Hurst Green
Open Jan–mid-Feb: weekends 11–4; mid-Feb–Oct: daily 10–6 (or dusk if sooner);
Nov–Jan: weekends 10–4.
One of the most famous castles in Britain, Bodiam was built in 1385 by Sir
Edward Dalyngrigge both as a defence and a comfortable home. He chose a site
in the valley of the River Rother overlooking the wharves on the river frontage
adjacent to Bodiam Bridge. A compact building, it is defended by a broad, water-
filled moat and boasts a defensive arrangement of towers linked by a curtain
wall. Enough of the interior survives to give an impression of castle life, and
there are spiral staircases and battlements to explore.

■14■ CARISBROOKE CASTLE ☎ 01983 522107
Carisbrooke, Newport, Isle of Wight PO30 1XY
1 mile SW of Newport off B3323
Open Mar–Sept: daily 10–6; Oct–Mar: daily 10–4
A Norman castle adapted from a Saxon fort, Carisbrooke is the only medieval
castle on the island. It is set on a hill 150 feet (46 metres) high, and the twelfth-
century keep is built on an artificial mound of around 60 feet (18 metres).
The keep overlooks the Elizabethan and Jacobean additions and the strong
castle walls. There are two medieval wells in the castle, one in the keep reached
by climbing 71 steps, the other housed in a sixteenth-century well-house in
the courtyard. A donkey traditionally drove the winding gear for the well, and a
team of donkeys now gives displays of the machinery working. Charles I was a
prisoner in the castle from 1647 to 1648, and the castle was the home of the
governor of the island. His lodge is now the Isle of Wight Museum.

■15■ DEAL CASTLE ☎ 01304 372762
Victoria Road, Deal, Kent CT14 7BA
SW of Deal town centre, follow signs from A2
Open Apr–Oct: daily 10–6 (5 in Oct); Nov–Mar: Wed–Sun 10–4

Built in the late 1530s by Henry VIII in response to a threat of invasion by the Catholic powers of Europe. It was originally designed to guard the Kent coast and formed an important link in a chain of coastal defences that stretched from Hull to Milford Haven in Wales. From the outside, Deal Castle shows all the characteristic features that distinguish Henry's fortresses. Dominating the centre is the circular keep with its lantern (the present lantern dates from the early eighteenth century but is on the site of the original). Attached to the keep are six semicircular bastions, or lunettes. These overlook a narrow courtyard and carry the main armoury of guns. North of the gatehouse bastion, part of the northern curtain wall still retains its original broad, rounded parapets. The crenellated battlements elsewhere form part of an extensive refurbishment of the castle undertaken between 1729 and 1732.

■16■ DOVER CASTLE ☎ 01304 201628
Dover, Kent CT16 1HU
On E side of Dover, from A2 or A20
Open Apr–Oct: daily 10–6 (5 in Oct); Nov–Mar: daily 10–4

One of Europe's mightiest fortresses, guarding the shortest sea crossing from France, its location overlooking the Strait of Dover gave it great strategic importance. Its shape was largely predetermined by the Iron Age hill fort that was here when Duke William of Normandy's forces constructed the first earthwork castle after their victory at the Battle of Hastings in 1066. During its medieval heyday, this was very much a frontier fortress. Under Henry II it was rebuilt to incorporate concentric defences and regularly spaced wall towers. By the 1250s its medieval defences had assumed the extent and shape they have today. After its importance decreased from the sixteenth century, the castle was modernised and its defences extended in the 1750s and again during the Napoleonic Wars. Further alterations and additional gun batteries added in the 1870s enabled the castle to retain the role of first-class fortress almost until the end of the nineteenth century. The castle was rearmed during both world wars and it retained a garrison until October 1958.

■17■ FORT BROCKHURST ☎ 023 9258 1059
Gunners Way, Gosport, Hampshire PO12 4DG
Off A32 in Elson on N side of Gosport
Open Apr–Sept: weekends and Bank Hols 10–6; Oct weekends 10–5

Fort Brockhurst is one of a remarkable line of five forts constructed in the middle of the nineteenth century. They were designed to protect Portsmouth Harbour and the naval installations on the Gosport Peninsula from attack by an invasion force, approaching from the north-west. The line superseded the eighteenth-century defences around Gosport, which were being made obsolete by the more powerful weapons coming into service with the armies and navies of Europe in the 1840s and 1850s. The fort today is largely unaltered. The main approach is through the keep. A rising drawbridge protected this from outside attack. Within the fort the large parade ground is divided by two earth gun ramps. The former Regimental Institute, which stands in the centre, was built some 40 years after completion of the rest of the fort.

■18■ HERSTMONCEUX CASTLE ☎ 01323 833816
Herstmonceux, Nr Hailsham, East Sussex BN27 1RN
Signposted off A271
Open Apr–Sept: daily 10–6; Oct: daily 9–5.30. Tours by arrangement, phone for details

Huge moated castle whose outside walls have changed very little since they were first built in the fifteenth century. The castle was built of brick, an unusual material for that time in Britain, and it is the oldest brick building of any note still standing in England. With its moat, towers and battlements, Herstmonceux looks every inch a medieval castle. In strategic terms, however, it is in a poor situation, and the brick walls would not have withstood bombardment by cannonballs for very long. The intention of Sir Roger Fiennes, who built it, was apparently to provide a stylish country house for himself, not a military fortress. The castle fell into ruin in the nineteenth century and was much restored in the twentieth; the present interior is much changed from the original.

■19■ **HEVER CASTLE** ☎ 01732 865224
Hever, Edenbridge, Kent TN8 7NG
Off B2026 Westerham–Maresfield road
Open Mar–Nov: daily 12–6
Dates from 1270, when the massive gatehouse, outer walls and the moat were first constructed. Two hundred years later the Bullen (or Boleyn) family added a comfortable Tudor dwelling-house inside the walls. Hever Castle was the childhood home of Anne Boleyn and was frequently visited by Henry VIII when he was courting her. In 1903 the American millionaire William Waldorf Astor bought the castle. He spent millions of dollars restoring it, building a Tudor village behind it and creating landscaped gardens complete with artificial lake.

■20■ **HURST CASTLE** ☎ 01590 642344
Milford-on-Sea, Keyhaven, Limington, Hampshire SO41 0QU
On Pebble Spit, S of Keyhaven. Go south on B3058 and follow brown signs from Milford.
Can take hourly ferry from Keyhaven (half-hourly in summer)
Open Apr–June and Sept: daily 10–5.30; July and Aug: daily 10–6; Oct: daily 10–4
Tudor castle built between 1541 and 1544 by Henry VIII as one of a chain of coastal fortresses. Extensively modernised during the Napoleonic Wars. Its defences were updated again in the 1850s and most spectacularly in the 1860s and 1870s by the addition of the two massive casemated wings that dominate their surroundings. The castle was garrisoned in both world wars. Visitors today can see the Tudor castle and its exhibition and an exhibition in the Victorian west wing on the defences of this area. The Victorian east wing has recently opened.

■21■ **LEEDS CASTLE** ☎ 01622 765400
Maidstone, Kent ME17 1PL
4 miles E of Maidstone, take M20 junction 8
Open Mar–Oct: daily 10–5; Nov–Feb: daily 10– 3
Set on an island, surrounded by a lake, Leeds Castle has often been described as the loveliest castle in the world. Originally a Norman stronghold, it was first built in stone by a Norman baron during the reign of William the Conqueror's son, Henry I, nearly 900 years ago. The barbican, fortified mill and gatehouse form part of its impressive defences, while the revetment walls and towers, rising sheer from the surface of the lake, are punctuated with arrow slits and murder holes. The castle became a royal palace and was home to six of England's medieval queens. Henry VIII, the most famous of its royal owners, was responsible for much of the castle's splendour and he spent lavishly on transforming it from a rugged fortress to a comfortable palace. Inside, the castle is decorated throughout with carved beams, Tudor stonework, fine wall-hangings and Flemish tapestries.

■22■ LEWES CASTLE ☎ 01273 486290
Barbican House Museum, 169 High Street, Lewes, East Sussex BN7 1YE
Off High Street. Lewes is accessed via A27, A26 and A275
Open all year: Mon–Sat 10–5.30, Sun and Bank Hols 11–5.30. Closes at dusk in winter
Begun soon after 1066 by William de Warenne as his stronghold in Sussex and
added to over the next 300 years, this splendid Norman castle is perched high
above the medieval streets of Lewes. A steep climb to the top of the keep and
the magnificent barbican are rewarded by spectacular views over the Sussex
countryside. The castle was restored and updated during Georgian times, and
Barbican House's elegant Georgian façade conceals a much older timber house.
This is now the home of the Museum of Sussex Archaeology.

■23■ PEVENSEY CASTLE ☎ 01323 762604
Castle Road, Pevensey, East Sussex BN24 5LE
Off Pevensey High Street – A259
Open all year: Mar–Sept daily 10–6; Nov–Mar: Wed–Sun 10–4
Remains of surviving medieval castle enclosed within the massive walls of
fourth-century Roman shore fort. It was here that William the Conqueror
landed in 1066, and he may have used the Roman fort as a shelter for his
invasion force. Interesting remains of an unusual keep, dungeons and the
Roman walls, which were repaired after William gave the castle to his half-
brother, can all be explored.

■24■ PORTCHESTER CASTLE ☎ 023 9237 8291
Castle Street, Portchester, Fareham, Hampshire PO16 9QW
M27 junction 11. On S side of Portchester off A27
Open Apr–Sept: daily 10–6; Oct: daily 10–5; Nov–Mar: daily 10–4
Norman keep built in one corner of a Roman fort that was constructed in the
late third century. The outer walls of the substantial Roman fort are very well
preserved and are among the most complete in Northern Europe. The keep was
the main stronghold of the castle and provided secure, defensible accommodation; it was later used as a prison. Another period of building followed in the
fourteenth century, when Richard II replaced many of the castle's earlier buildings with a palace which now stands almost complete except for its roof.
Extensive remains from all these periods can be seen.

■25■ ROCHESTER CASTLE ☎ 01634 402276
The Keep, Boley Hill, Rochester, Kent ME1 1SW
Take M2 junction 1 by Rochester Bridge, A2
Open Apr–Sept: daily 10–6; Oct–Mar: daily 10–4
One of the best-preserved Norman fortresses in Britain. Begun in the eleventh
century on the site of Roman fortifications, the massive five-storey square
keep was built in 1127. It is the tallest in Britain, measuring over 120 feet
(36 metres) high with walls that are 12 feet (3.6 metres) thick. Parts of the
castle walls are still intact, and inside can be seen the site of the banqueting
hall, Norman chapel and mural galleries.

■26■ SOUTHSEA CASTLE ☎ 023 9282 7261
Clarence Esplanade, Southsea, Hampshire PO5 3PA
From M275 follow brown signs
Open Apr–Oct: daily 10–5.30; Nov–Mar: Sat, Sun and school hols only 10–4. Additional
opening times for schools and parties

Built by Henry VIII between 1544 and 1545 to protect Portsmouth from possible French invasion. Its revolutionary design provided for the most efficient use of guns at a time when artillery had begun to dominate warfare. The castle was substantially altered to accommodate more guns and a larger garrison of 200 men in the early nineteenth century. The most significant addition of this period was an underground tunnel around the moat, which visitors can still enter. The castle was only withdrawn from active service in 1960.

■27■ SPITBANK FORT ☎ 01329 664286
Hill Head Road, Hill Head, Fareham, Portsmouth, Hants PO14 3JJ
Take M275 southbound. In town centre
Open May–Sept: Tue–Sun. Ferry departs from Historic Dockyard, Portsmouth, weather permitting (call 01983 564602 for ferry details)
This massive man-made island built in the sea, a mile (1.6 kilometres) from Portsmouth Harbour, is the only sea fort open to the public. It is a magnificent example of Victorian engineering and architecture. Set in the Solent, the solid granite walls are 15 feet (4.5 metres) thick at basement level, and beneath the sea 35 feet (10.6 metres) of solid stone was positioned by divers to form the foundations. Fresh water is obtained from a well 400 feet (122 metres) deep, with a capacity of 23,000 gallons (10,456 litres) per day. The fort consists of a maze of passages and rooms, with one passage over 400 feet (122 metres) long. Replicas of the huge 38-tonne guns and 800-pound (363-kilogramme) shells are displayed, with some original shell and cartridge hoists still in working order.

■28■ TONBRIDGE CASTLE ☎ 01732 770929
Castle Street, Tonbridge, Kent TN9 1BG
In town centre off High Street
Open Apr–Sept: Mon–Sat 9–5, Sun and Bank Hols 10.30–5; Oct–Mar: Mon–Fri 9–5, Sat 9–4, Sun 10.30–4
Good example of a thirteenth-century motte-and-bailey castle with a mighty gatehouse that is among the finest in England. The castle towers above the River Medway in the centre of Tonbridge. Constructed of local sandstone in the second half of the thirteenth century, the gatehouse not only offered living accommodation and a state room but also incorporated the latest features of castle design, making it well-nigh impregnable. Castle is currently being renovated and re-opens in autumn 2000.

■29■ TOWER OF LONDON ☎ 0207 709 0765
Tower Hill, London EC3N 4AB
Tube to Tower Hill or car park on Lower Thames Street
Open Mar–Oct: Mon–Sat 9–5, Sun 10–5; Nov–Feb: Tue–Sat 9–4, Sun and Mon 10–4
With over two and a half million visitors a year the Tower of London is Britain's best-known and most-visited fortress. At its heart is the original stone keep built by William the Conqueror to subdue London at the time of the Norman Conquest. Nine hundred years on, the original fort is now the White Tower and it is surrounded by buildings and fortifications that were added over the centuries. The medieval palace is made up of a group of buildings which were begun by Henry III and enlarged by his son Edward I, who created a watergate which enabled the monarch to enter the tower from the Thames. It's now known as Traitors' Gate because of the number of prisoners accused of treason who passed through it. The Tower is surrounded by massive defence walls, long sections of which can be walked round, and is the home to the Crown Jewels.

Leeds Castle

■30■ **WALMER CASTLE AND GARDENS** ☎ 01304 364288
Kingsdown Road, Walmer, Deal, Kent CT14 7LJ
On coast south of Walmer, off A258
Open Apr–Oct: daily 10–6; Nov–Dec and Mar: Wed–Sun 10–4; Jan–Feb: Sat and Sun 10–4
Built circa 1540 as one of a chain of coastal artillery forts by Henry VIII against
the threat of invasion by Europe's Catholic powers. From 1708 it became the
official residence of the Lords Warden of the Cinque Ports, a title dating from the
thirteenth century. The castle's martial appearance has been much modified by
the alterations of successive Lords Warden in transforming the imposing fortress
into a comfortable residence. The Duke of Wellington once held the post of Lord
Warden and also died here. His sparsely furnished bedroom, with many of his
personal possessions, can be seen. The current Lord Warden is the Queen Mother.

■31■ WINDSOR CASTLE　☎ 01753 831118
Windsor, Berkshire SL4 1NJ
Signposted from M4 junction 6 and M3 junction 3. Rail: Paddington–Windsor and Eton Central or Waterloo–Windsor Riverside
Open Mar–Oct: daily 9.45–5.15 (last admission 4); Nov–Feb: daily 9.45–4.15 (last admission 3). Changing of the Guard Apr–June: Mon–Sat 11; Jul–Mar: every other day excluding Sun – phone for details. Moat garden open in Aug
Largest inhabited castle in the world. Originally a wooden fort constructed by William the Conqueror and rebuilt in stone by Edward III. Almost every monarch since has made their own additions and alterations. Built around two main courtyards, the Lower Ward and the Upper Ward, with the Middle Ward in between, much of the present-day appearance is due to the restoration work of Sir Jeffrey Wyatville in the reign of George IV. The entrance through Henry VIII's gatehouse leads to St George's Chapel, one of the finest examples of perpendicular architecture in Britain. There is magnificent fan vaulting, intricate carving on the stalls and an impressive stained-glass west window containing glass that dates from 1503. On the south side of the Lower Ward are the houses of the Military Knights of Windsor. Their Horseshoe Cloisters were built in the fifteenth century in the half-timbered style. On the north wing of the Upper Ward are the state apartments, which contain fine paintings, furniture and works of art. The castle was severely damaged by fire in 1992. The restoration work cost over £35 million and took five years. The semi-state apartments are open from October to March.

■32■ YARMOUTH CASTLE　☎ 01983 760678
Quay Street, Yarmouth, Isle of Wight PO41 0PB
Next to car ferry terminal
Open Easter–Sept: daily 10–6 (or dusk if sooner); Oct: daily 10–5
When it was completed in 1547 as part of Henry VIII's system of coastal defences, Yarmouth Castle embodied all the very latest ideas in military engineering. The castle is square in plan with walls nearly 100 feet (30 metres) high; two drop straight down to the sea, and the other two were originally flanked by a moat. This was filled in in the late seventeenth century, and a house, now the George Hotel, was built over it. Yarmouth differs radically from Henry's earlier forts, which all had semicircular bastions fronting a higher, central tower.

⛫ EASTERN　　　　　　　　　　　　　　　　　**MAP 3**

■33■ FRAMLINGHAM CASTLE　☎ 01728 724189
Framlingham, Woodbridge, Suffolk IP13 9BP
On B1119 in Framlingham
Open: Apr–Oct: daily 10–6 (dusk in Oct); Nov–Mar: daily 10–4. Closed New Year's Day
Superb twelfth-century castle. From the outside it looks almost as it would have done when it was first built. This was mainly during Edward I's reign, and it was one of the earliest castles to use a surrounding curtain wall with towers spaced along it at intervals rather than a central keep. Today the continuous curtain wall links all thirteen of the original towers, and from it there are excellent views over Framlingham and its reed-filled mere. At different times in its history the castle has been a fortress, an Elizabethan prison, a poorhouse and a school. The seventeenth-century poorhouse is still standing inside the walls. The towers are adorned with Tudor chimneys and the many alterations and additions such as this have led to a pleasing mixture of historical styles.

■34■ HEDINGHAM CASTLE ☎ 01787 460 261
Castle Hedingham, Nr Halstead, Essex CO9 3DJ
Off B1058 in Castle Hedingham or off A1017 between Cambridge and Colchester
Open late Mar–Oct: daily 10–5
Huge 110-feet-high (33.5-metre-high) castle with walls 12 feet (3.6 metres) thick.
it is one of the most magnificent and best-preserved Norman keeps in England.
Built in 1140 by Aubrey de Vere, it was home to the de Veres, Earls of Oxford, for
550 years and is still owned by their descendants. A beautiful bridge, built in
around 1496 to replace the drawbridge, spans the dry moat leading to the inner
bailey and was the only access to the castle. The banqueting hall has a fine timbered ceiling and is reached from the first floor by a beautiful spiral staircase. A
good view of this impressive room can be obtained from the minstrel's gallery.

■35■ MOUNT FITCHETT ☎ 01279 813237
Stansted, Essex CM24 8SP
Off B1383 in village centre
Open mid-Mar–mid-Nov: daily 10–5
Believed to have been an early Iron Age fort and Roman, Saxon and Viking
settlement, what you see today is a reconstruction of the way it would have
looked in 1086, twenty years after the Norman Conquest. It's a 'living'
museum, with live animals roaming free and animated figures.

■36■ TATTERSHALL CASTLE ☎ 01526 342543
Tattershall, Lincoln, Lincolnshire LN4 4LR

Fred's
FAVOURITE

On S side of A153, 15 miles NE of Sleaford, 10 miles SW of Horncastle
Open Apr–Oct: Sat–Wed and Bank Hol Mons 10.30 –5.30; Nov–mid-Dec: 12–4
The impressive red-brick tower is all that remains of the castle, but it is still a
good example of the type of fortified house that appeared during the Wars of
the Roses. Unlike the great spartan castles of the Normans, these were much
more comfortable places to live in. The original castle was built by Robert de
Tatershale in 1231, but only traces remain. The red-brick keep, built by Ralph
Cromwell, now stands alone but was once inside the castle's inner ward.
Although Tattershall's plans follow those of twelfth-century castles, architectural
and domestic details still intact show that it was really more of a country house
than a castle. There is a decorative roof gallery, which is unusually large and
therefore vulnerable, deep window recesses and turret rooms. The carved stone
chimneypieces on each level are original, reinstated after being retrieved (an
American syndicate bought the castle after the estate was mortgaged and sold
the fireplaces; they were returned after a public outcry).

■37■ TILBURY FORT ☎ 01375 858489
Fort Road, Tilbury, Essex RM18 7NR
1 mile E of Tilbury off A126
Open Apr–Oct: daily 10–6 (5 in Oct); Nov–Mar: Wed–Sun 10–4 (dusk if sooner)
One of England's finest surviving examples of late seventeenth-century military
engineering, which replaced a smaller fort built during the reign of Henry VIII. It
was designed at a time when artillery had become the dominant weapon and was
therefore low-lying and largely earthen to withstand the shock of bombardment.
For its defence from landward attack, complicated outworks depending on a
double line of moats were provided. This form of defence in depth, based on
the bastion system, is extremely rare in this country, and Tilbury is the finest
surviving example of it. The fort was garrisoned until after the First World War.

🏰 CENTRAL　　　　　　　　　　　　　　　　　　　　　MAP 4

■38■　ASHBY-DE-LA-ZOUCH CASTLE　☎ 01530 413343
South Street, Ashby-de-la-Zouch, Leicestershire LE65 1BR
In Ashby-de-la-Zouch, off A511
Open Apr–Oct: daily 10–6 (5 in Oct); Nov–March: Wed to Sun 10–4
Impressive ruins of a late-medieval castle. The earliest remains are sections of
the walls of the hall, buttery and pantry, which appear to belong to the middle
of the twelfth century. In the course of the next two centuries these buildings
were rebuilt, and the kitchen and solar added to them. After the Wars of the
Roses, Edward IV granted Ashby to his Lord Chamberlain, William Lord
Hastings, who, between the years 1474 and 1483, added Hastings Tower, which
bears his name, and the chapel. These were the last additions of importance to
the castle, which was neglected after the Civil War.

■39■　BELVOIR CASTLE　☎ 01476 870262
Belvoir, Nr Grantham, Lincolnshire NG32 1PE
Between A52 and A607
Open Apr–Sept: Tues–Thurs and Sat, Sun and Bank Hol Mons 11–5
Although the home of the Dukes of Rutland for many centuries, the castle
visitors see today with its turrets, battlements, towers and pinnacles, is a
nineteenth-century Gothic fantasy. It was Robert de Todeni, William the
Conqueror's standard bearer at the Battle of Hastings, who built the first castle
on this site, but destruction caused in two Civil Wars and by a catastrophic fire
in 1816 made it necessary to replace it with the present building. Inside, the
Pre-Guard Room and the Guard Room have a suitably castle-like feel; the rest,
including the Grand Dining-Room, Picture Gallery, Libraries and Chinese
Rooms, are the rooms of a nineteenth-century country house. Among the
many treaures to be viewed are paintings by Van Dyck, Murillo and Holbein.

■40■　BROUGHTON CASTLE　☎ 01295 276070
Banbury, Oxfordshire OX15 5EB
2 miles W of Banbury on B4035 Shipston on Stour road
*Open Easter and mid-May–Jun: Wed and Sun 2–5; July and Aug: Thur, Bank Hol Sun
and Mon 2–5*
The original medieval manor house, of which much remains today, was built in
about 1300 by Sir John Broughton. It stands on an island site surrounded by a
3-acre moat. The castle was greatly enlarged between 1550 and 1600, at which
time it was embellished with magnificent plaster ceilings, splendid panelling and
chimneypieces, including one in the French style in the room known as the
King's Chamber. The chapel survives from the fourteenth century. Eighteenth-
century Gothic alterations, of which the gallery is the most interesting. Arms
and armour from the Civil War and other periods are on display in the Great
Hall. Today the castle is essentially a family home lived in by Lord and Lady
Saye and Sele and their family.

■41■　GOODRICH CASTLE　☎ 01600 890538
Goodrich, Ross-on-Wye, Herefordshire HR9 6HY
5 miles S of Ross-on-Wye off A40
Open Apr–Oct: daily10–6 (5 in Oct); Nov–Mar: 10–4
The castle stands above the River Wye and gives wonderful views. It was built

around 1150 and then expanded in the thirteenth and fourteenth centuries, using the red sandstone rock on which it stands, so that rock and castle seem to merge together. Its medieval buildings are still largely intact and are protected by wide and deep ditches cut into the rock. A Norman tower stands three storeys high, surrounded by high walls and round drum towers that were added in the thirteenth and fourteenth centuries. Inside the walls are the remains of three separate halls with attached residential suites arranged around a courtyard.

■42■ LUDLOW CASTLE ☎ 01584 873355
Castle Square, Ludlow, Shropshire SY8 1AY
1 mile from A49, in the centre of Ludlow. Road runs out at Castle
Open May–July and Sept: daily 10–5; Aug daily: 10–7; Oct–Dec and Feb–Apr: daily
10–4; Jan: Sat and Sun 10–4
Late-eleventh-century border stronghold of Marcher Lord Roger de Lacy. Enlarged into a huge fortified palace early in the fourteenth century by Roger Mortimer, who was then the most powerful man in England. Further major building work was carried out in the mid-sixteenth century, when the castle was virtually the capital of Wales. Although the castle is now a ruin, many of its buildings still stand, and its long history is reflected in the varied architecture that can still be seen in it – Norman, medieval and Tudor. From the huge outer bailey a bridge across the moat leads to the inner bailey, the oldest and most important part of the castle. Here there are substantial remains of the great tower gatehouse keep, the great chamber, the solar wing and the Chapel of St Mary Magdalene with its unusual circular nave.

Warwick Castle

■43■ **PEVERIL CASTLE** ☎ 01433 620613
Market Place, Castleton, Hope Valley, Derbyshire S33 8WX
On S side of Castleton, 15 miles W of Sheffield on A625
Open Apr–Oct: daily 10–6 (5 in Oct); Nov–Mar: Wed–Sun 10–4
Small late-Norman keep, dating from around 1176, perched on a site of remarkable
strength on the summit of a limestone crag. Originally founded soon after the
Norman Conquest by one of King William's most trusted knights, William Peveril.
It had an important role in guarding the Peak Forest lead-mining area. In 1155 it
became royal property and its defences were strengthened, notably by the addition
of the main tower or keep. Improvements were made to its living accommodation
in the thirteenth century. It declined in importance in the fourteenth century: in
1372 the castle passed to John of Gaunt, but from then on its story is of gradual
decay. Remains of the keep and parts of the curtain wall survive.

■44■ **ROCKINGHAM CASTLE** ☎ 01536 770240
Market Harborough, Leicestershire LE16 8TH
On A6003 2 miles N of Corby
Open Easter Sun–mid Oct: Thurs, Sun, Bank Hol Mons plus all Tues in Aug 1–5
Impressive combination of Tudor house and medieval fortress. The original
castle was built by William the Conqueror and continued to be used as a royal
residence until 1422. It then fell into disrepair until work started in the sixteenth century to convert the castle into a comfortable Tudor house. Parts of
the medieval castle remain, including the Norman walls and the remains of the
gatehouse added by Edward I. The castle is based around the medieval hall,
which was divided into two rooms with bedrooms above in 1553. After being
damaged in the Civil War, little building work took place until the nineteenth
century, when a major modernisation programme was undertaken. The
Georgian stables were removed, the towers castellated and a flag tower added to
the gallery wing. The work was done using old materials wherever possible, and
care was taken to preserve the principal features of the Tudor house.

■45■ **STOKESAY CASTLE** ☎ 01588 672544
Stokesay, Craven Arms, Shropshire SY7 9AH
7 miles NW of Ludlow off A49
Open Apr–Oct: daily 10–6; Nov–Mar: Wed–Sun 10–4
Despite its name, Stokesay is not really a castle. It is in fact England's oldest
moated, fortified manor house, more domestic in character than military.
Stokesay Castle has hardly altered since the late thirteenth century, and it is one
of the finest examples of this type of building in the country. The house was
built by a successful wool merchant who wanted to create a comfortable residence that would combine pleasing design with some defensive capabilities. As
with many early manor houses, the castle and the nearby church are now iso-
lated, the village of which they were once the focal point having either moved
or disappeared. A half-timbered gatehouse leads into a courtyard opposite the
main range of buildings. These are made up of a hall and a solar, or private
apartment, flanked by two towers. The roof of the great hall is thought to include
some of its original timbers, and in the solar there is a medieval stone fireplace.

■46■ **TAMWORTH CASTLE** ☎ 01827 709626
The Holloway, Tamworth, Staffordshire B79 7LR
Signposted off A51 and A5
Open all year: Mon–Sat 10–5.30, Sun 2–5.30 (last admission 4.30)

Typical Norman motte-and-bailey castle with curtain wall and shell keep, dating from the late twelfth century. Footpath over superb herringbone wall leads up to the keep and down to excavated thirteenth-century gatehouse, of which the lower part of the double tower survives. Numerous additions and alterations have been made to the castle. The banqueting hall, with its oak-timbered roof and wide tie beams, was added in the fifteenth century, and the warder's lodge at the entrance to the courtyard is Tudor. With the construction of the south wing in the early seventeenth century, the twelfth-century keep was turned into a country gentlemen's residence and that is what we see today.

■47■ **WARWICK CASTLE** ☎ 01926 406600
Warwick, Warwickshire CV34 4QU
M40 junction 15 then follow signs
Open all year: daily 10–6; (5 in Nov–Mar). Last admission ½ hour before closing
Magnificently preserved fourteenth-century castle with massive walls, towers and turrets, making this one of England's finest medieval castles. The mighty ramparts and fortifications of the castle remain largely unchanged from the Middle Ages. After the Norman Conquest it was part of a chain of command set up to subdue Saxon England, and by the late thirteenth century it had begun its rise to prominence as one of the great seats of power in the land. The towers and curtain walls that protect the courtyard date from a major restructuring plan carried out in the fourteenth and fifteenth centuries. The gatehouse and barbican are perfectly preserved along with all the towers. Caesar's Tower is a masterpiece of fourteenth-century military architecture. Occupying its lowest chamber is the dungeon. During Tudor times the castle took on more of the comforts of a home, and by the end of the eighteenth century basic work on the state rooms had finished and the castle was very much as we see it today. They include the state dining-room, which was built by some of eighteenth-century England's finest craftsmen. The largest room in the castle, the Great Hall, was built in the fourteenth century, rebuilt in the seventeenth and restored in 1871 after it had been badly damaged by fire. By the nineteenth century the castle had completed its transformation into a fine stately home, and in the Library, the Music Room, the Smoking Room and the Bedrooms there is a re-creation of a Victorian house party.

▟▙ WALES   MAP 5

■48■ **BEAUMARIS CASTLE** ☎ 01248 810361
Castle Street, Beaumaris, Anglesey LL58 8AP
Cross the Menai Bridge and follow signs to Beaumaris
Open: Mar–Oct: daily 9.30–6; Nov–Feb: Mon–Sat 9.30–4, Sun 11–4
Begun in 1295, this unfinished castle is the last and the largest of Edward I's Welsh fortifications. It is designed on a concentric plan with the main courtyard surrounded by a narrow enclosing ward and both in turn protected by a wide moat filled with a controlled supply of tidal water from the Menai Strait. Although building work went on for around thirty-five years, when it finally ceased in the 1330s the great towers of the inner ward were still without their top storeys while the turrets were never so much as begun. Because of this, the castle, with its low-lying, squat appearance, lacks the dramatic impact of Conwy, Caernarfon or Harlech (see entries). What makes Beaumaris impressive is its size and strength and the perfect symmetry of its design and water defences.

Caernarfon Castle

■49■ **CAERNARFON CASTLE** ☎ 01286 677617
Castle Ditch, Caernarfon, Gwynedd LL55 2AY
Take A55 and follow signs for Bangor, then follow second sign for Caernarfon
Open July–Oct: 9.30–6 (5 in Oct); Nov–late Mar: Mon–Sat 9.30–4, Sun 11–4
Begun in 1283 and still not completely finished when building work stopped in
around 1330, Caernarvon castle is one of Britain's most striking and famous
medieval buildings. With its nine polygonal towers, two great gatehouses and
walls of colour-banded stone, the castle was always intended to be much more
than a military fortification. When Edward I built it, he intended Caernarfon to
be his royal residence and seat of government for North Wales. Caernarfon stands
apart from his other Welsh castles in its sheer scale and the degree of its architectural finish. The castle plan is shaped like a figure eight divided into two
wards at the waist. Towers, gatehouses and curtain walls are very well preserved,
but all the courtyard buildings have disappeared except for their foundations.
The King's Gate and the Eagle Tower are particularly impressive, both giving
striking demonstrations of the strength of medieval fortifications in Britain.

■50■ **CAERPHILLY CASTLE** ☎ 029 2088 3143
Castle Street, Caerphilly, Caerphilly CF83 1JD
Can take A468 from Newport or A469 or A470 from Cardiff; rail station ¼ mile away;
accessible by bus from Cardiff
Open Mar–Apr: daily 9.30–5; May–Oct: daily, 9.30–6 (5 in Oct); Nov–Feb: Mon–Sat
9.30–4, Sun 11–4 (last admission ½ hour before closing)
Caerphilly Castle is the largest castle in Wales and one of the great strongholds
of medieval Europe. Concentrically planned, its massive stone and water
defences which gave it a strength barely surpassed by any other fortresses in
Britain, are formidable even today. Its strength lies in the scale of its monumental architecture coupled with the defensive qualities of the two lakes that surround it. It was built for Red Gilbert de Clare, the Marcher Lord of Glamorgan.
With its inner defences overlooking and commanding the lower outer ring of

walls, Caerphilly is a particularly fine example of the concentric or 'walls within walls' principle of fortification. Although allowed to fall into gradual decay from the mid-fourteenth century, it is still an impressive castle. The well-preserved Great Hall is an essentially fourteenth-century construction with a new roof put on in the 1870s.

■51■ CARDIFF CASTLE ☎ 029 2087 8100
Castle Street, Cardiff, CF10 3RB
From M4 or A470 follow signs to city centre, then follow castle signs
Open Mar–Oct: daily 9.30–6 (tours daily 10–5); Nov–Feb: daily 9.30–4.30 (tours daily 10–3.15)
Originally the site of a Roman fort, part of the Roman walls, bastions and north gate have been preserved. In the eleventh century, a Norman motte-and-bailey fortress was built on the site, which now dominates the castle grounds. The medieval Lords of Glamorgan added further fortifications and dwellings, but it was the third Marquess of Bute who transformed the interior of the castle building into the fantasy of today, full of stained glass, wall paintings, elaborate marble fireplaces and gilded ceilings. Together with his architect William Burgess, their medieval visions were also extended to the nearby Castell Coch on the outskirts of Cardiff, which acted as a hunting lodge for the Bute family.

■52■ CARREG CENNEN ☎ 01558 822291
Trapp, Llandeilo, Carmarthenshire SA19 6UA
M4 junction 49, then signposted
Open late Mar–Oct: daily 9.30–8; Nov–late Mar: daily 9.30–dusk
Dramatic ruins standing high on a remote cliff in the foothills of the Black Mountains. Carreg Cennen's site is spectacular. Perched high on a limestone crag some 300 feet (90 metres) above the valley of the River Cennen the castle is visible for miles around. It was built in the late thirteenth or early fourteenth century. Its nucleus is the inner ward, which is structurally the earliest part of the castle to survive. The barbican built against the front of the gatehouse was added later. Finally, the outer ward, of which little remains, was added, extending down the crag. Surviving remains include an interesting underground passage and cave which runs into the hill under the castle for about 50 yards (46 metres).

■53■ CHEPSTOW ☎ 01291 624065
Bridge Street, Chepstow, Monmouthshire NP16 5EY
Chepstow town centre, off A48 or M48
Open late Mar–Oct: daily 9.30–6 (5 in Oct); Nov–late Mar: Mon–Sat 9.30–4, Sun 11–4
Substantial remains of one of the earliest stone-built castles in Britain. Chepstow guarded the river crossing near the mouth of the Wye where the main coastal land route from southern England enters Wales. At its heart is the great tower built within a decade of 1066. The castle was then modified and expanded in successive stages throughout the Middle Ages and again in Tudor times and after the Civil War.

■54■ CHIRK CASTLE ☎ 01691 777701
Chirk, Wrexham LL14 5AF
7 miles S of Wrexham off A483, 1 mile N of Chirk village
Open late Mar–Oct: Wed–Sun and Bank Hol Mons 12–5
Built in the late thirteenth and early fourteenth centuries by Roger Mortimer to

maintain the conquests of Edward I in Wales, the castle has been lived in continuously ever since. The south wing had become a house by Tudor times, and the outline of the many Tudor gables can still be traced on the filling in carried out during the eighteenth century. The interior of the east wing, now a private house, was much altered during the nineteenth century by Augustus Welby Pugin. The west wing with its deep dungeon hollowed out of the rock, survives largely untouched since 1300. Entered through a hall by Pugin, the rooms are notable for their elaborate decorative work of the sixteenth to early nineteenth century. The park, crossed by Offa's Dyke, is entered from Chirk village past magnificent iron gates completed in 1721.

■55■ ·CILGERRAN CASTLE ☎ 01239 615007
Cilgerran, Ceredigion SA43 2SF
3 miles SE of Cardigan
Open Apr–late Oct: daily 9.30–6.30; late Oct–late Mar: daily 9.30–4.30
The castle is on the north side of the village of Cilgerran. Standing on the rim of a steep gorge in the Teifi Valley, with its mighty east and west towers standing clear of surrounding woodlands, the physical features of the site give a superb defensive position. Yet despite this, the castle was won and lost many times during its history. The castle, as it now stands, dates from the early thirteenth century when the Norman Baron William Marshall the Younger set about rebuilding an earlier castle that had stood on the site following a troubled period of capture and recapture from the Welsh. The castle's most striking surviving features are Marshall's powerful twin round towers and curtain wall, built to defend the castle's vulnerable side.

■56■ CONWY CASTLE ☎ 01492 592358
Conwy, District of Conwy LL32 8LB
In centre of Conwy

Fred's
FAVOURITE

Open late Mar–late Oct: daily 9.30–6; late Oct–late Mar: Mon–Sat 9.30–5,
Sun 11–4 (last admission ½ hour before closing)
The turrets and battlements of its castle dominate the picturesque walled town of Conwy. It is one of Edward I's chain of eight Welsh castles built between 1283 and 1287 under the direction of Master James of St George, the king's military architect. Conwy remains one of the most outstanding achievements of medieval military architecture. The distinctive elongated shape, with its two barbicans, eight massive towers and great bow-shaped hall, was determined by the narrow rocky outcrop on which the castle stands. The whole structure was designed to serve as a symbol of Edward's military domination and of civilian control. The castle is distinguished by the unity and compactness of so great a mass of building, with its eight almost identical towers, four on the north and four on the south. The view from across the River Conwy with Thomas Telford's nineteenth-century suspension bridge in the foreground is particularly impressive.

■57■ CRICCIETH CASTLE ☎ 01766 522227
Castle Street, Criccieth, Gwynedd LL52 0DP
Off A497 near Criccieth town centre
Open Apr–Sept: daily 10–6 (last admission 5.30)
Perched on a rocky coastal promontory above the little seaside resort of Criccieth, the ruins of the castle are dominated by the huge twin-towered gatehouse built by Llewellyn the Great in the 1230s. It was extended by Llewellyn the Last and

later remodelled by Edward I after he had captured it in the early fifteenth century. The castle was destroyed by Owain Glyn Dîor and was never rebuilt.

■58■ DENBIGH CASTLE ☎ 01745 813385
Castle Hill, Denbigh, Denbighshire LL1C 3NB
On hill above town centre
Open Apr–Oct: daily 9.30–6.30; Nov–Mar: daily 9.30–4.30
Denbigh Castle stands on the summit of a steep and prominent rock outcrop in the heart of the Vale of Clwyd. Begun by Henry de Lacy in 1282 with the support of Edward I, the ruins of the castle are dominated by the remains of the impressive triple-towered great gatehouse that was the main entrance to the castle. The castle is in the shape of a great oval which encircles one inner ward. There is a contrast between the west and south walls, where straight lines of walls connect poorly surviving semicircular towers, and the north and east walls, where shorter lengths of wall connect better surviving octagonal towers with many courtyard buildings set between them. The town itself is walled too.

■59■ HARLECH CASTLE ☎ 01766 780552
Castle Square, Harlech, Gwynedd LL46 2YH
Approach from A496
Open late Mar–Oct: daily 9.30–6 (5 in Oct); Nov–late Mar: Mon–Sat 9.30–4, Sun 11–4
Built between 1283 and 1289 by Master James of St George for Edward I, Harlech's spectacular location by the sea with the mountains of Snowdonia behind it have made it one of the most familiar castles in Britain. It is designed on a concentric plan with a small inner ward dominated by atwin-towered gatehouse and four round corner towers. The gatehouse is a magnificent construction which dominates the whole of the castle. Its inner façade is one of the most striking compositions of military architecture from thirteenth century Britain.

■60■ KIDWELLY CASTLE ☎ 01554 890104
5 Castle Road, Kidwelly, Carmarthenshire SA17 5BQ
Reached via A484
Open late Mar–early Oct: daily 9.30–6; Nov–late Mar: Mon–Sat 9.30–4, Sun 11–4
Basically a building of the late thirteenth and early fourteenth centuries, with some late-medieval and Tudor additions, the shape was heavily influenced by an earlier earth and timber castle built in around 1106. The earliest surviving parts of the stone castle are the defences of the inner ward, consisting of four round towers and curtain walls on the north, south and west sides. The main entrance to the castle in the Middle Ages was through the great south gate, which is the way the castle is entered today.

■61■ PEMBROKE CASTLE ☎ 01646 681510
Castle Terrace, Pembroke, Pembrokeshire SA71 4LA
At the W end of Main Street
Open Apr–Sept: daily 9.30–6; Mar and Oct: 10–5; Nov–Feb: daily 10.30–4.30
Pembroke Castle has a massive round keep, which is 75 feet high (23 metres) and 50 feet (15 metres) in diameter, which is the largest keep of its kind in the country. The Henry VII Tower is believed to be the birthplace of Henry Tudor. It was severely damaged during the Civil War, but most of it has been extensively restored. The most impressive of the castle's buildings is the gatehouse. In the Middle Ages this was an important residential part of the castle and, with its adjacent barbican tower, it forms a fortified unit larger than many complete castles.

A fine view of Conwy Castle from the medieval walls of the town

■62■ PENHOW CASTLE ☎ 01633 400800
Nr Newport NP6 3AD
On A48 between Newport and Chepstow
Open Good Fri–Sept: Wed–Sun and Bank Hols 10–5.15: Aug: daily 10–5.15; Oct–Easter:
Wed 10–5.15
Oldest inhabited castle in Wales, spanning 800 years of history. Originally a
small Border fortress, Penhow was the home of the Seymour family. The castle
has been set out to present a picture of life from the twelfth to the nineteenth
century. The ramparts, with views of three counties, are twelfth century, while
the Great Hall and minstrel's gallery are of the fifteenth. The kitchen shows life
in the seventeenth century, and there is a Victorian housekeeper's room.

■63■ POWIS CASTLE AND GARDENS ☎ 01938 554338
Powis Castle, Nr Welshpool, Powys SY21 8RF
1 mile S of Welshpool off A483
Open Apr–Jun: Wed–Sun 1–5; July–Aug: Tues–Sun 1–5; Sept–Oct: Wed–Sun 1–5.
Admission for groups outside these hours by prior arrangement
Perched on a rock above the garden terraces, the medieval castle was originally
built as a fortress by Welsh princes and is still inhabited after some 700 years.
The present castle dates from the late thirteeth century, when Edward I granted
Gruffydd ap Gwenwynwyn the barony of de la Pole. In 1587 the castle was
bought by Sir Edward Herbert, who added the long gallery and did much internal remodelling. There was further construction during the seventeenth to
nineteenth century, while the beginning of the twentieth saw extensive remodelling of the interior and exterior. Among these interior features are the panelling
and plasterwork, the carved late seventeenth-century staircase, and the state bedroom and ceilings and murals by Lanscroon. The late seventeenth-century formal
garden is still as it was when it was first laid out with four terraces, each nearly
200 yards (183 metres) long. Magnificently developed since 1700 and especially
in the twentieth century, it is now one of the finest gardens in Britain.

■64■ RAGLAN CASTLE ☎ 01291 690228
Raglan, Monmouthshire NP15 2BT
Signposted off A40
Open late Mar–late May: daily 9.30–5; late May–Oct: 9.30–6 (5 in Oct); Nov–late Mar:
Mon–Sat 9.30– 4, Sun 11–4
Remains of an impressive fifteenth-century castle built by Sir William ap Thomas
and his son William Herbert and remodelled by William, Earl of Worcester,
between 1549 and 1589. Despite demolition attempts during the Civil War,
much of its hexagonal-shaped great tower and state apartments still survive.
Raglan was one of the last true castles to have been built in England and Wales,
and it remains one of the finest late-medieval buildings in the British Isles. There
is a very pronounced French influence on the design of the castle, with highly
decorative features on the gatehouse towers and a double drawbridge arrangement of the keep, unique in Britain but common on the Continent.

■65■ RHUDDLAN CASTLE ☎ 01745 590777
Castle Street, Rhuddlan, Denbighshire LL18 5AD
3 miles south of Rhyl
Open 1 May–Sept: daily 10–5
Remains of the second of Edward I's great Welsh fortifications begun in 1277.
A protected river dock forms one side of the defences of this concentrically
planned castle, which is dominated by a distinctive diamond-shaped inner
ward. The west gatehouse, whose twin towers lack only their battlemented
parapets, is one of the best surviving features of the castle.

⛰ NORTH-WEST   MAP 6

■66■ APPLEBY CASTLE Ltd ☎ 017683 51402
Appleby-in-Westmorland, Cumbria CA16 6XH
M6 junction 38, then B6260 to Appleby
Open Jan–Easter and Oct–Dec exc Christmas: Sat and Sun 10.30–4; Easter–Sept:
daily 10–5
Extensively restored in the seventeenth century, the castle, which overlooks the
River Eden, still has a fine Norman keep. It began as a motte-and-bailey strong-
hold of timbered earthwork, and the banks and ditches that have survived are
now some of the most impressive examples of Norman engineering in England.
Lady Anne Clifford converted the property in 1635 into a fortified home, and it
remained as such for most of its history. In 1675 the castle was acquired by the
Earls of Thanet, and during their time the present staircase was added and the
building was refaced using dressed stone from nearby demolished castles.

■67■ DALTON CASTLE ☎ 019467 26064
Market Place, Dalton-in-Furness, Cumbria LA15 8AX

Fred's
FAVOURITE

Western end of Main Street of Dalton-in-Furness
Open Easter–Sept: Sat 2–5
Rectangular tower of limestone rubble with red sandstone dressing erected in
the mid-fourteenth century. Formerly the manorial courthouse of Furness
Abbey. After the dissolution of the abbey in 1537 it continued as a courthouse
for another 300 years. The interior has seen many alterations, the last and most
radical being that of 1856 when the three upper floors, accessible from a stone
spiral staircase, were replaced by a single upper room and an additional stairway.

■68■ **LANCASTER CASTLE** ☎ 01524 64998
Shire Hall Castle Park, Lancaster, Lancashire LA1 1YJ
2 minutes from Lancaster railway station
Open mid-Mar–mid-Dec: daily 10–5 (last admission 4, guided tours only)
Standing high above the river in the centre of the city on the site of a Roman fort, Lancaster Castle is a much-altered building which includes the Shire Hall, Crown Court and a prison. As it is still used as both a court of law and a prison, only certain parts of the interior can be viewed. The castle is made up of an interesting collection of medieval and Georgian buildings. The chief medieval remains are the gatehouse, which dates from around 1400, and the Norman keep, which was restored at the end of the sixteenth century. The Shire Hall and Crown Court, the latter of which cannot be viewed when the court is in session, have Gothic interiors. The thirteenth-century Hadrian's Tower contains a collection of prison equipment.

■69■ **SIZERGH CASTLE** ☎ 015395 60070
Sizergh, Nr Kendal, Cumbria LA8 8AE
3 miles S of Kendal, NW of A590/A591 interchange
Open Apr–Oct: Sun–Thur 1.30–5.30. Garden from 12.30.
Massive three-storey peel tower dating from around 1350, characteristic of Border refuges built to withstand Scottish raids. A close inspection of its north-western front reveals the various additions made through the centuries to the fortress at its heart. Adjoining the tower is a great Tudor hall, remodelled during Elizabethan times and again in the eighteenth century. An Elizabethan gabled corner block next to it has two long sixteenth-century wings which project to form a three-sided courtyard. The castle has some fine early-Elizabethan wood-work, including benches and panelling, with oak linenfold in the passage-room upstairs dating from Henry VIII's time. Five magnificent chimneys dated from 1563–75 are carved with remarkable skill. A number of Stuart relics are housed in the top floor of the peel tower, where an in-laid panel, dating from 1570–80, has recently been reinstated in the master bedroom.

⛰ NORTH-EAST   MAP 7

■70■ **ALNWICK CASTLE** ☎ 01665 510777
Alnwick, Northumberland NE66 1NQ
1 mile from Alnwick turn off on A1, signposted. Just off town centre on N side of Alnwick
Open Apr–Sept: daily 11–5 (last admission 4.15)
The Percy family has lived in Alnwick Castle since 1309, and it was described by the Victorians as the 'Windsor of the North'. On entering the castle, you are faced with a rather simple room, which gives you no clue as to the delights to come. The Grand Staircase is the first taste of splendour, each step made from a single piece of stone measuring 12 feet (3.6 metres) in length. The library is also impressive; grand in its appearance, it holds some 13,000 volumes. The interior throughout the castle is that of the Italian Renaissance, and there are also many fine paintings.

■71■ **BAMBURGH CASTLE** ☎ 01668 214208
Bamburgh, Northumberland NE69 7DF
On coast 6 miles E of Belford, off B1340 or B1342
Open Mar–Oct: daily 11–5 (last admission 4.30). Groups of fifteen or more by arrangement
An impressive castle set dramatically on a rocky outcrop towering above a wide

sandy beach on the Northumberland coast, Bamburgh Castle is a huge, square Norman castle with fine original Norman keep and other apartments restored in the late nineteenth century by Lord Armstrong. It has an impressive armoury on the first floor of the keep, with a smaller collection of armour on loan from the Tower of London. Although it follows the outline plan of the medieval hall, the magnificent Great or King's Hall is almost entirely a nineteenth-century creation that displays Victorian craftsmanship of a very high standard.

■72■ BOLTON CASTLE ☎ 01969 623981
Leyburn, North Yorkshire DL8 4ET
Off A684, signposted
Open Mar–early Nov: 10–5 (dusk if sooner; last admission 4.30)
This castle was designed around a rectangular courtyard, with a huge five-storey tower at each corner and two smaller towers on the north and south sides in 1399. Although it was defensive in nature, it was also a luxury dwelling in the Middle Ages. Each of the private apartments had its own garderobe, or toilet, with plumbing that was so sophisticated it was still in use in Victorian times. The castle stored and milled its own grain, brewed its own beer, made its own bread and had its own forge and all the facilities to sustain a castle under siege. In 1761 the north-east tower collapsed, weakened by artillery fire a century earlier, but the other three towers and curtain walls survive almost to their original height. Mary, Queen of Scots was imprisoned for six months here.

■73■ CHILLINGHAM CASTLE ☎ 01668 215359
Chillingham, Nr Wooler, Northumberland NE66 5NJ
12 miles N of Alnwick, signposted from A1 and A697
Open Easter–Sept: daily 12–5; closed Tue May–June and Sept. Phone for group bookings
Medieval fortress which has remained the home of the same family since the thirteenth century. Originally constructed in the twelfth century, it became a fully fortified castle in the fourteenth century and occupied a strategic position during Northumberland's border feuds. Decorative refinements were made in the sixteenth, eighteenth and nineteenth centuries, including the gardens and grounds laid out by Sir Jeffrey Wyatville. The castle has a jousting course, dungeon and torture chamber as well as antique furnishings, tapestries and armour.

■74■ CONISBROUGH CASTLE ☎ 01709 863329
Castle Hill, Conisbrough, South Yorkshire DN12 3BU
Off A630 between Doncaster and Rotherham
Open Easter–Sept: Mon–Fri 10–5, Sat and Sun 10–6; Oct–Mar: daily 10–4
Impressive white keep of twelfth-century castle, Conisbrough is the oldest circular keep in England. It is built of magnesium limestone and is supported by six buttresses, one of which contains a family chapel. The castle was the principal northern stronghold of the Earls of Surrey but lost its importance in the fifteenth century and fell into disrepair. It was restored in 1994 when two new floors and a new roof were put into the keep.

■75■ DURHAM CASTLE ☎ 0191 374 3864 (or 0191 374 3800, phoneline)
Palace Green, Durham DH1 3RW
Opposite cathedral
Open for guided tours: July–Sept, Easter and Christmas holidays, daily 10–12 and 2–4.30; Oct–Jun: Mon, Wed, Sat and Sun 2–4.30. Closed for private functions, phone first
Founded soon after the Norman Conquest, the castle has been rebuilt, extended

and adapted over a period of 900 years. As it stands today, the castle reflects its changing functions and displays a wide variety of architectural styles of different periods. Often these alterations reflected new standards and fashions in military and, increasingly, in domestic building and furnishing. From being a key fortress for the defence of the border with Scotland, it was transformed gradually in more peaceful times into a palace for the Bishops of Durham. Since 1837, soon after the foundation of the University of Durham, it has served as a residential college for many generations of students and dons.

■76■ HOUSESTEADS ROMAN FORT ☎ 01434 344363
Haydon Bridge, Northumberland NE47 6NN
2 miles NE of Bardon Mill on B6318
Open Apr–Oct: daily 10–6 (5 in Oct or dusk if sooner); Nov–Mar: daily 10–4
Housesteads Fort on Hadrian's Wall is the most complete example of a Roman fort in Britain. Stretching across much of northern England, the wall was built between AD122 and 128 by Emperor Hadrian to mark the frontier between the Roman Empire and the barbarians of Caledonia in the north. The line of forts and castles linked by the wall was rebuilt several times in the next three centuries and included Housesteads Fort, where a Roman infantry cohort was stationed. Remains of the commander's house, the hospital and the four gates can still be seen. The fort, perched high on its ridge overlooking the open Northumbrian countryside, was an addition to Hadrian's Wall, forming part of the second scheme for the frontier. In order to gain as much room as possible on the ridge, the north wall of the fort was pushed to the very edge of the escarpment. This entailed building deep foundations for the fort wall, and these can be seen below the threshold of the north gate, though they would have been covered by a ramp.

■77■ LINDISFARNE CASTLE ☎ 01289 389244
Holy Island, Berwick-upon-Tweed, Northumberland TD15 2SH
6 miles E of Beal across tidal causeway. Check tide times before crossing
Open Apr–Jun: Sat–Thur and Good Fri 1–5.30; July and Aug: Sat–Thur 11–5. Opening times dependent on tides
Sixteenth-century castle built to protect English ships using the sheltered anchorage of Holy Island. It was garrisoned until the end of the Napoleonic Wars and became a coast-guard station between 1840 and 1900, soon after which it fell into disrepair. The shell was then transformed into a private house by Edwin Lutyens for Edward Hudson, the founder and owner of *Countrylife* magazine. Inside the lower part of the building, he created a modern entrance hall of low arches on strong round piers, and passages hewn from the rock, leading to two exquisite vaulted chambers. On the upper floor, a long gallery links a series of bedrooms with beamed ceilings.

■78■ RABY CASTLE ☎ 01833 660202
PO Box 50, Staindrop, Durham DL2 3AY
1 mile N of Staindrop, off A688
Open May and Sept: Wed–Sun 1–5; Jun–Aug: Sun–Fri 1–5. Grounds same days, 11–5.30
The fortress is built around a courtyard and is surrounded by a moat which is now dry. Raby Castle was erected during Saxon times, but what we see today is substantially fourteenth century, with parts that have been added in nearly every century since. It was the stronghold of the powerful Nevill family until 1569, and the home of the Vane family since 1626. It has an impressive gateway,

nine towers, of which the tallest is 80 feet (24 metres), a vast medieval hall and a Victorian octagonal drawing-room. The fourteenth-century kitchen, with its collection of Victorian copper cooking utensils, was in use daily until 1954. The castle has a fine collection of paintings, a carriage collection and there are five acres of gardens and a further 200-acre (81-hectare) deer park.

■79■ SKIPTON CASTLE ☎ 01756 792442
Skipton, North Yorkshire BD23 1AQ
Take Skipton turning on A59 or A65 and follow brown signs
In centre of Skipton
Open Mar–Sept: Mon–Sat 10–6, Sun 12–6; Oct–Feb: Mon–Sat 10–4, Sun 12–4

Fred's
FAVOURITE

Dating from the twelfth century and still fully roofed, Skipton is one of the best-preserved and most complete medieval castles in England. The watchtower is the most imposing of the towers, and a ledge below the windows reveals the thickness (13 feet/4 metres) the walls. The rooms have been left largely unfurnished, giving a good idea of what they would have been like without the later ornamentation that has been added in many other castles that are as well preserved. Interesting medieval kitchen with baking ovens and serving hatch, banqueting hall, chapel, day-rooms and bedchambers. Dungeon steps lead down into the dark prison. The Conduit Court is at the heart of the castle, formed by a range of domestic buildings which have survived unaltered and intact from early Tudor times.

▟▙ SCOTLAND   MAP 8

■80■ ABERDOUR CASTLE ☎ 0131 668 8800
Aberdour, Fife KY3 0SL
In Aberdour, S of A921, N of harbour
Open Apr–Sept: daily 9.30–6.30; Oct–Mar: Mon–Wed and Sat 9.30–4.30, Thurs 9.30–12.30 Sun 2–4.30

Ruined E-plan tower house, consisting of a fourteenth-century keep and later wings and extensions, some of which are complete. A range of buildings and a bakehouse were added in the sixteenth century, and in around 1630 the castle was extended with the addition of a block, which is occupied by a long gallery. The castle has a walled courtyard within which a round turret survives. A terraced garden has been restored. Originally the castle belonged to the Mortimer family, but in 1342 the property passed to the Earls of Morton. The castle was abandoned in 1725 and was burnt out, then in 1844 the keep partially collapsed.

■81■ BLACKNESS CASTLE ☎ 01506 834807
Blackness, By Linlithgow, West Lothian EH49 7NH
4 miles NE of Linlithgow, on Firth of Forth, off A904
Open Apr–Sept: daily 9.30–6.30; Oct–Mar: Mon–Sat 9.30–4.30, Sun 2–4.30 (closed Thurs afternoons, Fri and Sun mornings in winter)

A grim and impressive courtyard castle which was used as the state prison. It was built in the fifteenth century but was much modified in later centuries for artillery. The main entrance is protected by a spur with caponier and gun platforms. The curtain wall dates partly from the fifteenth century, but it was massively strengthened for artillery in the sixteenth and seventeenth centuries. The oldest part of the castle, right in the centre, is the square, four-storey fifteenth-century keep. This was heightened between 1537 and 1542 and altered again later with the addition of a projecting round stair tower. From 1537, under Sir

James Hamilton of Finnart, work began on turning the castle into an artillery fort, making it one of the most formidable fortresses in Scotland. During Cromwell's invasion of Scotland in 1650 the castle suffered much damage and was not repaired again until the late 1660s. In the nineteenth century the castle was greatly altered to hold powder and stores and became the central ammunition depot for Scotland. In 1912 the castle was handed over to the state and major restoration work took place between 1926 and 1935.

■82■ BLAIR CASTLE ☎ 01796 481207

Blair Atholl, Pitlochry, Perthshire & Kinross PH18 5TL
7 miles NW of Pitlochry off A9
Open Apr–Oct: daily 10–6, opens 9.30 July and Aug, (last admission 5). By special arrangement at other times.
Blair Castle has seen three main stages of development: medieval, Georgian and Victorian. The oldest part is Cummings Tower, built in about 1270. In 1530 the third Earl extended the castle by building south from the tower to add a Great Hall, which now includes the dining-room, over a series of vaulted chambers. The next major change was begun in 1740 by the second Duke. In keeping with the mood of the times, the architect James Winter removed the turrets and castellations and remodelled the castle as a Georgian mansion, with pitched roofs, chimney stacks and fine interiors by the stuccoist Thomas Clayton of Edinburgh. A century later the seventh Duke put back the tower and the crenellations, built a new entrance hall and front gates, and finished it all off with a splendid ballroom. The north end was completely refurbished in 1998.

■83■ BOTHWELL CASTLE ☎ 01698 816894

Bothwell, Uddingston, Glasgow G71 8BL
About 3m NW of Hamilton, on minor roads off B7071
Open Apr–Sept: daily 9.30–6.30; Oct–Mar: Mon–Sat 9.30–4.30, Sun 2–4.30. Check winter dates
One of the largest and finest stone castles in Scotland. Bothwell Castle consists of what was once a magnificent moated round keep within a walled courtyard, which was defended by towers at the corners and by a gatehouse. The courtyard is enclosed by a strong thick curtain wall, which in some places rises to 60 feet (18 metres). Within the walls are the ruins of many buildings, including a hall, a chapel and the foundations of a large tower. Another tower is complete to the corbelled wallhead, and the prison tower and adjacent wall, which date from the thirteenth century, also remain. The magnificent round keep has a surrounding ditch partly hewn out of rock, 25 feet (7.6 metres) wide and 15 feet (4.5 metres) deep. The entrance to the keep is through a fine pointed doorway, originally reached by a drawbridge across the ditch.

■84■ BRAEMAR CASTLE ☎ 01339 741219

Braemar, Ballater, Aberdeenshire AB35 5XR
NE of Braemar on A93
Open Good Fri–Oct: Sat–Thur 10–6 (open Fri in July and Aug)
Impressive fortress built in 1628 by the Earl of Mar and used by Hanoverian troops after the Jacobite Rising of 1745. Later became the seat of the Farquharsons of Invercauld. It has an underground prison, a star-shaped defensive curtain wall, and a central round tower with a spiral staircase and barrel-vaulted ceilings. From outside it looks every inch a fortress; inside it is a living home filled with the furnishings and the decoration of 200 years of the Farquharsons' history.

■85■ **BRODICK CASTLE** ☎ 01770 302202
Brodrick, Isle of Arran KA27 8HY
Ferry from Ardrossan to Brodick. Castle is 2 miles N of Brodrick
Open 1 Apr or Good Fri–Oct: daily 11–4.30 (5 in July and Aug). Grounds open all year
The Victorian extensions to this medieval castle dominate its appearance. The earliest sections date from the thirteenth century, while the sixteenth century saw the addition of a simple rectangular baronial-style tower. In the middle of the seventeenth century Cromwellian troops added the battery to the east and extended the castle two bays to the west. The castle, standing on a 700-acre (283-hectare) estate with a 700-acre (283-hectare) woodland garden, became a base for the Hamilton family in the nineteenth century when the architect Gillespie Graham was commissioned to add a major extension to the west of the old tower.

■86■ **BRODIE CASTLE** ☎ 01309 641371
Brodie, Forres, Moray IV36 2TE
4 miles W of Forres off A96
Open Apr–Sept: Mon–Sat 11–5.30, Sun 1.30–5.30; Oct: Sat 11–5.30, Sun 1.30–5.30
Handsome gabled Scottish castle containing numerous treasures acquired by the Brodie family over the centuries, their association with this area going back to 1160. The oldest part is a sixteenth-century Z plan, with additions made in the seventeenth and nineteenth centuries after the damage in 1645 during the Montrose Campaigns.

■87■ **CAERLAVEROCK CASTLE** ☎ 01387 770244
Caerlaverock, By Dumfries, Dumfries & Galloway DG1 4RU
8 miles SE of Dumfries on B725
Open Apr–Sept: daily 9.30–6.30; Oct–Mar: Mon–Sat 9.30–4.30, Sun 2–4.30
Impressive castle, on a triangular site surrounded by a moat and most famous for being beseiged by Edward I in 1300. The gatehouse has two tall round towers pierced by many gunloops. It was reached by a drawbridge over the moat. The gatehouse has a vaulted basement, and a tall stair-tower was added in the late fifteenth century. The Nithsdale Lodging, which was built in the courtyard in 1638, is a fine Renaissance range with two large chambers on the first floor over barrel-vaulted cellars. One of the round towers, Murdoch's Tower, remains to its full height, but the other was demolished to its foundations. The curtain wall on this side was also demolished.

■88■ **CASTLE FRASER** ☎ 01330 833463
Sauchen, Inverurie, Aberdeenshire AB51 7LD
Off A944 16 miles W of Aberdeen
Open Good Fri–Easter Mon, May–June and Sept: daily 1.30–5.30; July and Aug 11–5.30; Oct: Sat and Sun 1.30–5.30
One of the grandest of the Scottish baronial tower houses. The elaborate Z-plan design was constructed between 1575 and 1635 and was the work of two families of master masons, Bell and Leiper. The upper storeys contain turrets, gables, chimneys, balustrades, decorative stonework and coats of arms set high on the walls. The castle has the air of a French château but is very much a Scottish building, constructed out of local granite as a reflection of family pride. The interior was remodelled in 1838, and decoration and furnishings of that period survive in a number of rooms. A formal garden has been re-created in the old walled garden.

■89■ CASTLE MENZIES   ☎ 01887 820982
Weem, Aberfeldy, Perthshire & Kinross PH15 2JD
1 mile from Aberfeldy on B846
Open Apr–mid-Oct: Mon–Sat 10.30–5, Sun 2–5 (last admission 4)
Z-plan tower house consisting of a central block with flanking towers at diagonally
opposite corners. Erected during the sixteenth century, it remained the seat of the
chief of the Menzies clan until 1918. There are indications that the upper storey
and roof were altered in 1577 when the sculptured dormers were added to
complete the building as it now stands. Additional apartments were built on to
the north side in the early eighteenth century, at which time considerable alterations were made to the interior and a new entrance was made in the south wall.

■90■ CAWDOR CASTLE   ☎ 01667 404615
Cawdor, Nairn, Highland IV12 5RD
S of Nairn on B9090 between Inverness and Nairn
Open May–mid-Oct: 10 –5.30 (last admission 5)
Massive fortress made up of fourteenth-century keep, which was fortified in the
fifteenth century, and impressive additions dating mainly from the seventeenth
century. There are lots of winding stairs, low doorways and ancient passageways in this castle, which is for ever associated with Shakespeare's *Macbeth*. The
design of the tower is typical of Scottish constructions, with basement and top
storey vaulted for fire-resistance and strength. It has thick walls, thin windows
and a staircase that could be hauled into the house if necessary. The castle has
very little decoration or frivolity in its design; it was here to serve a purpose.

■91■ CRAIGNETHAN CASTLE   ☎ 01555 860364
Lesmahagow, Lanarkshire ML11 9PL
4 miles WNW of Lanark off A72
Open daily: 9.30–6.30 (4.30 in Oct and Nov) exc Christmas and Boxing Day (closed
Thurs afternoon, Fri and Sun mornings in winter)
One of the earliest castles built to withstand artillery. A strong tower was surrounded by a curtain wall on three sides with a massive thick rampart protecting
the landward side. The ruined main tower is squat and rectangular, with a
corbelled-out parapet, open round corners and a machicolation over the entrance.
The entrance leads through a large lobby on the first floor to the hall and to a
turnpike stair by the guard-room. There were large flanking towers, only one of
which survives, and a thick rampart that has been completely destroyed. The
bases of another flanking tower and of the gatehouse survive on one side. The
outer courtyard consists of an enclosing wall with a gatehouse, a corner tower
and another tower incorporated into a seventeenth-century house.

■92■ CRATHES CASTLE   ☎ 01330 844525
By Banchory, Aberdeenshire AB31 5QJ
On A93, 3 miles E of Banchory
Open Apr–Oct: daily 11–5.30 (last admission 4.45)
The castle, built in the second half of the sixteenth century, is a typical Scottish
baronial tower house of the district and time, plain below but turreted in its
upper part. Crathes is best known for the decorative work of its interior, especially for its splendid painted ceilings, with their legendary figures, and for the
ribbed and carved ceiling of the Long Gallery, unique in Scotland for being of
oak. Crathes is one of the most beautiful and best-preserved sixteenth-century
castles in Scotland and has been lived in by the same family for over 350 years.

■93■ CRICHTON CASTLE ☎ 01875 320017
Crichton, Pathhead, Midlothian CH37 5QH
Off A68 2 miles SW of Pathhead
Open Apr–Sept: daily 9.30–6.30; Oct and Nov: Mon–Sat 9.30–4.30,
Sun 2–4.30

Crichton Castle

A large and sophisticated castle that consists of buildings from the fourteenth
to sixteenth centuries. The oldest part is a fourteenth-century keep, which originally had three storeys. The basement was vaulted and had a pit prison. A stair
led up to the hall and the entrance on the first floor, and another turnpike stair
led to the floors above. In the fifteenth century a new gatehouse was added,
and then further ranges enclosing the courtyard. A particularly impressive block
was added by the Earl of Bothwell between 1581 and 1591, which has a façade
of faceted stonework in an Italian style.

■94■ CULZEAN CASTLE AND COUNTRY PARK ☎ 01655 884455
Maybole, South Ayrshire KA19 8LE
12 miles S of Ayr on A719, 4 miles W of Maybole
Open Castle: Apr–Oct: daily 10.30–5.30. Country park all year: daily 9–sunset
Apart from some nineteenth-century alterations the castle as it is seen today is
the work of Robert Adam. It combines Georgian symmetry and romantic mock
fortification with some Italianate elements. Adam designed and built the castle
in three stages. The first was the conversion of the existing sixteenth-century
tower house into an elegant and comfortable mansion facing southwards. The
second involved the replacement of the old domestic buildings on the north
side with a wing of rooms along the rim of the cliff. These include a unique
round drawing-room with windows sheer above the sea. In the third stage, the
old courtyard which still survived between the new mansion and the clifftop
wing, became the site of the Oval Staircase.

■95■ DEAN CASTLE COUNTRY PARK ☎ 01563 574916
Kilmarnock, North Ayrshire 1KA 3XB
Signposted from A77 Kilmarnock bypass
Open Easter–Oct: daily 12–5; Nov–Mar: Sat and Sun 12–5. Park all year: dawn–dusk
Fine castle set within a 200-acre country park. It is made up of a fourteenth-
century (around 1360) keep and a fifteenth-century palace. With its 10-feet-thick

(3-metre-thick) walls, it was designed for defence rather than comfort. The ground floor has neither windows nor outside doors, and a ladder would have had to be used to reach the first-floor door. The palace was built in the 1460s and this was designed for comfort. Defence was not ignored in its construction, and it has a tower which has projecting battlements. The courtyard was protected by a high wall known in Scotland as a barmkin. The present gatehouse was built between 1935 and 1936 when the castle was restored. However, it is carefully copied from real sixteenth-century buildings and includes details like windows of half wooden shutters and half leaded glass. The overall design and the decorative gunloops were copied from the gatehouse built at Tolquhoun Castle, Aberdeenshire, in the 1580s.

■96■ DOUNE CASTLE ☎ 0131 668 8600
Castle Road, Doune, Stirling FK16 6EA
8 miles SE of Callender on A84
Open Apr–Sept: daily 9.30–6.30; Oct–Mar: Mon–Sat 9.30–4.30, Sun 2–4.30.
Check winter dates
Restored fourteenth-century courtyard castle with two strong towers linked by a lower range. These buildings form two sides of a courtyard; the other sides are enclosed by a high curtain wall. The larger gatehouse, or Lord's Tower, is rectangular in plan, with an arched entrance to the castle through the basement. It has a semicircular tower projecting at one corner and rises to five storeys. The tower has vaulted cellars in the basement and a fine vaulted hall on the first floor with a magnificent double fireplace and a gallery. The kitchen has an enormous arched fireplace, an oven and drains. Above this were more private chambers, including a suite used by Mary Queen of Scots.

■97■ DRUM CASTLE ☎ 01330 811204
Drumoak, Banchory, Aberdeenshire AB31 3EY
Off A93, 3 miles W of Peterculter, 8 miles E of Banchory
Open Easter–May: daily 1.30–5.30; Jun–Aug: daily 11–5.30; Sept: daily 1.30–5.30;
Oct: Sat and Sun 1.30–5.30. Gardens as castle: 10–6
The great square tower house is one of the oldest in Scotland. It is believed to have been built in 1286 by the royal mason, Richard Cementarius. The square keep, which is noteworthy for its unusually high battlements, has three vaulted storeys. The first, which was once the Great Hall, was converted into a library in about 1845. Above is a large upper hall, from which a wooden staircase allows access to the battlements. A brewhouse was added to the tower's north wall during the thirteenth century, and a very fine Jacobean mansion house was built on by the ninth laird in 1619. Later changes included the addition of a central door and steps to the south front of the mansion in about 1800, and the construction in 1875 of a door on the north front within the courtyard.

■98■ DRUMLANRIG CASTLE ☎ 01848 330248
Thornhill, Dumfries & Galloway DG3 4AQ
3 miles N of Thornhill off A76
Open May–Aug: Mon–Sat 11–4, Sun 12–4
Pink sandstone castle built between 1679 and 1691 by William Douglas and set on a hill (drum) at the end of a long (lang) ridge (rig). It is built around an open courtyard, with a circular staircase tower in each corner. On the outside there is a square tower at each of the corners. Drumlanrig is one of the first examples of Renaissance building in Scottish domestic architecture.

■99■ DUNVEGAN CASTLE ☎ 01470 521206
Macleod Estate Office, Dunvegan House, Dunvegan, Isle of Skye IV55 8WF
25 miles from Portree on A850
Open mid-Mar–Oct: daily 10–5.30; Nov–mid-Mar: daily 11–4
Fortress stronghold set on a rock on the shores of the sea loch of Dunvegan in
north-west Skye. For nearly 800 years Dunvegan Castle has been the home of
the chiefs of clan MacLeod. The castle is unique in Scotland, the same family in
unbroken succession having made their home in it under the same roof since
the beginnings of recorded history. Today the castle has a unified design with
Victorian dummy pepperpots and defensive battlements running the whole
length of the roofline. Underneath this 'romantic restoration' there remains a
series of complete buildings, each of a different date. These include parts of
Leod's original fort, dating from around 1200, and the fourteenth-century keep.
The Fairy Tower is a typical example of a traditional Scottish castle tower with a
steeply pitched roof set within its battlements. Other buildings date from the
seventeenth and eighteenth centuries. Still in frequent use today by the family,
and beautifully well kept, are the dining-room and library.

■100■ EDINBURGH CASTLE ☎ 0131 225 9846
Castle Hill, Edinburgh EH1 2NG
In Old Town at top of Royal Mile
Open Apr–Sept: daily 9.30–6; Oct–Mar: daily 9.30–5
(last admission ¼ hour before closing)

Huge fortress which dominates Edinburgh's skyline. Edinburgh Castle stands on
the precipitous 435-feet- (133-metre)-high crag of Castle Rock, the core of an
extinct volcano, which is a formidable natural defence. The oldest building
within the castle grounds is the twelfth-century St Margaret's Chapel on the
rock's summit, but most of the present castle evolved later during its stormy
history of sieges and wars. The most important part of James IV's sixteenth-
century Great Hall to survive is its hammerbeam roof, which looks like an
upturned ship's hull. During James IV's reign this was the main banqueting
chamber. Following Cromwell's invasion of Scotland in 1650, the castle became
a garrison fortress and much of its look today reflects this. After the restoration
of the monarchy in 1660, the castle continued to develop as a garrison, and new
army buildings began to spread out from the Upper Ward. There were further
extensive alterations in Victorian times, and building work, carefully designed to
blend with the existing structure, continued until well into the twentieth century.

■101■ EDZELL CASTLE ☎ 01356 648631
Edzell, By Brechin, Angus DD9 7UE
6 miles N of Brechin on B966
Open Mar–Sept: daily 9.30–6.30; Oct–Mar: Mon–Sat 9.30–4.30, Sun 2–4. Check winter
dates (last admission ½ hour before closing)
Sixteenth-century tower house, later enlarged and extended with ranges
around a courtyard. The L-plan tower, at one corner of the main courtyard,
replaced an older castle. It rises to four storeys and a garret, and has open
rounds at all corners and small projecting half-rounds in the middle of each
wall. The entrance, reached through an arched doorway from the courtyard,
leads to the vaulted basement. An L-shaped gabled range of three storeys was
added in the sixteenth century. This is now in ruins, but it once contained
comfortable chambers. The large garden is surrounded by a wall with many
interesting carvings.

■102■ **FORT GEORGE** ☎ 01667 462777
Ardersier, Inverness, Invernesshire IV1 2TD
6 miles W of Nairn off A96 near Ardersier; nearest rail station is Nairn, buses run
from Inverness
Open Apr–Sept: daily 9.30–6.30; Oct–Mar: Mon–Sat 9.30–4.30, Sun 2–4.30
(last admission ¼ hour before closing)
Built on a barren spit of land jutting into the Moray Firth, Fort George is one
of Europe's mightiest artillery fortifications. The fort was built by the
Hanoverian King George II after the defeat of Bonnie Prince Charlie and his
Jacobite army at Culloden as the ultimate defence against any further unrest.
The fort's elaborate eighteenth-century bastioned defences and original
barracks, guard-rooms, artillery blocks, workshops, ordnance stores, provision
stores and chapel all survive intact. With a perimeter of almost a mile
(1.6 kilometres) Fort George covers an area of 42 acres (17 hectares). Despite
taking twenty-one years to complete and costing £1 billion at today's prices,
Fort George never saw active service. The historical barrack-rooms have been
reconstructed to show what living conditions would have been like a century
after the fort's completion.

■103■ **FYVIE CASTLE** ☎ 01651 891266
Fyvie, Turriff, Aberdeenshire AB53 8JS
Off A947, 8 miles S of Turriff
Open Easter, May–Jun and Sept–Oct: daily 1.30–5.30; July–Aug: daily 11–5.30; Oct: Sat
and Sun 1.30–5.30
Large L-plan tower house with long wings. The main block is known as the
Seaton Tower, and three large towers, the Preston, Meldrum and Gordon
towers, each refer to the families who lived in them. The building is adorned
with fine corbelling, turrets, steep roofs and dormer windows. The oldest part
dates from the thirteenth century, and the castle is an excellent example of the
Scottish baronial style of architecture. The interior was created by the first
Lord of Leith, and Fyvie reflects the opulence of the Edwardian era. The
grounds were designed as landscaped parkland at the beginning of the
eighteenth century.

■104■ **GLAMIS CASTLE** ☎ 01307 840393
Estates Office, Glamis, Forfar, Angus DD8 1RJ
5 miles W of Forfar on A94
Open Apr–mid-Nov: daily 10.30–5.30 (10 in July and Aug, 4 last two weeks in Nov;
last admission 4.45)
Turreted and battlemented castle, the family home of the Earls of Strathmore
and the childhood home of the Queen Mother. The present castle dates from
the fifteenth century, although there is known to have been a building here
for many centuries. Duncan's Hall is one of the oldest parts, a reminder of the
death of King Duncan in Shakespeare's *Macbeth*. Other notable rooms are
the chapel, with its painted panels, and the drawing-room. There are also fine
collections of china, pictures, tapestries and furniture. In the late seventeenth
century the castle had outer defences of walls and towers enclosing formal
parterres. These were swept away in 1772–5 with the intention of remodelling
the park in the fashion of Capability Brown. The result is that the grounds
resemble the surroundings of an English Palladian mansion, contrasting
strongly with the rugged, ancient castle which dominates the park.

Glamis Castle

■105■ **HUNTINGTOWER CASTLE** ☎ 01738 627231
Huntingtower, By Perth, Perthshire & Kinross PH1 3JL
3 miles NW of Perth off A85
Open Apr–Sept: daily 9.30–6.30; Oct–Mar: Mon–Sat 9.30–4.30, Sun 2–4.30. Check winter dates
Well-preserved castle consisting of three phases of building. The oldest part is a fifteenth-century rectangular keep which has three storeys and a garret, with open rounds at the angles. Nearby, but not touching, was built a sixteenth-century L-plan tower house, consisting of a main block of four storeys and a wing rising a storey higher. Towards the end of the sixteenth century, a connecting range of three storeys was built, containing a stair for both the keep and the tower. The basement of the keep is vaulted, and the entrance was at first-floor level reached by external stairs. Some of the rooms have fine painted ceilings, mural paintings and plasterwork, as well as decorative beams in the hall.

■106■ **HUNTLY CASTLE** ☎ 01466 793191
Huntly, Aberdeenshire AB54 5BP
In Huntly on A96
Open Apr–Sept: daily 9.30–6.30; Oct–Mar: Mon–Sat 9.30–4.30, Sun 2–4.30. Check winter dates
Magnificent ruin of a mainly sixteenth- and seventeenth-century castle. The fifteenth-century rectangular keep has a large round tower at one end and a smaller, circular tower at the opposite corner. The upper storey of the keep was remodelled in the late sixteenth century with decorative stonework and new windows. A large adjoining courtyard had ranges of buildings on two sides. From the entrance, a straight stair leads down to the vaulted basement. The floor above is also vaulted and contains two cellars and a kitchen with a private chamber. The hall, on the main first floor, was a fine chamber but was later subdivided and the fireplace removed.

■107■ INVERARAY CASTLE ☎ 01499 302203
Inveraray, Argyll & Bute PA32 8XE
Close to A83
Open Apr–June and Sept–Oct: Sat–Thur 10–1 and 2–5.45, Sun 1–5.45; July and Aug:
Mon–Sat 10–5.45, Sun 1–5.45 (last admission ¼ hour before closing)
Classical mansion with corner towers and turrets. The present building designed
by Roger Morris and Robert Mylne in the style of a castle, was erected between
1741 and 1785 to replace a traditional fortified keep, and it marks the start of
more settled times in the country. On display are the famous Armoury Collection,
French tapestries and fine examples of Scottish and European furniture.

■108■ KELLIE CASTLE ☎ 01333 720271
By Pittenweem, Fife KY10 2RF
On B9171, 3 miles NW of Pittenweem
Open Easter and May–Sept: daily 1.30–5.30; Oct: Sat and Sun 1.30–5.30 (last admission
4.45). Gardens: all year 9.30–dusk
Although called a castle, Kellie is in fact a noteworthy example of lowland
Scottish domestic architecture. The house seen today was completed in about
1606, the last stage in development from a single tower dating from around
1360. The interior is particularly noteworthy for its painted panelling and plas-
terwork ceilings and for the ceiling painting in the Vine Room. A mural by
Phoebe Anna Traquair has recently been uncovered.

■109■ LOCHLEVEN CASTLE ☎ 0131 668 8800
By Kinross, Perthshire & Kinross KY13 7AR
On island in Loch Leven, accessible by boat from Kinross, off M90
Open Apr–Sept: Mon–Sat 9.30–6.30, Sun 2–6.30 (last admission 6)
Small fifteenth-century rectangular keep at one corner of a fourteenth-century
courtyard. The five-storey keep has a corbelled parapet. The courtyard has a
small round tower, with gunloops at one corner; the entrance is through an
arched gateway. The courtyard enclosed ranges of buildings, including a hall
and kitchen, but these are now in a ruinous state. The original entrance was at
second-floor level and leads to the hall through a hooded arch. The chamber
above the hall has an oratory with an altar shelf.

■110■ NEIDPATH CASTLE ☎ 01721 720333
Peebles, Borders EH45 8NW
1 mile W of Peebles on A72
Open Apr–Sept: Mon–Sat 11–5, Sun 1–5 (last admission 4.40)
Fourteenth-century stronghold, with walls 11 feet (3.3 metres) thick, occupying
a spectacular position on the River Tweed. The castle was converted into a
tower house in the seventeenth century. It contains a pit prison and a rock-hewn
well, Queen Mary's room, where Mary Queen of Scots stayed, and Laigh Hall,
with displays of tartan. The Great Hall has batiks depicting the 'Life of Mary
Queen of Scots'. Fine views from the parapets. The castle is set in a beautiful
wooded gorge of the River Tweed.

■111■ STIRLING CASTLE ☎ 01786 450000
Upper Castle Hill, Stirling FK8 1EJ
At the head of Stirling's old town
Open Apr–Sept: daily 9.30–6.30; Oct–Mar: 9.30–5 (last admission ¼ hour before closing)
Perhaps the grandest of all Scottish castles. Sitting on top of a rock 250 feet

(76 metres) high, Stirling Castle occupies a strategic position which has ensured it has always played an important part in Scottish history. It is a courtyard castle dating in part from the twelfth century, but much of what remains today is from the fifteenth and sixteenth centuries. It is entered through the eighteenth-century outer defences and sixteenth-century walls, of which the Prince's Tower and gatehouse survive. The gatehouse leads to the Lower Square, which is bordered on one side by the King's Old Building and on the other by the gable of the Great Hall. The King's Old Building contained royal chambers over a vaulted basement which were reached by a turnpike stair. A road leads between this and the hall to the Upper Square, which includes the Chapel Royal and the Great Hall built during the reign of James IV.

■112■ THIRLESTANE CASTLE ☎ 01578 722430
Lauder, Borders TD2 6RU
Off A68 in Lauder
Open Easter and mid-Apr–Oct: 11–5 (last admission 4.15)
The castle's main keep was built in 1590 by the Maitland family, the Earls of Lauderdale, who lived in the castle from the twelfth century. Some splendid plasterwork ceilings may be seen in the seventeenth-century state rooms. Former nurseries now house a sizable collection of antique toys and dolls, while in the south wing there are several interesting displays illustrating Borders life.

🏰 NORTHERN IRELAND **MAP 9**

■113■ CARRICKFERGUS CASTLE ☎ 028 9335 1273
Marine Highway, Carrickfergus, Co. Antrim BT38 7BG
On the N shore of Belfast Lough, 11 miles from Belfast via M2
Open Apr–Oct: Mon–Sat 10–6, Sun 2–6 (12 in Jun–Aug); Nov–Mar: Mon–Sat 10–4, Sun 2–4 (last admission ½ hour before closing)
Well-preserved medieval castle, situated on a rocky headland overlooking Belfast Lough. The main part of the castle was built by John de Courcy in the late twelfth century and includes the inner ward, small bailey and massive four-storey keep 90 feet (27 metres) high. Two new curtain walls were added in the thirteenth century: the first, in around 1210, so that the approach over the rock could be protected as well as the eastern approach over the sand, which was exposed at low tide, the second added to enclose the remainder of the promontory to form an outer ward, thus doubling the area of the castle. In the sixteenth and seventeenth century, improvements were made to accommodate artillery gun ports and embrasures for cannons.

■114■ ENNISKILLEN CASTLE ☎ 028 6632 5000
Castle Barracks, Enniskillen, Co. Fermanagh BT74 7HL
24 miles SW Omagh on A32
Open May–Sept: Mon and Sat (and Sun in July and Aug) 2–5, Tues–Fri and Bank Hols 10–5; Oct–Apr: Mon 2–5, Tues–Fri 10–5
Set on the banks of the River Erne, the castle was home to the Gaelic Maguire chieftains back in the fifteenth century. In the middle of the vast array of buildings is the main castle. To the south of the main castle is the watergate, with its two eye-catching turrets. The name watergate is a little misleading as there was never a gateway there. The rectangular three-storey keep in the centre of the castle complex incorporates the battered base of the Maguire Tower House.

CHAPTER

2

HOUSES AND PALACES

One of my earliest adventures into building was when I still lived at home with my mum and dad. I lived in a row of terraced houses similar to those in *Coronation Street* and we had a chimney stack which had four pots on it. Only one of these pots was actually in use, and that was the one for the back kitchen fire and the back boiler. The other three just dripped water down the walls of our bedrooms – and next door's as well. So good old Fred, who was newly trained as a joiner and a roof mender, among other things, decided that he would take the old chimney stack down and build a new one for his mother. I set off with brand-new Accrington bricks accompanied by various comments, like 'What's he doing?' because it was a bit unusual to see a seventeen-year-old lad knock his mother's chimney down and build another one.

I didn't have any real design or plans for it, but as I built it I kept getting another idea about what I wanted it to look like, and when it was completed it turned out to be a most handsome thing. It has stood there now for some forty years. When my mother died, my brother and I sold the house. The people who live in it now decided they wanted to knock the chimney down, but the local authority put a preservation order on it. So it is still there to this day, and looking just as good as the day that I built it.

Ever since I was a lad, then, I've been interested in building and building techniques and in that great range of skills that go into building a house. They're skills that have been around for a long time – since way back into the Middle Ages and even before that. Ightham Mote is one of the oldest and loveliest of medieval manor houses to have survived in England. It was never a grand place, and it has stood largely unchanged for over 650 years. One of the reasons for this is that its successive owners were people like squires, sheriffs and Members of Parliament, and they were all fairly indifferent to

The fine Elizabethan town house, Plas Mawr, in Conwy, North Wales

changes in fashion, so they expanded the house as their needs dictated, making it more comfortable but retaining the basic shape and style of the buildings. When they did add to them, it was always in a manner that was sympathetic to the medieval origins of the house. The history of the house is quite complicated, but it has become possible in recent years to trace it in much greater and more reliable detail because the National Trust, in the course of repairs that have been carried out, has had to take sections apart and, in doing this, they've unearthed some clues about its construction.

A moat surrounds all four wings of the house, and all of its walls drop straight down to the waters of the moat. Within these four wings there is a lovely open courtyard. When you first look at it, the house looks as though it was all built at the same time, but it's actually the product of six centuries of development. The main entrance to the house is on the west front and, with its central gatehouse tower, it's got a bit of a castellated appearance. A manor of a reasonable size like this required some sort of formal entrance which also did duty to guard the main approach.

From the outside the east front is the most complex of the four fronts because it was constructed and reconstructed at many different periods, and the builders didn't think twice about breaking through earlier walls to light a room or to insert a bank of chimneys, or build upwards into a third storey or outwards on to ledges that had been left vacant. All this was done in what appears to be a fairly haphazard sort of way, without the help of any architect's drawings. The north front is more regular because a lot of it was constructed all at the same time in about 1480. The south front, which was built in the late fifteenth or early sixteenth century, is the most photographed of all the fronts because it looks the most genuine. But looks can be deceptive, and its attractiveness is due partly to a twentieth-century fake.

What makes Ightham Mote very interesting at the moment is the restoration work that is being done there. It is the largest conservation project ever undertaken by the National Trust on a building of this age, and right from the start the Trust decided to retain as much as it could of the original material, where it hadn't decayed beyond redemption. When it did have to provide new stone for the sections that were most badly weathered, care was taken to avoid excessive smoothness in the finished appearance and, when it was repairing the interior surface of the walls for replastering, traditional laths were used to follow the undulations of the timber frame.

Where it was necessary to cut away sections of the frame where the wood had been eaten away by moisture, woodworm or dry rot, the new oak was fitted to the old by imitating medieval carpentry joints. The window glass, some of which has survived since the fifteenth century, has all been set in new strips of lead, and wherever possible the metal window bars that support the glass were repaired and treated against rust, rather than renewed. The work will be going on until at least 2002 and it gives a very good opportunity to find out how a medieval house was built.

Ightham Mote is quite a modest house. At the other end of the scale, Hampton Court is the biggest and most impressive palace of Tudor England. The first buildings at Hampton Court belonged to the Knights Hospitalers of St John of Jerusalem, but in 1514 a ninety-nine-year lease on the estate was taken by Thomas Wolsey, Archbishop of York, and Chief Minister to Henry VIII. By 1515 Wolsey had been appointed both a cardinal and Lord Chancellor of England, and he began a building programme that turned his new country seat into a home that was fit for a man of his status. One of

Plenty of chimneys to keep me busy at Hampton Court Palace

the best surviving parts of Wolsey's Hampton Court is the vast outer Base Court that was built to house his guests. The main shape of the court, which had forty guest lodgings arranged around the court-yard, still remains.

Throughout the 1520s, Wolsey used his residence for pleasure and for affairs of state, but by 1528 he had fallen out of favour with the king because he couldn't secure the Pope's consent to Henry's divorce from Catherine of Aragon. He was forced to hand over Hampton Court to the king, and within six months Henry began his own building programme. In just ten years Henry VIII spent more than £62,000 rebuilding and extending Hampton Court. This was a vast sum at the time, equivalent to approximately £18 million today.

By the time the palace was finished in about 1540, it was one of the most modern sophisticated and magnificent palaces in England, complete with real tennis courts, bowling alleys, pleasure gardens for recreation, a hunting park of more than a thousand acres (over 400 hectares), kitchens covering 36,000 square feet (3,345 square metres), a fine chapel, a vast dining-room, a Great Hall, and multiple garderobes or toilets, which could sit twenty-eight people at a time.

Hampton Court remained much as it was in Henry's day until William III came to the throne in 1689. William then commissioned Sir Christopher Wren to rebuild Hampton Court. William liked the site and the good hunting, but he thought, by this time, that the buildings needed replacing if they were to provide a suitable substi-tute for Whitehall Palace, which was his principal residence. Wren's original plan was to demolish the entire Tudor palace, except the Great Hall, which he intended to keep as the centre of the new northern approach. Neither the time nor the money proved to be available for this ambitious plan, and Wren had to be content with rebuilding the king's and queen's main apartments, on the south-east side of the palace, on the site of the old Tudor lodgings. What we see today is largely the way the palace would have looked after William's alterations and extensions had been completed. Hampton Court is one of our grandest palaces, a place that really was fit for a king.

If you want to see the way that lesser mortals used to live, Culross in Fife is a perfectly preserved example of a seventeenth-century Scottish burgh with little houses, roofed with red pantiles, lining narrow cobbled streets. The height of the burgh's prosperity was reached during the life of one man, Sir George Bruce, who was granted the lease on collieries around Culross in 1575. Between then and his death fifty years later, Bruce pioneered many innovations in coal-mining and built himself a very successful business. Culross Palace, which was built for him, is a unique example of a merchant's house of the early seventeenth century. The word 'palace' isn't really right for it because the house is not grand enough to be a palace, and it was certainly never a royal residence. Original title deeds refer to the building as the great lodging, and it certainly would have been the most impressive house in the area at the time, with space for a courtyard, stableblock and garden.

Visiting Culross, in Fife

The decline of Culross's prosperity was a very gradual process that took place over the next two centuries, and as a result there was very little change. The palace was lived in until the middle of the nineteenth century, then it fell into neglect. In 1932 it was bought for £700 by the National Trust for Scotland, and by the outbreak of the Second World War the Trust had bought over twenty other properties in Culross. Their condition can be judged from their cost: nine of the buildings were bought for £168. After the war the work of restoration continued, and Culross began to emerge in its role as one of Scotland's showplaces.

The palace itself is the main attraction. Its ornate dormer windows, crow step gables and pantiled roofs create a very strong impression of the seventeenth century. One of the features of the house is the splendid painted decoration of some of the rooms. At the time the palace was built, wall-coverings were expensive and painted wood panelling provided a less costly method of decoration. It was a style that was typical in Scandinavia and the Low Countries, which had extensive trade with Scotland in the sixteenth and seventeenth centuries. Another feature of the house is its barrel-vaulted ceilings: the way in which these were constructed can be seen because there's a place where the woodwork inside the roof trusses is all visible. Living in this house must have been a bit draughty, though, because they had glass only in the top half of the windows; the bottom half was shuttered and when daylight arrived they opened the shutters.

Outside the palace the burgh's present appearance is the result of restoration work by the Trust aimed at achieving modern living standards in the houses while preserving the characteristic architecture of the place. If you want to get a feel for what a small town would have been like in olden days, this small royal burgh on the north shore of the Forth provides a good view of Scottish domestic life in the sixteenth and seventeenth century when Culross was a thriving community.

Not far from Culross is one of Scotland's most historical palaces. Falkland Palace was the hunting palace of the Stuart dynasty, but it was damaged by fire while occupied by Cromwell's troops and allowed to fall into ruin. In 1887 the third Marquess of Bute, a great Victorian patron of the arts, rebuilt and restored much of the palace. In his Victorian restoration work, Lord Bute inserted a course of red sandstone to indicate where his reconstruction work began, and to leave no doubt as to the identity of the original masonry. All the Victorian restoration work was done in a way that was sympathetic to the style created by James V when he transformed the original medieval castle of Falkland into an elegant and sophisticated Renaissance palace. Lord Bute's restoration work on the chapel, for example, reflects the magnificence of early-seventeenth-century Scottish royal interiors.

The part of Falkland Palace that I like best of all are those bits that the Marquess of Bute restored when he arrived on the scene. Some of the work he did is very splendid. There is some lovely oak panelling, beautiful doors and carvings reputedly of his family and children. He must have been a very vain man, because everything has the letter 'B' on it, and a bit of a dandy as well, because in his study there are lots of paintings of him modelling suits. Falkland Palace is well worth a visit to look at the woodwork if, like me, you like joinery.

Whether building magnificent new country houses or just restoring older houses and castles, the nineteenth century was a time of great activity. The Industrial Revolution brought a great surge in house-building as wealthy industrialists put their wealth into great country houses. Cragside in Northumberland is the creation of the first Lord Armstrong; innovator, engineer and gunmaker. Built on a bare and rugged hillside near Rothbury in Coquetdale, it was the most remarkable house of its day. In the 1880s it had hot and cold running water, central heating, fire alarms, telephones, a hydraulic passenger lift and, most remarkable of all, it was the first house in the world to be lit by hydroelectricity. It is not surprising that it was described in its day as the 'palace of a modern magician'. The house began as a comparatively small one. It was built between 1863 and 1866 for Sir William Armstrong, as he then was, as a weekend retreat to get him away from his armaments and engineering business in Newcastle. The architect of the original house is unknown, but in 1869 Armstrong called in Norman Shaw to turn Cragside into a proper country mansion.

At first Armstrong wanted Shaw only to add to the house's existing north end, and not to improve or replace it, but gradually Shaw gave himself a bit more scope to bring in his own ideas, and by the gradual additions that he made over the next fifteen years the house came to assume the wild, picturesque outline that it has today. Even so, in all the time that he worked at Cragside, Shaw was never given the free hand that he really wanted. Perhaps the great industrialist's independence and the fact that his brief was to extend an existing house prevented the creation of the unified architectural masterpiece that Shaw had in mind for the house. Armstrong had a very hands-on approach, and the work was done not by a building contractor but by local masons working under the direct supervision of Armstrong.

But it is as much for the technology as its architecture that Cragside is distinguished. Armstrong used his hydraulically powered machines at Cragside to help with domestic chores and also to impress prospective customers and visiting dignitaries. The whole place was really his shop window. Many of his installations survive and can be seen on the 'Power Circuit', a circular walk through the house and grounds.

William Henry Fox Talbot was another great nineteenth-century innovator. It was his discoveries that formed the basis of all modern photography. His family home, like many country houses, started its life as a religious institution, which was acquired by a wealthy family at the time of the Dissolution of the Monasteries and turned into a Tudor mansion. At Lacock Abbey we see how, in houses such as this, the original features of the abbey, like the cloisters, were incorporated into the design of the house. Lacock has the cloisters and several rooms of the Augustinian nunnery that was founded in the thirteenth century. The Tudor house has an unusual octagonal tower and courtyard of domestic buildings as well as additions from the eighteenth and nineteenth centuries including a Gothic hall.

Before the Reformation there were usually anything from fifteen to twenty-five nuns at Lacock. After Henry VIII took it over in

Lacock Abbey, Chippenham, Wiltshire

1539, he sold it to a courtier, William Sharrington. Courtiers like Sharrington were in a good position to buy the monastic buildings that had been appropriated by Henry; but how was he going to be able to live there? The abbey buildings that he had bought consisted of a church and large rooms for the nuns. They were cold and uncomfortable, and it certainly wasn't the kind of place where a wealthy courtier would want to live. This was a problem that was arising all over the country, as buyers tried to think of ways of making use of old monastic buildings that had been taken over by Henry and sold to them. At some places, like Buckland Abbey, the church itself was converted into a house with the addition of walls, ceilings and floors. William Sharrington didn't do this. Instead he demolished the church, converted the first floor-rooms of the nunnery, then built a tower and a stable court. It was this building that put Sharrington's mark on Lacock, turning it into a Tudor building stuck on to a medieval church building. But not all the medieval monasteries taken over by Henry VIII were turned into houses, as we shall see in Chapter Three when we look at places of worship.

PLACES TO VISIT

■115■ BUCKLAND ABBEY ☎ 01822 853607
Buckland Abbey, Yelverton, Devon PL20 6EY
Signposted from A386 S of Tavistock
Open Apr–Oct: daily exc Thurs 10.30–5:30; Nov–Mar: Sat and Sun 2–5
Although now better known as the home of Sir Francis Drake, Buckland was originally a small but influential Cistercian monastery. Built in the thirteenth century, it was the last of seventy-six medieval Cistercian abbeys to be built in England and Wales. The cavernous Great Barn still stands as a reminder of Cistercian farming activity. The abbey metamorphosed from a medieval monastery into a Tudor home. At Buckland you can see Drake memorabilia, including his famous drum and standards, and examples of Tudor plasterwork can be seen in the Great Hall and a newly decorated plasterwork ceiling in the Drake Chamber.

■116■ CASTLE DROGO ☎ 01647 433306
Drewsteignton, Exeter, Devon EX6 6PB
5 miles S of A30 Exeter to Okehampton road, via Crockernwell
Open Easter or Apr–Oct: Sat–Thurs 11–5.30 (last admission 5)
This granite castle, built between 1910 and 1930 for the self-made millionaire Julius Drewe, is the work of the architect Edwin Lutyens. Drewe had traced his ancestry to a twelfth-century Norman baron, Drogo de Teign, and this provided the inspiration for Lutyens's unique design, which combines the austerity of a medieval castle with the comfort of a family home. The interior was intended for comfortable and elegant living, with an interesting kitchen and scullery and elaborately appointed bathrooms. The castle is complemented by formal gardens on three levels which Lutyens also helped create.

■117■ COMPTON CASTLE ☎ 01803 875740
Compton, Marldon, Devon TQ3 1TA
At Compton, 1 mile N of Marldon off A380
Open Apr–Oct: Mon, Wed and Thurs 10–12.15 and 2–5
The two portcullised entrances, handsome battlements and angular towers on the north front give Compton Castle an almost fairy-tale appearance. It was built in three distinct periods (the early fourteenth, fifteenth and sixteenth centuries) and remained in the Gilbert family for 600 years. The house is surrounded by a massive wall 24 feet (7 metres) high, and the towers have interior shafts that provided an early if rudimentary form of sanitation. The reconstructed hall is full of Gilbert mementoes, and the old kitchen, probably built in around 1520, has an open fireplace which extends for its full width. A magnificently built eighteenth-century barn of limestone and thatch stands beside the house.

■118■ CORSHAM COURT ☎ 01249 701610
Corsham, Wiltshire SN13 0BZ
4 miles W of Chippenham off A4
Open mid-Mar–Sept: Tues–Sun and Bank Hol Mons 11–5; Oct–mid-Mar exc Dec: Sat and Sun 2–4.30. Admission for groups outside these hours by arrangement
Elizabethan house dating from the late sixteenth century. It was bought by Paul

Methuen in the mid-eighteenth century to house a collection of sixteenth-
and seventeenth-century Italian and Flemish paintings and statuary. In the
mid-eighteenth century the house was enlarged and received a second collection (purchased in Florence) in the mid-nineteenth century. The architects
involved in the alterations to the house and the park were Capability Brown in
the 1760s, John Nash in 1800 and Thomas Bellamy between 1845 and 1849.
Brown set the style: he rebuilt the gateway but retained the Elizabethan stables,
riding school and the gabled stone front, and he doubled the gabled wings at
either end. Inside, he designed the east wing as state room picture galleries.
Nash's work has now largely disappeared, but Bellamy's can still be seen, notably
in the hall and staircase. The state rooms, including the music room and dining-
room, provide the setting for the outstanding collection of over 150 paintings,
statuary, bronzes and furniture. The gardens, designed not only by Capability
Brown but also by Repton, contain herbaceous borders, secluded lawns, a rose
garden, stone bathhouse and the Bradford Porch.

■119■ **COTEHELE** ☎ 01579 351346
St Dominick, Saltash, Cornwall PL12 6TA
S of A390 between Callington and Tavistock
Open Apr–Oct: Sat–Thurs 11–5 (4.30 in Oct). Garden: 11–5. Mill: as House plus Fri 1–5
Remarkable early-Tudor mansion house that has hardly changed in 300 years.
Built between 1485 and 1627 in granite and slatestone around three courts,
on the foundations of an earlier house, it contains some Cromwellian armour,
fine furniture and tapestries. Charles I is said to have slept in the Jacobean
Tower in the north-west corner of the building; and in the South Room, one of
the bedrooms, there are squints which enabled the occupants to see what was
happening in the hall and chapel below. The impressive medieval hall is 40 feet
(12 metres) long, and the late fifteenth-century chapel has a barrel-vaulted
ceiling with oak ribbing and a fine carved oak screen. In the grounds there is a
medieval barn, and alongside the path leading to Cotehele Quay is an old dovecote shaped like a giant beehive. The gardens have terraces and several
attractive eighteenth- and nineteenth-century buildings.

■120■ **FORDE ABBEY** ☎ 01460 221290/220231
Forde Abbey, Chard, Somerset TA20 4LU
From A358 and B3167 S of Chard follow signs for Forde Abbey
Open Apr–Oct: Wed, Sun and Bank Hols 1–4.30; also Thurs in May–Aug. Gardens same as
House: 10–4.30
Forde Abbey started its life as a twelfth-century Cistercian monastery and was
reconstructed in the perpendicular style by the last abbot. In the mid-seven-
teenth century, Edmund Prideaux, attorney-general to Oliver Cromwell bought
the abbey and began changing it into a 'palazzo' – for which its monastic layout
was particularly well suited. Prideaux's classical additions, which are seen at their
best in the Saloon, blend remarkably well with the earlier monastic buildings.

■121■ **KINGSTON LACY HOUSE** ☎ 01202 883402
Wimborne Minster, Dorset BH21 4EA
On B3082 1 mile NW of Wimborne
Open Mar–Oct: Sat–Wed 12–5.30; Nov and Dec: Fri–Sun 11–4. Grounds: daily 11–6
Sir Roger Pratt designed this magnificent house in the seventeenth century for
Sir Ralph Bankes. Originally it was surrounded by formal gardens, then in the
eighteenth century the park was landscaped. Sir Charles Barry altered the

house in the nineteenth century, encasing the original brick exterior in stone. Barry's fine marble staircase is a particularly impressive feature of the house. Splendid interior decoration, much of which was acquired or commissioned in Italy. Excellent collection of paintings including works by Titian, Rubens, Murillo and Jan Brueghel the Elder. The Golden Room or Spanish Picture Room is the most dramatic room in the house and is Kingston Lacy's best-known room. It is very heavy in style, with walls that are hung in gilded leather.

122 KNIGHTSHAYES COURT ☎ 01884 254665

Tiverton, Devon EX16 7RQ
2 miles N of Tiverton off A396
Open Mar–Oct: Sat–Thurs 11–5.30 (4.30 in Oct)
One of the many large country houses built by the Victorians in the boom years of agricultural and industrial development between the 1860s and early 1870s. Its architect, William Burges, was primarily a designer and a builder of churches. As a very young man he became interested in Gothic architecture, which was to become his lifelong obsession. As a Gothic revivalist architect, Burges chose to create an extravagant imitation of a medieval vaulted hall. As in great medieval houses, the hall is preceded by a screens passage made of teak and partly glazed. Many rooms are open to the public, displaying paintings and furnishings, and the fine garden features a paved garden, an azalea dell, kitchen garden (currently being restored) and the Douglas Fir Walk.

123 LACOCK ABBEY ☎ 01249 730227

Lacock, Chippenham, Wiltshire SN15 2LG
3 miles S of Chippenham, just E of A350
Open Abbey Mar–Oct: Wed–Sun 1–5.30. Grounds, cloisters and museum of photography Mar–Oct: daily 11–5.30
Interesting amalgamation of medieval nunnery and Tudor house with eighteenth-century Gothic additions. Lacock Abbey was founded in 1232 for the Augustinian canonesses and taken over by Henry VIII at the Dissolution of the Monasteries. It was sold to Sir William Sharrington, who demolished the church but incorporated the fine thirteenth-century cloisters and several rooms of the nunnery into his new house. These are still largely intact, and can be viewed along with the unusual octagonal tower and the courtyard of domestic buildings that make up the fine Tudor part of the house. The hall and dining-room were altered in the 1750s, contributing much to the house's present Gothic appearance. It was here that William Henry Fox Talbot (1800–77) made important discoveries that are the basis of modern photography.

124 LANHYDROCK ☎ 01208 73320

Lanhydrock, Bodmin, Cornwall PL30 5AD
2½ miles SE of Bodmin, follow signposts from A30 or A38
Open Apr–Oct: Tues–Sun and Bank Hol Mons 11–5.30. Gardens all year: daily 10–dusk
Built by the Robartes family in the seventeenth century, Lanhydrock was almost entirely destroyed by fire in 1881, leaving only the gatehouse and the Long Gallery, with its extraordinary plasterwork ceiling depicting scenes from the Old Testament. It was rebuilt by the second Baron Robartes, who retained the outward appearance using local granite in a neo-Jacobean style. Internally, the house was modernised to late-nineteenth-century style. Today visitors can see forty-nine rooms, from servants' rooms to the grandeur of the dining-room, all reflecting Victorian life.

■125■ LONGLEAT ☎ 01985 844400
Longleat, Warminster, Wiltshire BA12 7NW
Entrance on A362 Warminster–Frome
Open House Apr–Oct: daily 10–6; Nov–Mar: daily 10–4. Safari Park open Apr–Oct: daily 10–5. Other attractions Apr–Oct: 11–5.30
Majestic Elizabethan house, built for Sir John Thynne between 1559 and 1580 and decorated in the Italian Renaissance style in the late nineteenth century. It was built using the then newly popular Italian style, and it breaks with older tradition in the regularity of its plan and the uniformity of its four fronts. Inside, only the Great Hall, with its stone floor and hammerbeam roof, belong to Sir John's time. The corridors and the main staircase date from alterations made between 1801 and 1811. The Italianate decoration and matching furnishings of many of the rooms, including the former Long Gallery, are the work of Italian craftsmen who were employed by the fourth Marquess of Bath in the 1870s. In the eighteenth century Capability Brown was employed to lay out the formal gardens, orangery and terraces. The sixth Marquess of Bath has turned the inner section of his estate into a wildlife park.

■126■ MOMPESSON HOUSE ☎ 01722 335659
The Close, Salisbury, Wiltshire SP1 2EL
On N side of Choristers Green near High Street Gate
Open Apr–Oct: Sat–Wed 12–5.30 (last admission 5)
The epitome of a Queen Anne town house, Mompesson House was built in around 1701 for Charles Mompesson. It is remarkable chiefly for its superb interior moulded plasterwork, especially in the staircase hall, which dates from the 1740s and includes flowers, fruit and the head of Midas with asses' ears! The brick-built back of the house is much less grand than the elegant Georgian façade of the front. The house later became the home of the Townsend family for nearly 100 years. There is an important collection of English eighteenth-century drinking glasses, together with fine eighteenth-century furniture especially assembled for the house.

■127■ MONTACUTE ☎ 01935 823289
Montacute, Somerset TA15 6XP
4 miles W of Yeovil, S of A3088
Open Apr–Oct: Wed–Mon 12–5.30 (last admission 5). Grounds open all year from 11
Elizabethan house built of local golden Ham Hill stone in the late sixteenth century by Sir Edward Phelips, a successful lawyer and Member of Parliament who became Speaker of the House of Commons. It is one of the best preserved of Elizabethan mansions and has been described as 'the most beautiful Elizabethan house in England'. Internally, it preserves much of its original decoration and, although the original furnishings have long vanished, the house contains many fine examples of seventeenth- and eighteenth-century furniture, panelling and tapestries. The Long Gallery, measuring 172 feet (52 metres), is the longest of its kind to survive and has recently been re-decorated. It houses portraits of the Tudor and Jacobean courts, on loan from the National Portrait Gallery.

■128■ PARNHAM HOUSE AND GARDENS ☎ 01308 862204
Beaminster, Dorset DT8 3NA
½ mile S Beaminster off A3066
Open Apr–Oct: Tues–Wed, Sun and Bank Hol Mons 10–5
Magnificently restored Tudor mansion set in lovely grounds. Later alterations to

its exterior include mock battlements and pinnacles added in the early nineteenth century. The interior, including the Great Hall, is largely the result of twentieth-century reconstruction. If you're interested in woodwork, Parnham also houses a furniture workshop and a school for wood craftsmen.

■129■ SALTRAM HOUSE ☎ 01752 336546
Plympton, Plymouth, Devon PL7 1UH
3 miles E of Plymouth, between A38 and A379
Open Mar–Oct: Sun–Thurs and Good Fri 12–5. Gardens as House (plus Sat and Sun in Mar): 10.30–5.30
Classical façade, built in the mid-eighteenth century, masks the remains of a large Tudor house. Saltram is Devon's largest country house. Although the exterior is plain, the interior is noteworthy for its grand saloon and dining-room, which were completed in 1768 by Robert Adam. The great kitchen, still in use until 1962, includes a Victorian range as well as a display of cooking utensils. In the grounds there is an orangery by the woodcarver Henry Stockman, completed in 1775 and rebuilt after a fire in 1932. There is also a garden house known as 'Fanny's Bower', a chapel which is thought to be a conversion of a medieval barn, an eighteenth-century stable block and a little building known as 'the castle' which Adam is thought to have designed.

■130■ SHERBORNE CASTLE ☎ 01935 813182
Cheap Street, Sherborne, Dorset DT9 3PY0
½ mile E of Sherbourne off B3145
Open Apr–Oct: Tues, Thurs, Sat, Sun and Bank Hols 12.30–5 (last admission 4.30). Admission of groups outside these hours by appointment
Built by Sir Walter Raleigh in 1594 and set amid beautiful parkland with a lake created in 1753 by Capability Brown, Sherborne Castle has been a family home since 1617 when the diplomat Sir John Digby acquired the castle and added four new wings to Raleigh's original building. Tudor, Jacobean and Georgian styles are all to be found here. State rooms, a collection of pictures, porcelain and furniture and Raleigh's original Tudor kitchen and cellars are among the things to be seen.

■131■ STOURHEAD HOUSE ☎ 01747 841152
Stourton, Warminster, Wiltshire BA12 6QD
3 miles NW of Mere off B3092
Open Mar–Oct: Sat–Wed and Bank Hol Mons 12–5.30 or dusk. Gardens same: 9–7 or dusk
Palladian-style villa, commissioned by the banker Henry Hoare I and built between 1721 and 1724 by Colen Campbell. Classical stone building with grand porticoed entrance front on the east side. The main additions to the house were made in the 1790s when Sir Richard Colt Hoare commissioned Thomas Atkinson to build two projecting wings for his books and his picture collection. Further additions were made in 1840 when the portico was built to Campbell's original design. The library is a splendid room, with a barrel-vaulted ceiling; its furniture, including a fine flight of library steps, was made by Thomas Chippendale the Younger in the early nineteenth century. Stourhead Garden is one of the most famous examples of the early eighteenth-century English landscape movement. It was begun by Henry Hoare I, but its magnificent landscaping is largely the work of his son, Henry Hoare II, who was more interested in the grounds than in the house itself. His tastes in architecture are to be seen in the temples and the other buildings set around the lake, designed by Henry Flitcroft.

■132■ TORRE ABBEY ☎ 01803 293593
The Kings Drive, Torquay, Devon TQ2 5JE
On Torqauy seafront next to the Riviera Centre
Open Apr–Nov: daily 9.30–6 (last admission 5)
Founded as a monastery in 1196, the abbey became a country house and the
residence of the Cary family for nearly 300 years. Beneath the house are the
undercrofts, hushed and cool ancient rooms, unchanged since the monks went
about their business. As well as the medieval monastic remains, which include
a great barn, guest hall and gatehouse, the house has over twenty historical
rooms, a beautiful family chapel, a splendid collection of paintings and Torquay
terracotta.

■133■ WILTON HOUSE ☎ 01722 746729
Estate Office, Wilton, Salisbury, Wiltshire SP2 0BJ
3 miles W of Salisbury on A30
Open Apr–Oct: daily 10.30–5.30 (last admission 4.30)
Built on the site of an abbey, the Tudor origins of the house can still be seen in
the tower that survived a fire in 1647. It is now incorporated into the splendid
seventeenth-century house, which is based on designs by Inigo Jones. Gothic
cloisters were added in the early nineteenth century by James Wyatt. The most
famous of the six state rooms are the double and single cube rooms with their
fabulous painted ceilings. Wilton boasts a world-famous art collection of over
200 paintings. There is also a reconstructed Tudor kitchen and a Victorian
laundry.

■134■ WOLFETON HOUSE ☎ 01305 263500
Wolfeton, Dorchester, Dorset DT2 9QN
1½ miles from Dorchester on A37 towards Yeovil, follow Historic House signs
Open May–Sept: Sun, Tues, Thurs and Bank Hol Mons 2–6
Fine Grade 1 listed medieval and Elizabethan house, dating from 1480. The two
unmatched round towers of the gatehouse date back even further, possibly to
the fourteenth century. The south front of the main house remains mostly
intact; internally, there are fine pictures and furniture of the seventeenth century. The chapel has a simple fireplace and a timber ceiling which date from the
sixteenth century, and a series of carved panels dating from 1510 show the
signs of the zodiac.

🏛 SOUTH-EAST   MAP 2

■135■ APPULDURCOMBE HOUSE ☎ 01983 852484
Wroxall, near Ventor, Isle of Wight PO38 3EW0
1 mile from Wroxall on B3327
Open mid-Feb–Jun and Oct–mid-Dec: daily 10–4; Jun–Sept: daily 10–6 (last admission 5)
Built early in the eighteenth century by Sir Robert Worsley in the short-lived
architectural style of English baroque. It was enlarged and altered some seventy
years later by his great-nephew, Sir Richard, who also appointed Capability
Brown to landscape the grounds. From 1909, Appuldurcombe was unoccupied
and fell into decay, but since the 1950s it has been in the care of English
Heritage, which has carried out a lengthy programme of repair, and in 1986 a
number of the rooms were reroofed and their windows replaced. An owl and
falcon centre exists on the grounds.

■136■ BASILDON PARK ☎ 01189 843040
Lower Basildon, Reading, Berkshire RG8 9NR
Between Pangbourne and Streatley 7 miles NW of Reading off A329
Open Apr–Oct: Wed–Sun and Bank Hol Mons 1–5.30. Closed Good Fri
Lovely Palladian-style mansion built in golden Bath stone. Classical front with
a splendid central portico joined by one-storey links to separate pavilions.
Basildon Park was built by John Carr of York for Sir Francis Sykes between
1776 and 1783. Inside there are delicate neoclassical-style plasterwork decora-
tions on the walls and ceilings. The grand staircase and the Octagon Drawing-
Room, with its fine pictures and furniture and three big windows overlooking
the River Thames, are particularly elegant and impressive. Small formal garden
and pretty terrace garden overlooking the grounds.

■137■ BEAULIEU ☎ 01590 612345
John Montagu Building, Beaulieu, Brockenhurst, Hampshire SO42 7ZN
Off B3054 between Hythe and Lymington
Open May–Sept: daily 10–6; Oct–Apr: daily 10–5
Sixteenth-century house in beautiful setting on the Beaulieu River. Lord
Montagu's ancestral home since 1538, the house was once the gatehouse of a
great abbey that stood here, and the ruins of some of the monastic buildings are
seen in the grounds. The monastic origins of the house can be seen in
features like its fan-vaulted ceilings. The current entrance hall was used as a
billiard-room during the nineteenth century. Today it displays pictures and
objects relating to four generations of the Montagu family. Re-created Victorian
kitchen and private dining-room with linenfold panelling. Upper drawing-room
and anteroom, formerly chapels in the great gatehouse, still display the religious
origins in their architecture. The piscina where the priest washed the altar
vessels is still present. Beaulieu is also home to the National Motor Museum.

■138■ BROADLANDS ☎ 01794 505010
Romsey, Hampshire SO51 9ZD
S of Romsey. Take M27 junction 3 and A3057 or M27 junction 2 then A31, signposted
Open mid-Jun–Aug: daily 12–5.30 (last admission 4)
Elegant Palladian house in lovely Capability Brown-landscaped setting beside
the River Test. Historic home of Lord Mountbatten. The eighteenth-century
grace of its Georgian exterior is complemented by its elegant interior. Domed
hall with coffered ceiling decorated with plasterwork reminiscent of snowflakes.
Sculpture Hall displays pieces from the Broadlands' collection of ancient Greek
and Roman marbles. Several beautiful rooms including the Wedgwood Room,
with neoclassical friezes and mouldings reminiscent of Wedgwood pottery, the
saloon, with its delicate white and gold neoclassical decoration, and the dining-
room, where Van Dyck paintings are displayed.

■139■ BUCKINGHAM PALACE ☎ 0207 839 1377
Buckingham Palace, London SW1A 1AA
Victoria, Green Park or St James Park Underground
Ticket office open July–Oct: daily 9–4. Check on 24-hour info line: 0207 799 2331
Official London residence of Her Majesty The Queen. Eighteenth-century
Buckingham House was bought from the Crown in 1762 for George III. It was
remodelled by John Nash for George IV in 1820s. The first monarch to make
Buckingham Palace her home was Queen Victoria, who added the east front
and made some modernisations. Since that time very few alterations have been

made to the palace. Each August and September the state rooms are open to the public. These rooms, which are used for state and official entertaining, occupy the main west front overlooking the garden. They are all decorated with works of art from the Royal Collection. One of the greatest attractions is George IV's state rooms, built in the 1820s.

■140■ **CHARTWELL** ☎ 01732 868381
Mapleton Road, Westerham, Kent TN16 1PS
2 miles S of Westerham (A25), fork left off B2026
Open Apr–Oct: Wed–Sun and Bank Hol Mons 11–5 plus
Tues in July and Aug

Chartwell

The home of Sir Winston Churchill from 1924 until the end of his life. The house has been left as it was in his lifetime with rooms containing pictures, maps and personal mementoes. The house itself is Victorian, with lovely terraced gardens sloping down to the lake offering stunning views over the wield of Kent.

■141■ **CLANDON PARK** ☎ 01483 222482
West Clandon, Guildford, Surrey GU4 7RQ
At West Clandon on A247
Open House Apr–Oct: Tues–Thurs and Sun 11.30–4.30. Garden all year: daily 9–dusk
Built in the 1730s for the second Lord Onslow by the Venetian architect Giacomo Leoni, this grand mansion is like an Italian villa in the English countryside. The exterior is red brick, but distinguished on its main west front by a central section of white stone and a white stone portico, and complemented by a white stone ballustrade surrounding the roof of the entire building. Internally, the main feature is its magnificent two-storey Marble Hall, with its superb white plasterwork ceiling. The marbling of the lower columns and the skirting had been thought to be original but in fact was probably done for the fourth earl in 1879. It has been carefully toned to correspond with the different marbles used in the chimneypieces. The house has one oak and one stone staircase, which seem to have been of equal importance, on either side of the hall.

■142■ **CLAYDON HOUSE** ☎ 01296 730349
Middle Claydon, Buckingham, Buckinghamshire MK18 2EY
In Middle Claydon, 13 miles NW of Aylesbury off A413, 3 miles SW of Winslow
Open Apr–Oct: Sat–Wed 1–5 (last admission 4.30)
Although originally late Tudor/early Jacobean, most of the house dates from
the eighteenth century, when it was remodelled by Sir Thomas Robinson for
the second Earl Verney. The rather sober-looking exterior gives no clue to the
splendours inside in the form of extravagant rococo carvings and plasterwork.
Ceilings, cornices and walls are adorned with delicately carved fruits, flowers,
animals and birds – the work of Luke Lightfoot, a highly skilled stonemason
and woodcarver. His Chinese Room is particularly impressive. There is also a
magnificent staircase with plasterwork by John Rose. The earl's ambitious decorating schemes bankrupted him and he had to sell the house. His successor
demolished two-thirds of the house, and today only a relatively small amount
of its former glories can be seen.

■143■ **FIRLE PLACE** ☎ 01273 858335
Nr Lewes, East Sussex BN8 6LP
Off A27 Eastbourne to Brighton road SE of Lewes
Open Easter and mid-May–Sept: Sun, Wed, Thurs Bank Hol Mons 2–5
Originally a Tudor manor house built by Sir John Gage and home of the Gage
family for over 500 years, Firle Place's Tudor core was extensively remodelled in
the eighteenth century. Its treasures include important European and English
Old Master paintings and furniture and fine Sèvres porcelain.

■144■ **GOODWOOD HOUSE** ☎ 01243 755048
Goodwood, Chichester, West Sussex PO18 0PX
3 miles NE of Chichester, signposted from A27
Check opening times. Recorded information on 01243 755040
Original Jacobean hall, now known as the Long Hall, was built by the thirteenth
Earl of Northumberland as a hunting lodge between 1616 and 1617. It was
remodelled between 1729 and 1730 to give the exterior the classical appearance
seen today. Two great wings were added between 1800 and 1806. Recent
extensive renovations have returned the interiors to their Regency splendour.
Sumptuous drawing-rooms, dining-rooms, reception rooms and ballroom with
beautiful collections of furnishings and art, including paintings by Canaletto,
Stubbs and Van Dyck and a fine collection of Sèvres porcelain.

■145■ **HAM HOUSE** ☎ 0208 940 1950
Ham Street, Richmond, Surrey TW10 7RS
On the S bank of Thames W of A307 at Petersham. Tube or rail to Richmond, then 371 bus
Open Mar–Oct: Sat–Wed 1–5 (last admission 4.30). Check other dates
Red-brick house, built in the shape of a shallow U with projecting wings on the
north or entrance front. Ham House was built in 1610 during the reign of James I.
Much of the interior was remodelled between 1637 and 1639, creating the Great
Staircase, one of the earliest examples of pierced panelwork in England, and a
suite of state rooms on the first floor. The house was redecorated by the Duke and
Duchess of Lauderdale in the 1670s. The duke was a member of Charles II's government and a great follower of fashion. Much of this decoration is intact in
many of the rooms, offering a rare picture of seventeenth-century fashions. The
most attractive rooms are not the great rooms so much as the little 'closets' leading
off them. All are full of furniture and pictures and have richly decorated walls.

■146■ HAMPTON COURT PALACE ☎ 0208 781 9500

Hampton Court Palace, Surrey KT8 9AU

M3 junction 1, then A308 towards Kingston
Open mid-Mar–mid-Oct: Mon 10.15–6, Tues–Sun 9.30–6; mid-Oct–mid-Mar: check dates

One of the largest and most sumptuous palaces of Tudor England and a royal residence until the eighteenth century, Hampton Court was begun by Cardinal Wolsey in 1514 and handed over to Henry VIII after his fall in 1529. The Great Gatehouse, the large Base Court and the Clock Court are what remain of Wolsey's original palace, with the adaptations that were made by Henry VIII. Henry expanded it, adding the hammer-beamed Great Hall, the fan-vaulted ceiling of Anne Boleyn's Gateway, the astronomical clock, immense kitchens, real tennis courts and the Great House of Easement, a multiple garderobe (lavatory) to seat twenty-eight people! The present east and south wings replaced original Tudor courtyards when William III and Mary II commissioned Sir Christopher Wren to build a baroque palace. Between 1838, when Queen Victoria opened the palace to the public, and 1851 the Great Hall, Great Gatehouse and the whole of the west front were re-Tudorised. Sash windows, introduced in the eighteenth century, were removed and new casement windows in a Tudor style inserted. Work continued between 1875 and 1900, restoring large parts of Henry VIII's palace. Highlights include the State Apartments, the Great Hall, the Chapel Royal and the Tudor kitchens.

■147■ HATFIELD HOUSE ☎ 01707 262823

Hatfield, Hertfordshire AL9 5NQ

Off A1000, 2 miles from A1(M) junction 4. Opposite Hatfield railway station
Open Apr–Sept: Tues–Thurs (guided tours) 12–4, Sat and Sun 1–5 plus Bank Hols 11–5

One of the largest Jacobean mansions in the country. Magnificent house built of red brick with stone dressings. Hatfield House was built by Robert Cecil between 1607 and 1611 to replace an older palace where Queen Elizabeth I spent much of her childhood. The south front (the original main entrance) has a clock tower and a loggia attributed to Inigo Jones. Inside there are fine examples of Jacobean craftsmanship including the carved oak Grand Staircase, a screen and minstrels' gallery in the Great Hall, a beautiful chimneypiece in King James's Drawing-Room and rare stained glass in the private chapel. There are collections of armour, fine furniture, paintings and items associated with Elizabeth I. The surviving part of the old palace, where the queen lived, can be seen in the grounds, and the gardens, run organically, include a Tudor Knot garden.

■148■ HIGHCLERE CASTLE ☎ 01635 253210

Newbury, Berkshire RG20 9RN

4 miles S of Newbury off A34
Open July–Sept: daily 11–5 (2.30 on Sat). Last admission 4

Designed by Charles Barry in 1842 this pinnacled Gothic mansion is reminiscent of the Houses of Parliament, which Barry was building at the same time. Highclere Castle provided the perfect setting for the third Earl of Caernarvon, who was one of the great hosts of Queen Victoria's reign, to entertain his guests. Capability Brown helped design the gardens. Today the castle is a treasure house with Old Master paintings, and portraits by Van Dyck and eighteenth-century painters. Napoleon's desk and chair, rescued from St Helena, sit with other eighteenth-century furniture. The fifth Earl of Caernarvon discovered the tomb of Tutankhamun, and the castle houses a unique exhibition of some of his archaeological finds, which come to light in the castle only in 1988.

■149■ IGHTHAM MOTE ☎ 01732 811145

Mote Road, Ivy Hatch, Sevenoaks, Kent TN15 0NT
6 miles E of Sevenoaks off A25, 2 miles S of Ightham off A227
Open Apr–Oct: Mon, Wed–Fri, Sun, Bank Hol Mons and Good Fri 11–5.30
Ightham Mote is one of England's oldest and loveliest moated medieval manor
houses. It has stood for 650 years, dating from 1340. The moat surrounds the
four wings of the house, the walls on all four sides dropping vertically into the
water, and containing within them a secluded, cobble-floored courtyard. The
Great Hall, with its magnificent roof, dates from the 1340s and still forms the
heart of the house. The house was lived in continuously until 1985, and it is
particularly interesting to see the way in which successive owners have adapted
the rooms and made them more comfortable in a manner that has always been
sympathetic to the medieval origins of the house. Sections of the house are now
being taken apart to cut away and replace hidden decay in the largest conservation project ever undertaken by the National Trust.

■150■ KNEBWORTH ☎ 01438 812661

Knebworth Park, Knebworth, Hertfordshire SG3 6PY
A1 junction 7, then Stevenage South, A602
Opening times vary. Phone first. Tours out of hours by arrangement
Home of the Lytton family since 1490, the original Tudor manor house was
transformed in early Victorian times by the writer Edward Bulwer-Lytton into
the spectacular High Gothic fantasy house of today, complete with turrets,
griffins and gargoyles. The interior contains many different styles, including the
Regency elegance of Mrs Bulwer-Lytton's bedroom; the Victorian medievalism
of the state drawing-room; the Edwardian designs of Sir Edwin Lutyens in the
entrance hall, dining-parlour and library; and a superb Jacobean banqueting
hall with a fine early-seventeenth-century screen and gallery, a seventeenth-
century plaster ceiling and magnificent neoclassical wood panelling. The house
is surrounded by 250 acres (151 hectares) of parkland and a 25-acre (10 hectares)
formal garden.

■151■ KNOLE ☎ 01732 450608

Knole, Sevenoaks, Kent TN15 0RP
S of Sevenoaks just E of A225
Open Apr–Oct: Wed–Sat 12–4; Sun, Bank Hol Mons and Good Fri 11–5
A simple manor house when it was bought in 1456 by Thomas Bourchier
Archbishop of Canterbury, Knole is now one of the finest and one of the largest
English mansions. Bourchier set about transforming it into a palace, which was
given to Henry VIII a hundred years later. Henry extended it further with
additions that included the Green Court, through which the building is now
approached. In the middle of the sixteenth century Queen Elizabeth I granted
the lease on the house to her cousin, Sir Thomas Sackville. Sir Thomas spent a
great deal refurbishing the property, making it the largest house in England. He
employed builders, plasterers, upholsterers and glaziers, including 300 craftsmen he brought over from Italy. Knole had three Long Galleries, whereas most
Elizabethan houses had only one. The Great Staircase is one of the best of its
time. The state rooms are rich in architectural detail from the seventeenth and
eighteenth centuries, with fine portraits and furniture. Many have kept their
original fittings, and the seventeenth-century furniture is outstanding. Outside
there are 26 acres (10½ hectares) of formal gardens set within 1,000 acres
(405 hectares) of parkland.

■152■ MARBLE HILL HOUSE ☎ 0208 892 5115
Richmond Road, Twickenham, Middlesex TW1 2NL
Off A316; train to St Margaret's Station or Tube to Richmond, then bus
Open Apr–Sept: daily 10–6 (5 in Oct); Nov–Mar: Wed–Sun 10–4
Built as a country retreat on the Thames at Twickenham for Henrietta Howard, one of King George II's mistresses. Relatively modest in size, with a classically plain exterior. The Great Room, which was used to entertain guests, is the most impressive room in the house. There is a strong sense of period style at Marble Hill, with the sparseness of the furnishings making it a good place at which to take note of architectural and decorative features, such as wooden mouldings, plaster reliefs and fireplaces.

■153■ MICHELHAM PRIORY ☎ 01323 844224
Upper Dicker, Hailsham, East Sussex BN27 3QS
2 miles W of Hailsham, signposted from A22 and A27
Open Mar–Oct: Wed–Sun 10.30–5 (daily in July and Aug, 4 in Mar and Oct)
Enclosed by a medieval moat, the remains of the beautiful Augustinian priory, which was founded in 1229, were incorporated into a Tudor mansion. Today the Elizabethan house is set on a moated island surrounded by lovely gardens. It is approached through a fourteenth-century gatehouse which spans the longest medieval moat in the country. In the gardens are a working water-mill, herb and cloister gardens, a smithy, rope museum and an Elizabethan Great Barn.

■154■ OSBORNE HOUSE ☎ 01983 200022
East Cowes, Isle of Wight PO32 6JY
1 mile SE of East Cowes off A3021
Open House Apr–Oct: daily 10–5. Tours out of hours by arrangement
Osborne House was Queen Victoria's favourite country home and the place where she died in 1901. An external view of the house shows an open court-yard, behind which there is the flag tower and three-storey pavilion where Queen Victoria and her family lived. The queen's private study, bedroom and closet can all be seen. The highly decorated walls reflect Prince Albert's liking for the Italian Renaissance acquired during his visit to Italy in 1838. High on the walls are reduced plaster copies of reliefs from classical friezes, including the Elgin Marbles from the Parthenon, Athens.

■155■ OSTERLEY PARK ☎ 0208 568 7714
Isleworth, Middlesex TW7 4RB
M4 junction 3 via Thornbury Road on N side of A4. Syon Lane railway station, Osterley Underground
Open Apr–Oct: Wed–Sun and Bank Hol Mons 1–4.30
Osterley Park was built around 1577 by the financier Sir Thomas Gresham. It was transformed from 1761 into a highly fashionable villa by Adam for the Child family. Osterley Park is now one of the great showpieces of Robert Adam's decorative style, retaining to this day his neoclassical interiors and the furniture he designed for them. The rooms were intended for show rather than comfort, and each piece of furniture is placed against the walls where Adam intended.

■156■ PENSHURST PLACE AND GARDENS ☎ 01892 870307
Penshurst, Tonbridge, Kent TN11 8DG
Leave A21 at Hildenborough and Weald exit, then follow signs
Open Mar: Sat and Sun 11–6; Apr–Oct: daily 11–6. Grounds as house: 10.30–6

Built of local sandstone, the mediaeval manor house, with its magnificent
Great Hall, dates from 1341, when it was constructed for John de Pulteney. It is
widely regarded as one of the finest and most complete examples of fourteenth-
century domestic architecture in England, and the Great Hall, with its vast
chestnut roof and rare octagonal hearth, has been described as one of the
world's finest rooms. Each century since the fourteenth has made its own
contribution to Penshurst, and architecturally it combines the work of at least
eight periods. In 1552 it passed into the hands of Sir William Sidney, and the
house has remained in this family since.

■157■ **PETWORTH HOUSE**   ☎ 01798 342207
Petworth, West Sussex GU28 0AE
In centre of Petworth
Open Apr–Oct: Sat–Wed and Good Fri (plus Fri in July and Aug) 1–5.30
(last admission 4.30)
Petworth House dates from 1150 but was extensively remodelled during the
seventeenth century, and all that survives of the medieval building is the chapel
and parts of the basement. The great main front, some 300 feet (91 metres)
long, looks out across superb parkland. The Marble Hall was built as the main
entrance to the house and features a black and white marble floor and decora-
tively carved woodwork. The Grand Staircase has a wall-painting by Laguerre.
Petworth houses the National Trust's finest collection of paintings and sculptures.
The painter, Turner used the Old Library as his studio, and, though not open to
the public, some of his works can still be seen here. The servants' quarters are
in a separate building connected to the main house by a tunnel, along which all
the food had to be hurriedly carried. The parklands surrounding Petworth were
the creation of Capability Brown.

■158■ **POLESDEN LACEY**   ☎ 01372 458203
Great Bookham, Dorking, Surrey RH5 6BD
2 miles S of Great Bookham off A246
Open Apr–Oct: Wed–Sun 1.30–5.30; Bank Hol Mons 11–5.30

Polesden Lacey

Regency villa extensively remodelled in 1906–9. Tucked away on the fringe of the North Downs, it is a low sprawling house, yellow-stuccoed and white-painted, set above sloping lawns. The villa was built in the 1820s for Joseph Bonsor by Thomas Cubitt. After various alterations and enlargements throughout the nineteenth century, the house was purchased by the Hon. Mrs Ronald Grenville and her husband. It was converted by Mewes and Davis, the architects of the newly built Ritz Hotel, into a house fit for royalty and, in fact, King George VI and Queen Elizabeth the Queen Mother spent their honeymoon here. There are extensive grounds, including a walled rose garden and landscaped walks.

■159■ THE PRIEST HOUSE ☎ 01342 810479
North Lane, West Hoathly, West Sussex RH19 4PP
4 miles W of Wych Cross (A22)
Open Mar–Oct: daily 11–5.30 (Sun 2– 5.30). Evening visits by arrangement
Originally an early-fifteenth-century timber-framed farmhouse with a central open hall. It was most probably built for the priory of St Pancras in Lewes. Stone chimneys and a ceiling in the hall were added during the modernisation in Elizabethan times. The Priest House has been open as a museum since 1908, and here you can see its furnished rooms. These include a kitchen with a fireplace and collection of ironwork and utensils. There is also a collection of seventeenth- and eighteenth-century domestic furniture, needlework and household items. A cottage and herb garden also exists.

■160■ ROYAL PAVILION ☎ 01273 290900
4–5 Pavilion Buildings, Brighton, East Sussex BN1 1EE
Central Brighton, on the main road
Open June–Sept: daily 10–6; Oct–May: daily 10–5
Famous seaside palace of George IV. One of the most exotically beautiful buildings in Britain. Originally a simple farmhouse, in 1787 architect Henry Holland created a neoclassical villa on the site. From 1815 to 1823, the pavilion was transformed by John Nash into its current distinctive Indian style, complete with Chinese-inspired interiors. The music room and banqueting room, built by Nash and designed by the Crace brothers and Robert Jones respectively, show a chinoiserie style. Magnificent decorations and furnishings have been re-created in an extensive restoration programme. The gardens have also been restored to conform to the original Regency plan.

■161■ STOWE ☎ 01280 813650
Buckingham, Buckinghamshire MK18 5EH
4 miles N of Buckingham
Open Easter and summer school holidays: Mon–Fri 2–5, Sat, Sun and Bank Hols 12–5.
Phone first to check times
Former home of the Dukes of Buckingham and now a major public school. The house, originally late seventeenth century, was altered and enlarged during the ownership of Sir Richard Temple, later Viscount Cobham, between 1697 and 1749 and again in the 1770s by his nephew and successor, Earl Temple, who continued to expand and embellish both the house and gardens to make Stowe one of the most majestic houses of the eighteenth century. The south front was designed by Robert Adam, and the grounds, which are regarded as one of the greatest achievements of eighteenth-century picturesque landscaping, were designed by Vanbrugh, Bridgeman, Kent and Capability Brown.

■162■ SYON HOUSE ☎ 0208 560 0883
Syon Park, London Road, Brentford, Middlesex TW8 8JF
Off A315, via Park Road, Isleworth. Kew Bridge rail station, then bus 237 or 267 to
Brentlea Gate or Gunnersbury Underground
Open Apr–Oct: Wed, Thurs, Sun and Bank Hol Mons 11–5
Built during the sixteenth century, Syon House contains some of Robert Adam's
famous interiors and stands within parkland landscaped by Capability Brown.
Set in the grounds is Charles Fowler's Great Conservatory with a spectacular
central dome. Adam's instructions were to 'create a place of Graeco-Roman
splendour', and the Great Hall is dominated at either end by statues and
antique classical busts. The Red Drawing-Room is spectacular, with its extravagantly decorated ceiling and walls hung with crimson Spitalfields silk. The Long
Gallery is some 136 feet (41 metres) long and displays the genius of Robert
Adam magnificently. The gardens at Syon are equally spectacular.

■163■ WADDESDON MANOR ☎ 01296 653211
Waddesdon, Aylesbury, Buckinghamshire HP18 0JH
On A41 between Bicester and Aylesbury
Open Apr–Oct: Thurs–Sun, Bank Hol Mons, Wed in July and Aug 11–4
Huge mansion of Bath stone built at the end of the nineteenth century by
Baron Ferdinand de Rothschild in the style of a sixteenth-century château.
Rothschild employed the distinguished French architect Destailler to design
the house, while another Frenchman, Laine, was in charge of landscaping the
gardens and terrace. The baron was a great collector, and the house was
designed to accommodate his fine collection of eighteenth-century French
furniture, Sèvres porcelain, English portraits and other decorative arts.

■164■ WEST WYCOMBE PARK ☎ 01494 513569
West Wycombe, Buckinghamshire HP14 3AJ
At West Wycombe, S of A40, 2 miles W of High Wycombe
Open House and Gardens June–Aug: Sun–Thurs 2–6. Gardens only Apr–May: Sun and Wed
Eighteenth-century house which cannot be put into any neat architectural
pigeonhole. The patchwork of different styles in the architecture and decoration
of the house reflect the enthusiasm and the ever-changing tastes of Sir Francis
Dashwood, who remodelled the house in the mid-eighteenth century from the
Queen Anne house built by his father. It has hardly been touched since his death
and remains a reflection of his tastes. The most important influences on him were
his Grand Tour and visits he made to Italy. Many artists and craftsmen were
employed: skilled plasterers created lively rococo ceilings, artists painted ceilings
and walls, including the 'Banquet of the Gods' after Raphael and the Carracci in
the music room. The house is elaborately decorated in a classical style. Externally,
the best-known feature is the double colonnade to the south front filling the
space between two wings, recently attributed to the Italian Giovanni Servandoni.

■165■ WOBURN ABBEY ☎ 01525 290666
Woburn, Bedfordshire MK43 0TP
8 miles NW of Dunstable on A4012, M1 junctions 12 or 13
Open Apr–Sept: Mon–Sun 11–4; Jan–Mar and Oct: Sat and Sun 11–4
The palatial mansion is the home of the Duke of Bedford. The house dates from
1744 and was originally a Cistercian abbey. It was remodelled in 1802 by Henry
Holland. Sumptuous interiors containing a valuable art collection, with paintings
by Canaletto, Rembrandt, Van Dyck, Gainsborough and many others. There is

Woburn Abbey

also an extensive collection of eighteenth-century furniture, both French and English. Fourteen state apartments are on view, and the private apartments are shown when not in use by the family. The house stands in 3,000 (1214 hectares) acres of parkland, famous for its varieties of deer.

⛰ EASTERN   MAP 3

■166■ ANGLESEY ABBEY ☎ 01223 811200
Lode, Cambridge CB5 9EJ
6 miles NE of Cambridge on B1102
Open late Mar–mid-Oct: Wed–Sat and Bank Hol Mons 1–5. Gardens all year: Thurs–Sun
Manor house built in 1600 on the site of an Augustinian priory. Characteristic Elizabethan features include five bays with square-headed mullioned and transomed windows and a typical two-storeyed Jacobean porch. Most of the ecclesiastical buildings of the priory were destroyed at the time of the Reformation, but the Chapter House survived and was converted into the main domestic dwelling. From 1926 onwards Lord Fairhaven largely remodelled the interior and made a number of additions. He added a fourth bay to the Common Room block and threw the bridge across the drive to link with new picture galleries. The house contains the famous Fairhaven collections of paintings and furniture and is surrounded by 99 acres (40 hectares) of landscape garden and arboretum.

■**167**■ **AUDLEY END HOUSE** ☎ 01799 522842
Audley End, Saffron Walden, Essex CB11 4JF
M11 junction 8 or 10 to B1383, then signposted; 1½ miles W of Saffron Walden
Open Apr–Sept: Wed–Sun 11–6 (last admission 5). Oct: guided tours only 10–3
Originally a great Jacobean house built between 1603 and 1614 by the first Earl
of Suffolk, Audley End fell into decline when Suffolk fell out of favour with the
king. It was given a new lease of life in the second half of the eighteenth century by Sir John Griffin, who created an elegant suite of reception rooms with
the help of the architect Robert Adam. In the Great Hall the main focus is the
large Jacobean oak screen, with decorative carving and wooden panelling to the
walls and ceiling. Above all, though, the interiors which can be seen today
reflect the taste of the third Lord Braybrooke, whose interest in the early history
of the house led him, in the 1820s, to create a series of opulent rooms in a
romantic Jacobean style. The chapel is a rare example of late-eighteenth-century
Gothic style, with all its furniture intact.

■**168**■ **BELTON HOUSE** ☎ 01476 566116
Grantham, Lincolnshire NG32 2LS
Off the A607, 3 miles N of Grantham
Open Apr–Oct: Wed–Sun and Bank Hols 1–5.30. Closed Good Fri. Check other dates.
Built between 1685 and 1688 for 'Young' Sir John Brownlow, the house was
modernised towards the end of the eighteenth century by James Wyatt. The
house is a classic English country house containing fine plasterwork and woodcarving, as well as important collections of paintings, furniture, tapestries and
silverware.

■**169**■ **BURGHLEY HOUSE** ☎ 01780 752451
Stamford, Lincolnshire PE9 3JY
1 mile SE of Stamford, signposted from A1 and all approaches
Open Apr–early Oct: daily 11–4.30 (closed one day in Sept)
The finest example of later Elizabethan architecture in England, built between
1565 and 1587 by Queen Elizabeth's most able and trusted adviser, William
Cecil. The house has eighteen state rooms open to visitors, featuring elaborate
decorations, furnishings and ornate plasterwork, with almost 400 paintings on
display. The Old Kitchen, with its vaulted ceiling, is one of the few remaining
rooms at Burghley which reminds us that the house was built during Tudor
times. The chapel contains important pieces of furniture, among which are two
mahogany pulpits that follow a design by Chippendale. The Bow Room was
decorated by Laguerre in 1697, who painted the walls with scenes of Cleopatra
and Mark Antony, and scenes from classical mythology on the ceiling.

■**170**■ **DODDINGTON HALL** ☎ 01522 694308
Lincoln, Lincolnshire LN6 4RU
On B1190 5 miles SW of Lincoln; signposted off A46 Lincoln bypass
Open May–Sept: Wed, Sun and Bank Hol 2–6. Gardens open Mar and Apr: Sun 2–6
Superb late-Elizabethan mansion, designed by the great architect Robert
Smithson, set in flat Lincolnshire countryside. The hall itself is within the village
and is closely surrounded by seventeenth-century brick outbuildings, all of
which have been converted into private housing. In contrast with the traditional Tudor layout, where everything faces defensively inwards, Doddington
projects itself proudly outwards. Inside the house there are beautiful textiles,
porcelain and furniture reflecting over 400 years of family occupation.

■171■ ELIZABETHAN HOUSE ☎ 01493 855746
4 South Quay, Great Yarmouth, Norfolk NR30 2QH
On quayside
Open May–September: Sun–Fri 10–5
Built in 1596 by Benjamin Cooper, a wealthy merchant, the house has many
unique and interesting architectural features, including fine wooden panelling,
elaborate wooden carvings and an outstanding moulded ceiling dating from
around 1603. The unusual entrance passage was originally an open narrow lane,
called a Yarmouth row, and was enclosed to form part of the house some time in
the seventeenth century. Different owners have made changes and additions to
the house, and a nineteenth-century marble floor and early Flemish and Dutch
stained glass can be seen. The house has been specially set out to show what life
was like for a wealthy Elizabethan family and their servants.

■172■ FELBRIGG HALL ☎ 01263 837444
Felbrigg, Cromer, Norfolk NR11 8PR
2 miles SE of Cromer on B1436
Open end Mar–Oct: Sat–Wed 1–5. Gardens as Hall: 11–5
With its fine Jacobean front, Felbrigg has grown gradually over more than three
centuries. The south front was built by Sir John Wyndham for his son Thomas
and was dramatically altered by his son William Windham I. In the 1680s he
added the new west wing, employing William Samwell as his architect. Famed
for its rococo plasterwork and 'Grand Tour' paintings, its beautiful rooms still
contain the furniture, books and paintings bought by four generations of the
Windham family and their successors. The simple domestic offices of the
eighteenth century are also well preserved. Walled garden with interesting
octagonal dovecote, and icehouse in woods.

■173■ GAINSBOROUGH OLD HALL ☎ 01427 612669
Parnell Street, Gainsborough, Lincolnshire DN21 2NB
A631 to Gainsborough; signposted from Trent Bridge
Open all year: Mon–Sat 10–5, Sun 2–5.30. Closed Sun Nov–Easter
One of the hidden gems of Lincolnshire and one of the best-preserved medieval
manor houses in the country. Built by Sir Thomas Burgh in around 1460, architecturally it has changed very little over the years, being mainly a timber-framed
building giving it its characteristic black and white striped appearance. On the
north-east corner there is a brick tower, and at the centre is the Great Hall, with
its vast arched roof, where Richard III and Henry VIII once banqueted. The
kitchens remain virtually unchanged since the time of the royal visitors.

■174■ GRIMSTHORPE CASTLE ☎ 01778 591205
Grimsthorpe, Bourne, Lincolnshire PE10 0NB
8 miles E of Colsterworth on A151
Open Easter Sun–Sept: Sun, Thurs and Bank Hols 2–6; Aug: Sun–Thurs 1–6
Rising majestically from the flat landscape of south Lincolnshire, the principal
front of Grimsthorpe is the last masterpiece of the baroque architect Sir John
Vanbrugh. The grandeur of Grimsthorpe is emphasised by the arcaded central
portion of the front and the pairs of giant columns surmounted by trophies.
Inside the monumental Vanbrugh Hall superimposed arcades reflect the grand
style of the exterior of the house. Full-length Grisaille paintings and Rosenburg
statues are located within the arches. Staircases rise behind arcaded screens each
end of the hall leading to the state rooms on the first floor. The State Dining Room,

lit by a Venetian window, occupies Vanbrugh's north-east tower. A most impressive house, containing many paintings and lavish Continental furnishings.

■**175**■ **HOLKHAM HALL** ☎ 01328 710227
Holkham, Wells-next-the-sea, Norfolk NR23 1AB
Follow signposts from A149 2 miles W of Wells-next-the-sea
Open Jun–Sept: Sun–Thurs 1–5; Bank Hol Sun and Mon 11.30–5
A majestic stately home, situated in a 3,000-acre (1214-hectares) park on the Norfolk coast, this Palladian-style mansion was built between 1734 and 1762 by Thomas Coke, first Earl of Leicester. Holkham's most celebrated feature is its exquisite Marble Hall, rising to the full height of the building, with fluted columns copied from the Temple of Fortuna Virlis in Rome and a ceiling design from an idea by the seventeenth-century architect Inigo Jones. The richly and splendidly decorated state rooms contain Greek and Roman statues brought back by the first earl from his Grand Tour of Europe, fine furniture, and paintings by Rubens, Van Dyck, Claude, Poussin and Gainsborough. Throughout this magnificent home there are exquisite furnishings and artworks on display.

■**176**■ **ICKWORTH HOUSE PARK** ☎ 01284 735270
Horringer, Bury St Edmunds, Suffolk IP29 5QE
2 miles S of Bury St Edmunds off A143
Open Easter–mid-Jun and early Sept–Oct: Sat and Sun 11–5; mid-Jun–early Sept: daily 12–5. Check other times
One of the National Trust's most unusual and surprising properties, Ickworth is an Italianate house and gardens set within beautiful English parkland designed by Capability Brown. The present house dates from 1795 and features an extraordinary central rotunda with wings curving from it, which was designed to house treasures collected from all over Europe by Frederick Hervey, fourth Earl of Bristol and Bishop of Derry. Massive classical entrance hall, with giant columns, black marble fireplace and marble sculpture. Magnificent state rooms, displaying Old Masters, including works by Titian, Velasquez and Gainsborough, Georgian silver and Regency furniture. There is also a Pompeiian room, with *trompe l'oeil*.

■**177**■ **KENTWELL HALL** ☎ 01787 310207
Long Melford, Sudbury, Suffolk CO10 9BA
Off A134 N of Sudbury
Open Easter–mid-Jun: Sat and Sun 11–5; mid-Jun–early Sept: daily 12–5. Check times
Mellow red-brick E-shaped Tudor mansion surrounded by a broad moat. Externally little altered, with many of the sixteenth-century service areas intact; internally, changes in a variety of styles made by successive owners, including the present family, can be seen. There is a unique brick-paved mosaic Tudor rose maze, and fine gardens including many clipped yews – some 30 feet (9 metres) high – as well as an ancient walled garden, with a large herb garden and potager. It also has the largest tree sculpture in England. The farm has rare breeds of animals and a collection of timber-framed buildings.

■**178**■ **LAYER MARNEY TOWER** ☎ 01206 330784
Layer Marney, Colchester, Essex CO5 9US
Off B1022 SW of Colchester
Open Apr–early Oct: Sun–Fri 12–5
The tallest and most elaborate Tudor gatehouse in the country, built by Henry, first Lord of Marney, in the early years of Henry VIII's reign. East Anglia

features some of the finest brick buildings in the country, as there was little or no stone available. The window and parapet detail in terracotta was a new Italian idea, and, architecturally, Layer Marney Tower is renowned for its use of terracotta, a buff colour chosen so that the window mullions and tower decoration would resemble stone.

■179■ OXBURGH HALL ☎ 01366 328258
Oxburgh, Swaffham, Norfolk PE33 9PS
7 miles SW of Swaffham E of A134
Open Apr–Oct: Sat–Wed 1–5; Bank Hol Mons 11–5
Quintessential moated manor house. Oxburgh Hall, built in 1482 by the Bedingfeld family, who still live there, is a square brick mansion defended by a moat and a castellated gatehouse. The distinctive gatehouse, with its turret rooms and spiral staircase, is a rare untouched example of fifteenth-century architecture and brickwork. The King's Room inside the gatehouse, named after a stay by Henry VII in 1487, also remains intact. Seventeenth-century embossed leather covers two staircase walls. The rooms show the development from medieval austerity to Victorian comfort and include an outstanding display of embroidery done by Mary Queen of Scots during her captivity. The nineteenth-century library has a fireplace by Pugin.

■180■ SANDRINGHAM ☎ 01553 772675
The Estate Office, Sandringham, Norfolk PE35 6EN
Off A148, 8 miles NE of King's Lynn
Open Easter–mid-July and early Aug–Oct: daily 11–4.45. Opening times subject to change: telephone for details
Grand and imposing country home of Her Majesty the Queen set in 60 acres (24 hectares) of wooded grounds. Queen Victoria bought the estate for her son, Prince Edward, who commissioned London architect A. J. Humbert to design his new home in 1870. Fronted in red brick and dressed with sandstone, the neo-Jacobean-style house has a gabled roof and picturesque turrets. It was expanded by the addition of a ballroom in 1883 and partly rebuilt after a fire in 1891. All the main rooms used by the Royal Family when in residence are open to the public, and there are collections of porcelain, jade, quartz, enamelled Russian silver, gold and bronzes on display. Museum of vintage Royal Family cars.

🏛 CENTRAL   MAP 4

■181■ ATTINGHAM PARK ☎ 01743 709203
Attingham Park, Shrewsbury, Shropshire SY4 4TP
4 miles SE of Shrewsbury off A5
Open Apr–Nov: Fri–Tues and Good Fri 1.30–5; Bank Hol Mons 11–5
An imposing entrance front with massive portico, colonnades and pavilions greet the visitor to Attingham. The house was constructed around an earlier building, but most of what is seen today dates from the eighteenth and early-nineteenth centuries. George Stuart designed the house, with the more 'masculine' rooms on the left of the entrance hall and the more 'feminine' rooms on the right. The entrance hall itself is elaborately decorated to imitate marble. Other notable decorations can be seen in the boudoir, the Italian-style drawing-room and the Red Dining-Room. Nash, who made early use of curved cast iron and glass for the ceiling, designed the picture gallery.

■182■ BADDESLEY CLINTON HOUSE ☎ 01564 783294
Rising Lane, Baddesley Clinton, Knowle, Solihull, West Midlands B93 0DQ
Off A4141 SW of Knowle
Open Mar–Oct: Wed–Sun and Bank Hol Mons 1.30–5. Grounds 12–5. Check other dates
Described as 'the perfect medieval manor house' the present building dates
predominantly from the mid-fifteenth century. The wide moat surrounding it
may have encircled the earlier fortified manor house of the Clintons. The grey-
stone entrance front, approached across the moat by a Queen Anne bridge,
was erected by the Bromes, who inherited the estate in about 1438. The
entrance tower, with its tall porch and fine Elizabethan window to light the
great parlour, were alterations made by the Ferrers family who owned the
house from 1509. Henry Ferrer was proud of his ancestry and began the tradition at Baddesley of armorial glass, which has continued until the present day.
The Elizabethan fireplaces were theirs, as presumably were the numerous
hiding places or 'priest holes', including one below the level of the moat
constructed by Nicholas Owen, the leading 'hide' builder.

■183■ BLENHEIM PALACE ☎ 01993 811325
Woodstock, Oxfordshire OX20 1PX
On A44 at Woodstock
*House open mid-March–Oct: daily 10.30–5.30 (last admission 4.45). Park all year:
daily 9–6.30*
One of the finest examples of English baroque architecture. The palace, set in
2,100 acres (850 hectares) of parkland landscaped by Capability Brown, was
designed by Sir John Vanbrugh. Home of the eleventh Duke of Marlborough and
birthplace of Sir Winston Churchill, it was built for John Churchill, first Duke of
Marlborough in recognition of his great victory over the French at the Battle of
Blenheim in 1704. The military associations are never far away; entry to the
park is by the Triumphal Gate, and the Victory Column stands at the beginning
of a long avenue of trees. The artificial lake is crossed by Vanbrugh's Grand
Bridge. The palace itself was conceived by Vanbrugh in his most elaborate
manner, aiming to create a national monument rather than a comfortable home.
The building is made up of a central block linked by curved colonnades to a
kitchen courtyard and a stable courtyard. Interiors are lavish, with tapestries,
paintings, sculpture and fine furniture, set in magnificent gilded state rooms.
Most noteworthy are the Great Hall and saloon with their painted ceilings and
marble doorcases, the state rooms and the Long Library, with its stucco ceiling.

■184■ BOLSOVER CASTLE ☎ 01246 823349
Castle Street, Bolsover, Nr Chesterfield, Derbyshire S44 6PR
6 miles E of Chesterfield on A632
Open Apr–Oct: daily 10–6 (5 in Oct); Nov–Mar: Wed–Sun 10–4
Early-seventeenth-century country house built on the site of a medieval castle.
Perched on a ridge overlooking the Vale of Scarsdale, the medieval castle
dominated the landscape. By the late sixteenth century the military value of
the site had declined, but the potential of the site for the building of a mock-
medieval country house was fully appreciated. Sir Charles Cavendish replaced
the medieval keep with a fairy-tale tower house of rooms stacked on top of one
another. In contrast, the medieval defences along the ridge were replaced by a
linear sequence of state rooms, the Terrace Range for entertaining and admiring
the view. The Riding School Range, added in the 1630s, completed the complex,
which survives today as a rare example of a 'Cavalier Pleasure Palace'.

■185■ CANONS ASHBY HOUSE ☎ 01327 860044
Canons Ashby, Daventry, Northamptonshire NN11 3SD
Signposted from A5, on B4525
Open Apr–Oct: Sat–Wed 1–5 or dusk if sooner
Manor house built around 1550, added to in the 1590s and altered in the 1630s and again around 1710, since when it has been largely unaltered. Home of the Dryden family since the sixteenth century. Within the house, Elizabethan wall-paintings and outstanding Jacobean plasterwork are of particular interest. A formal garden includes terraces, walls and gate piers of 1710. There is also a medieval priory church, part of the original Augustinian priory from which the house takes its name. Interesting wine cellars and romantic pebble court.

■186■ CHARLECOTE PARK ☎ 01789 470277
Wellesbourne, Warwick CV35 9ER
1 mile W of Wellesbourne, 5 miles E of Stratford-upon-Avon, signposted from A429 and B4086
Open mid-Apr–Nov: Fri–Tues 11–5
Charlecote lies close to the River Avon at the heart of an ancient deer park and has been transformed several times over the centuries by the Lucy family. The present house was built in the 1550s when Thomas Lucy inherited the estate that had been in his family since at least the twelfth century. During the eighteenth century the house was comprehensively modernised, but when George Hamilton Lucy inherited it in 1823 he decided to turn the clock back and re-create Charlecote as it had been in its Elizabethan heyday. The house has remained the same since. A fully equipped Victorian kitchen and brewhouse complement the principal rooms, which are richly decorated and furnished.

■187■ CHATSWORTH ☎ 01246 582204
Chatsworth, Bakewell, Derbyshire DE45 1PP
8 miles N of Matlock off B6012
Open mid-Mar–Oct: daily 11–5.30 for House and 11–6 for Garden
One of the great stately homes of Britain. Work began in 1686 to replace the Elizabethan mansion of 1552. It was designed for the Duke of Devonshire by William Talman (among others), who was also responsible for the baroque interiors. The design of the house has evolved over the years with only the chapel and State Dining-Room (1690s) and the Great Dining-Room and Sculpture Gallery (1820s) remaining virtually unaltered since they were built. Also, the upper part of the magnificent Painted Hall has not been changed since it was painted in 1692–4 by Louis Laguerre, but the ground floor and stairs have been altered several times. The Great Staircase leads to the chapel, which contains four marble columns hewn from a single block quarried on Sheldon Moor, a few miles away. The house contains an outstanding collection of art displayed in twenty-six richly furnished rooms.

■188■ COUGHTON COURT ☎ 01789 762435
Alcester, Warwickshire B49 5JA
2 miles N of Alcester on A435
Open Apr–late Sept: Wed–Sun 11.30–5. Also open Bank Hol Mons and Sat and Sun in Mar and Oct and Tues in July and Aug. Telephone for details
Coughton Court has been the home of the Throckmorton family since the fifteenth century. The early Tudor gatehouse is the most substantial part that remains from this time. It is now flanked by Gothic wings built in the late

eighteenth century. A wide archway leads through to the rectangular courtyard with its Elizabethan half-timbered north and south wings. Protestant rioters destroyed the east wing in 1688.

■189■ **DEENE PARK** ☎ 01780 450223
Deene, Nr Corby, Northamptonshire NN17 3EW
Off A43 NE of Corby
Open Bank Hol Suns and Mons in Easter, May and Aug: 2–5; June–Aug: Sun 2–5
The house was built over six centuries and grew from a substantial medieval manor house into a Tudor and Georgian mansion. The Great Hall has an elaborate hammerbeam roof and stained-glass windows showing the arms of the Brudenells and other related families. The Tapestry Room holds a tapestry of Joseph greeting his brothers which dates from before 1629 and was made in Brussels, the ceiling dates from around 1600 from a design by Serlio, and the furnishings are mostly seventeenth century. King Henry VII's Room is a rare example of an early-Tudor room, with its original fireplace and linenfold panelling. Throughout this house there are many paintings and beautifully furnished rooms. Gardens surround the property, and a canal flows past the house under a stone bridge with seventeenth-century balusters.

■190■ **DYRHAM PARK** ☎ 01179 372501
Dyrham, Wiltshire SN14 8ER
S of M4 junction 18 at Dyrham (A46)
Open House late Mar–Oct: Fri–Tues 12–5.30. Park all year exc Christmas: 12–5.30
A fine William and Mary house built for William Blathwayt, Secretary of War and Secretary of State to William III. Between 1692 and 1704 he completely rebuilt and transformed the manor house that had stood on this site since Tudor times. The house is an excellent example, on a medium scale, of baroque planning. The east front, approached through the deer park, was designed, with the orangery by Talman, in 1698. The rooms have not changed much since they were furnished by Blathwayt; some are panelled in cedar and Virginia walnut, and one still has its original leather wall-hangings.

■191■ **EASTNOR CASTLE** ☎ 01531 633160
Eastnor, Ledbury, Herefordshire HR8 1RL
2 miles E of Ledbury on A438
Open Easter–Oct: Sun and Bank Hol Mons 11–5; July and Aug: Sun–Fri 11–5

Fred's **FAVOURITE**

Magnificent Georgian castle with towers at each corner and castellated terraces descending to a beautiful lake. Eastnor Castle, built by the second Baron Somers between 1810 and 1824, is dramatically situated in a 500-acre estate in the Malvern Hills. In the nineteenth century the size and splendour of a country house were the most obvious indications of the standing and fortune of any family, and the whole place is a massive exercise in medievalism. The style proposed by the architect, the young Robert Smirke, was Norman revival. From a distance, Eastnor was intended to create the impression of an Edward I-style medieval fortress guarding the Welsh Borders. The interiors were kept simple and in keeping with the medieval style of the building, which is seen at its best in the Red Hall, dining-room, and staircase hall. In 1849 Pugin decorated the drawing-room in the High Gothic revival style. More lavish embellishments were added in the 1860s and 1870s by Charles, third Earl Somers. The castle now houses a collection of armour, tapestries, furniture and paintings. Lavish Italianate and Gothic interiors have recently been restored.

Eastnor Castle

■192■ **FORD GREEN HALL**   ☎ 01782 233195
Ford Green Road, Smallthorne, Stoke-on-Trent, Staffordshire ST6 1NG
In Smallthorne on B5051 Burslem–Endon road
Open all year exc Christmas and New Year: Sun–Thurs 1–5
Timber-framed house built in 1624 for Hugh Ford. The house is the product of several centuries of alterations and additions to the original building, carried out by successive owners. By the late sixteenth century, as standards of living in England began to rise, many new houses were being built, and Ford Green is a fairly typical example of the type of luxurious new home, complete with upper floors and chimneys, which replaced the old-fashioned and smoky medieval halls. At Ford Green it is thought that the present timber-framed building may have been added to an earlier house of this kind which has since been destroyed.

■193■ **HADDON HALL**   ☎ 01629 812855
Bakewell, Derbyshire DE45 1LA
2 miles S of Bakewell on A6
Open Apr–Sept: daily 10.30–5; Oct: Mon–Thurs 10.30–4.30
Battlemented Haddon Hall has hardly changed for 400 years, and it is one of the most complete and best-preserved medieval manor houses in England.

Building started in the twelfth century, and there has been very little added
to it since the reign of Henry VIII. Its owners, the Dukes of Rutland, moved to
Belvoir Castle in around 1700 and left their old family home unoccupied and
unaltered for over 200 years. The stone buildings are all grouped around two
courtyards, each on a different level. The oldest part is the painted chapel; the
kitchen and the banqueting hall, with its minstrels' gallery, date from the fourteenth century; the Long Gallery, which was added in the seventeenth century,
leads to beautiful terraced rose gardens. After that there were no further
changes or additions, and no other medieval house has withstood the test of
time so triumphantly. The full beauty of Haddon Hall is best appreciated from
the gardens.

■194■ **HALLS CROFT** ☎ 01789 204016
Old Town, Stratford-upon-Avon, Warwickshire CV37 6BG
In town centre
Open mid-Mar–mid-Oct: Mon–Sat 9.30–5, Sun 10–5; mid-Oct–mid-Mar: Mon–Sat 10–4,
Sun 10.30–4
House displaying all the essential characteristics of half-timbered buildings
common in Stratford-upon-Avon in Shakespeare's time. Built on a stone foundation, the structure is of substantial oak timber framing and lath and plaster,
with a tiled roof of many gables surmounted by picturesque chimney stacks.
The northern portion of the building dates from the early sixteenth century: the
lower storey has close-set timber framing, and the overhanging upper floor rests
on shaped brackets carved from upright posts. This was evidently the original
house, a small, compact dwelling with outbuildings at the rear, which was
enlarged at the beginning of the seventeenth century. The present entrance
hall, staircase and landing were built at that time to link the original house with
rooms added on the south side at the front and with an improved kitchen at
the rear. During the eighteenth and nineteenth centuries further additions were
made, such as the bay windows to the frontage and the insertion of larger
windows in various rooms, which seriously weakened the structure. The rooms
are now finished in the style of a middle-class Tudor home.

■195■ **HANBURY HALL** ☎ 01527 821214
School Road, Hanbury, Droitwich, Worcestershire WR9 7EA
4 miles E of Droitwich, 1 mile N of B4090, 1 mile W of B4091
Open House Apr–mid-Oct: Sun–Wed 2–6. Gardens same, 12.30–6
The present substantial brick house was purchased in 1631 by an unknown
architect and was completed in 1701 for Thomas Vernon, a successful barrister.
The formal gardens laid out at the same time by George London were broken
up in the late eighteenth century as they were no longer fashionable but have
now been recreated. The orangery dates from soon after 1732. The outstanding
feature of the interior is James Thornhill's painted staircase, with its great
classical scenes, which dates from around 1710. Thornhill also carried out the
ceiling paintings in the Long Room.

■196■ **HARDWICK HALL** ☎ 01246 850430
Doe Lea, Chesterfield, Derbyshire S44 5QJ
M1 junction 29 and follow tourist signs
Open Apr–Oct: Wed, Thurs, Sat, Sun and Bank Hol Mons 12.30–5 (last admission 4.30)
Complete late-Elizabethan mansion built by Bess of Hardwick in 1597 after the
death of her fourth husband, the Earl of Shrewsbury. Architecturally important

for the innovations introduced by Bess and her architect Robert Smythson, particularly the use of glass in the building, with great expanses of windows, which shows the wealth of the family. Domestic arrangements had servants' quarters on the ground floor, family apartments on the first floor and state rooms on the second. Magnificent stone staircase soars up through the centre of the house, Long Gallery and High Great Chamber, which has been described as 'the finest room not only in England but in all Europe'.

■197■ **KEDLESTON HALL**   ☎ 01332 842191
Derby, Derbyshire DE22 5JH
5 miles NW of Derby, signposted from A38/A52 roundabout
Open late Mar–Oct: Sun–Wed 12–4.30; Nov and Dec: Sat and Sun 12–4
Regarded by many as the finest Robert Adam mansion in the country, Kedleston has been the home of the Curzon family for over eight centuries. When their original house was demolished at the end of the seventeenth century the architect Matthew Brettingham gave the house its present-day plan of a main block and two wings linked by corridors. The imposing north front was added by James Paine, and it wasn't until 1760 that Robert Adam appeared on the scene. He built the south front and designed most of the interior, including the Marble Hall, which is regarded as one of the most splendid rooms in Europe. The house has notable collections of seventeenth-century Dutch and Italian paintings, eighteenth-century furniture, china and Indian works of art collected by Lord Curzon when he was viceroy of India. The large park has several buildings by Adam, including a boathouse and a bridge over the lake.

■198■ **MARY ARDEN'S HOUSE**   ☎ 01789 204016
Station Road, Wilmcote, Stratford-upon-Avon, Warwickshire CV37 9UN
3 miles NW of Stratford-upon-Avon off A3400
Open mid-Mar–mid-Oct: Sat 9.30–5, Sun 10–5; mid-Oct–mid-Mar: Mon–Sat 10–4,
Sun 10.30–4
Tudor farmstead, home of William Shakespeare's mother, mostly dating from the early sixteenth century with an old stone dovecote and farm buildings. The timbered frontage of the house is of striking size and proportions. The outer walls are of substantial timber framing standing on a stone foundation about 3 feet (0.9 metres) from the ground. The timber came from the Forest of Arden, and the stone was quarried in Wilmcote. The timbers are set close together at the front of the house, but at the back the framing is at wider intervals, forming large panels that were originally filled in with clay on a wattle foundation. The roof is covered with hand-made tiles and has pretty dormer windows. Inside the farmhouse, the rooms maintain the atmosphere of a Tudor homestead with typical pieces of period farm furniture and utensils. The kitchen has a paved stone floor, small leaden windows and raftered ceiling.

■199■ **OLD COLEHURST MANOR**   ☎ 01630 638833
Sutton-upon-Tern, Market Drayton, Shropshire TF9 2JB
1 mile from A41 in Colehurst
Open Mar–Oct: Tues–Fri, Sun and Bank Hols 11–5 and all day Sat and Mon
by appointment
Built in around 1580 and restored recently over a seven-year period. The house has been painstakingly taken apart and rebuilt using wattle and daub and traditional building and carpentry skills There are rose, herb, seventeenth-century pot and salad gardens and a formal Elizabethan knot garden.

■200■ THE OLD HOUSE ☎ 01432 260694
High Town, Hereford, Herefordshire HR1 2AA
In centre of Hereford in pedestrian area
Open Apr–Sept: Tues–Sun plus Bank Hol Mons 10–5 (4 on Sun)
Good example of the timber framed dwellings typical of this Borders area.
The Old House is a three-storey town dwelling with an attic, central stone and
brick chimney stack, original stone-tiled roof, cleft-oak and hazel with daub infill
panels, including much lavishly decorated carvings and jettied second floor.
The house's structural and decorative features provide some evidence as to the
wealth of the original owner; the second floor juts out over the other floors –
a well-known technique to increase floor space inside, when available ground
space was at a premium; projecting bay windows are supported on carved brackets, and the bargeboards under the eaves are carved with heads and stylised flora
and fauna. The craftsmen involved were encouraged and allowed to display their
skills, using time and materials that only a fairly wealthy person could afford.
Although many of the basic features of the Old House are of the original 1621
construction, many alterations and restoration projects have taken place over
the years which have changed the building's character. The interior shows the
domestic arrangements of an early-seventeenth-century house.

■201■ ROUSHAM HOUSE ☎ 01869 347110
Rousham, Nr Steeple Aston, Bicester, Oxfordshire OX6 3QX
W of Bicester off B4030
Open House Apr–Sept: Wed–Sun and Bank Hol Mons 2–4.30. Garden all year: 10–4.30
Attractive seventeenth-century mansion built by Robert Dormer. A Royalist
garrison in the Civil War, it had shooting holes cut into its doors. Sir Robert's
successors, who were Masters of Ceremonies at court for eight reigns, embellished Rousham by employing court artists and architects. William Kent and
Roberts of Oxford also decorated rooms during the eighteenth century. The
house contains over 150 portraits and other pictures and also much fine
contemporary furniture. The gardens, by William Kent, are his only work to
survive unspoiled. Extending to over 30 acres, with the River Cherwell flowing
through them, they include classical buildings, cascades, statues, fine walled
gardens and herbaceous borders, a small parterre and views over the river.

■202■ SHAKESPEARE'S BIRTHPLACE ☎ 01789 204016
The Shakespeare Centre, Henley Street, Stratford-upon-Avon, Warwickshire
CV37 6QW
In centre of Stratford-upon-Avon
*Open mid-Mar–mid-Oct: Mon–Sat 9–5, Sun 9.30–5; mid-Oct–mid-Mar: Mon–Sat 9.30–4,
Sun 10–4*
The greater part of this timber-framed house was built in the late fifteenth or
early sixteenth centuries using local materials: timber from the Forest of Arden
and blue-grey stone from Wilmcote. The house consists of a low foundation
wall of stone on which is erected a framing of oak beams. The spaces between
the timbers are filled in with wattle and daub, and the structure is consolidated
by a massive stone chimney stack in the centre and a raftered roof. On the
lower frontage of the building, the timbers are the early close-studded variety,
about 9 inches (23 centimetres) wide and the same distance apart, with rectangular patterns in the upper storey. Though now detached, the house originally
formed part of a continuous frontage of houses and shops. The buildings on
either side were knocked down in 1857 to reduce the risk of fire. The rooms are

furnished in Elizabethan and Jacobean style (currently being redisplayed). The timber-framed walls and raftered ceiling of the living-room illustrate the extent to which timber was used in the construction of houses of this period.

■203■ SHUGBOROUGH   ☎ 01889 881388
The Shugborough Estate, Milford, Nr Stafford ST17 0XB
6 miles E of Stafford on A513
Open Easter–late Sept: daily 11–5; Oct: Sun 11–5
Set on the edge of Cannock Chase, Shugborough is an eighteenth-century classical house set in a beautiful 900-acre landscaped park. The present house was started in 1693 and has been greatly altered by successive generations of the Anson family. Between 1745 and 1748 the house was extended to feature rococo plasterwork by Vassali and further improved towards the end of the eighteenth century by the well-known architect Samuel Wyatt. These improvements included the addition of eight massive Ionic columns forming the grand portico. The gardens and park are home to a variety of monuments, including the Chinese House, Tower of Winds and Triumphal Arch.

■204■ SNOWSHILL MANOR   ☎ 01386 852410
Snowshill, Broadway, Worcestershire WR12 7JU
3 miles S of Broadway; turn off A44 Broadway bypass into Broadway village
Open Apr–late Oct: Wed–Sun (and Mon in July and Aug) and Bank Hol Mons 12–5.
Garden as House 11–5. Last admission 4.15
Cotswold manor house with a seventeenth-century façade. It dates mainly from around 1500; it was altered and enlarged in around 1600 and given its classical south front in about 1700. The last owner was Charles Paget Wade (1919–51), whose hobby was collecting anything and everything. The result is a house that is full of fascinating objects, including musical instruments, Japanese armour, clocks, toys, bicycles, oriental masks and spinners' and weavers' equipment.

■205■ SUDBURY HALL   ☎ 01283 585305
Sudbury, Uttoxeter, Derbyshire DE6 5HT
6 miles E of Uttoxeter, at junction of A50 and A515
Open Easter–late Oct: Wed–Sun and Bank Hols except Good Fri 1–5.30
Sudbury is largely the creation of George Vernon, who succeeded to the estate in 1660. He immediately began to rebuild the old manor house of his ancestors in a style that combined old-fashioned Jacobean features with carved stone, wood and plasterwork in the up-to-date classical style of Sir Christopher Wren's churches. The decoration of the interior carried on for many years, with the final touches coming in the 1690s with Louis Laguerre's baroque murals and painted ceilings to the staircase, saloon and other rooms. Few changes have been made to the building apart from the addition of a servants' wing in the late nineteenth century, which now houses a Museum of Childhood.

■206■ WALCOT HALL   ☎ 0171 5812782
Lydbury North, Shropshire SY7 8AZ
3 miles E of Bishop's Castle on B4385
Open House: by appointment. Arboretum Apr–Oct: Fri–Sun 12–4.30.
Georgian house built for Lord Clive of India on the site of a seventeenth-century house that was originally constructed for the Walcot family. Although it has been reduced in size to suit present-day requirements, its aspect is as intended by Chambers – a perfect Georgian elevation, with parapet walls and sash windows.

It has a freestanding ballroom, a stableyard with matching twin clock towers and an extensive walled garden. There is an arboretum, beautiful lakes and woodlands on the estate as well as an ice house, meat safe and dovecote.

🏛 WALES   MAP 5

■207■ ABERCONWY HOUSE ☎ 01492 592246
Castle Street, Conwy, Conwy LL32 8AY
At junction of Castle Street and High Street in Conwy
Open late Mar–Oct: Wed–Mon 10–5 (ast admission 4.30)
Medieval merchant's house with furnished rooms showing daily life from different periods in its history. The date of its building is uncertain, part of it is probably fourteenth century and certainly the whole house is not later than early sixteenth century and the arch to one of the ground-floor doorways (now a window) is thought to date from the fourteenth century. The ground floor, which was probably a shop or storeroom, is now some 2 feet (0.6 metres) below street level as a result of successive pavings and repavings of the street. On the first floor there is an oriel window with window seats and a fine old fireplace. The roof construction over the main room on the second floor shows the simple but skilled craftsmanship involved.

■208■ BODELWYDDAN CASTLE ☎ 01745 584060
Bodelwyddan, Denbighshire LL18 5YA
Adjacent to A55 near St Asaph
Open Apr–Oct: Sat–Thurs 11–5; Nov–Mar: Tues–Thurs and Sat and Sun 11–4
Eighteenth-century country home of Sir William Williams, Speaker of the House of Commons. Transformed into the present-day mock castle by Sir John Hay in the early nineteenth century. The towers, arches and castellations were all added by the famous architects Welsh and Hansom. Its interior reflects various periods and design styles from the nineteenth century and provides an appropriate setting for a collection of portraits and photography from the National Portrait Gallery, furniture from the Victoria and Albert Museum and sculpture from the Royal Academy. Visitors can enjoy the 'hands-on' galleries of Victorian parlour games, puzzles and optical illusions.

■209■ CASTELL COCH ☎ 029 2081 0101
Forrest Farm Industrial Estate, Whitchurch, Cardiff CF4 7YS
Near Tongwynlais, off A470, 5 miles NW of Cardiff
Open Apr–late May: 9.30–5; late May–late Oct: daily
9.30–6.30 (5 in Oct); Nov–Mar: daily 9.30–4, Sun 11–4
Late nineteenth century fairy-tale castle, designed for the third Marquess of Bute by William Burgess. The original thirteenth-century castle provided the inspiration for Burges's romantic vision of the Middle Ages. The castle has three round towers with conical roofs, along with a drawbridge and portcullis. The inside of the castle is lavishly decorated and furnished in Gothic style with a number of murals, giltwork, statues and carvings. The most spectacular room is probably Lady Bute's bedroom, which has a domed ceiling painted on the theme of Sleeping Beauty.

Castell Coch

■210■ ERDDIG HALL ☎ 01978 355314
Erddig, Wrexham LL13 0YT
2 miles S of Wrexham, signposted off the A483 and A525
Open late Mar–Oct: Sat–Wed and Good Fri 12–5 (4 in Oct)

Erddig Hall

Fascinating house dating from the seventeenth century with eighteenth-century
additions. Erddig is of particular interest because of the unusually close relation-
ship that existed between the family of the house and their servants. A mason
called Thomas Webb built the central portion of the house between 1684 and
1687, and John Mellor, who bought the property in 1716, added wings in 1724,
which he may well have designed himself. He is responsible for the state rooms,
with their splendid furniture which is thought of as Erddig's outstanding
feature. James Wyatt was associated with the stone facing of the west front in
the 1770s, and Thomas Hopper designed the neoclassical dining-room in 1826.
Erddig has a range of outbuildings and domestic rooms complete with contemporary equipment. A unique picture of the domestic history of the house is
given by the beautiful and evocative range of outbuildings, which include
kitchen, laundry, stables, bakehouse, sawmill, smithy, joiner's shop and servants'
hall. There is a large walled garden which has been restored to its eighteenth-
century formal design.

■211■ PENRHYN CASTLE ☎ 01248 353084
Bangor, Gwynedd LL57 4HN
1 mile E of Bangor at Llandegai on A5122
Open late Mar–Oct: Wed–Mon 12–5 (11 in July and Aug)
Dramatic neo-Norman castle between the Menai Strait and the mountains of
Snowdonia built by Thomas Hopper between 1820 and 1845 for the wealthy
Pennant family who had made their fortune from slate-mining. The castle
virtually obliterated the earlier Gothic house that had been built here in around
1800 by Samuel Wyatt. Hopper was allowed a free hand in designing the house,

and with both interior and exterior he achieved the spacious yet solidly massive effect that was his highly personal interpretation of Norman architecture. The extraordinarily grand staircase and extravagant stone carvings create an almost cathedral-like effect. At the same time, modern details included a hot-air heating system and water closets. The castle contains fascinating mock-Norman furniture, panelling and plasterwork, all designed by Hopper, and some unusual examples of craftsmanship in slate, such as a carved slate bed made by locals for Queen Victoria's visit in 1859. She refused to sleep in it, as she said it would be like sleeping in a tomb. The castle also has an industrial railway museum and a Victorian terraced walled garden.

■212■ **PLAS MAWR**   ☎ 01492 580167
High Street, Conwy
Signposted in town centre
Open Apr–end Oct: Tues–Sun 9.30–6.00
Perfect Elizabethan jewel, tucked away within the walls of Conwy. Plas Mawr is one of the best-preserved Elizabethan town houses in Britain, famous for the quality and quantity of its plasterwork decoration, which has been faithfully restored. The house is furnished and laid out to show what life was like for the Tudor gentry and their servants at a time when the creation of increased wealth among merchants and the gentry meant that private homes could be furnished and decorated lavishly.

■213■ **TUDOR MERCHANTS HOUSE**   ☎ 01834 842279
Quay Hill, Tenby, Pembrokeshire SA70 7BX
Signposted in Tenby
Open Easter–Sept: Thurs–Tues 10–5 (1 on Sun); Oct: Thurs, Fri, Mon and Tues 10–3, Sun 12–3
A late-fifteenth-century town house, characteristic of the area and of the time, when Tenby was a thriving trading port. It's the kind of house a reasonably successful Tudor merchant might have owned, living on the first and second floors and doing his trading on the ground floor. Fine ground-floor chimney at the rear of the house and original scarfed roof trusses survive. The remains of early frescos can be seen on three interior walls, and the house is furnished to re-create family life in the Tudor period.

🏚 NORTH-WEST   MAP 6

■214■ **ADLINGTON HALL**   ☎ 01625 820875
Macclesfield, Cheshire SK10 4LF
5 miles N of Macclesfield on A523
Open throughout the year to groups by prior arrangement only
Adlington Hall is a manor house, the home of the Leghs since 1315. The east wing and two sides of the courtyard were built in the typical black and white Cheshire style in 1581. Internally, the Great Hall features a hammerbeam roof richly moulded, and two heavily carved oak trees remain, their roots in the ground, supporting the east end of the hall. Spectacular murals in the Great Hall date from 1705. The south front and west wing, containing the dining-room and drawing-room, were added between 1749 and 1757 and are built of red brick with a stone portico with four Ionic columns. The gardens were landscaped in the style of Capability Brown in the eighteenth century.

■215■ CAPESTHORNE HALL ☎ 01625 861221
Macclesfield, Cheshire SK11 9JY
A34 S of Alderley Edge
Open Apr–Oct: Sun, Wed and Bank Hols Hall 1.30–5.30 (last admission 3.30), Gardens and Chapel 12–5.30
Distinctively turreted, red-brick, eighteenth-century Jacobean-style hall looking out over 100 acres (40 hectares) of Cheshire parkland. Within it there is a fine collection of paintings, sculptures, furniture and tapestries. Close to the house is a chapel dating from 1719, where services are still held.

■216■ DALEMAIN ☎ 01768 486450
Penrith, Cumbria CA11 0HB
On A592 SW of Penrith
Open Easter–early Oct: Sun–Thurs 10.30–4
Part medieval, part Tudor and part Georgian house. Dalemain was originally a medieval peel tower, which was added to in Tudor times and completed in 1745 when the imposing Georgian façade was added. Behind this façade, the surprise of Dalemain is its sheer variety. It's a real hotchpotch whose evolution has been dictated sometimes by domestic or agricultural demands and sometimes by the fashion of the day. As a result, parts of the house are a glorious confusion of winding passages, quaint little stairways and unexpected rooms, which include a Victorian nursery and a housekeeper's room. It also has splendid oak panelling, Chinese wallpaper, Tudor plasterwork and fine Queen Anne and Georgian furniture. Outside there is a sixteenth-century cobbled courtyard, gardens and a deer park.

■217 LEVENS HALL ☎ 01539 560321
Kendal, Cumbria LA8 0PD
5 miles S of Kendal on A6
Open Apr–mid-Oct: Sun–Thurs, Gardens 10–5, House 12–5 (last admission 4.30)
Elizabethan mansion built on to a thirteenth-century peel tower. Levens Hall is noted for its fine plasterwork and panelling. The house, which has been in the ownership of the Bagot family for over 700 years, contains fine furniture and the earliest English patchwork dating from around 1708. Its most remarkable feature is the topiary garden, laid out in 1694 and little changed since then.

■218■ LITTLE MORETON HALL ☎ 01260 272018
Congleton, Cheshire CW12 4SD
On A34, 4 miles S of Congleton
Open mid-Mar–Oct: Wed–Sun and Bank Hol Mons 11.30–5;
(last admission 4.30) Nov–mid-Dec: Sat and Sun 11.30–4. Guided tours daily

Fred's FAVOURITE

Idyllic moated half-timbered manor widely regarded as one of the finest examples of timber-framed architecture in Britain. Built in the mid-fifteenth century and gradually extended over the next 150 years, the house has survived almost unchanged since then. On the outside its timbers are arranged in a rich variety of patterns, giving the house its characteristic black and white patchwork effect. The house rises to three storeys with a spectacular Long Gallery at the top. Through the gatehouse there is a lovely courtyard with two-storey bay windows in one corner, and throughout there are rare wall-paintings and intricate carvings and woodwork. The carpentry, plasterwork, painting and glazing skills of the Tudor craftsmen can all be appreciated here.

■219■ RUFFORD OLD HALL ☎ 01704 821254
Rufford, near Ormskirk, Lancashire L40 1SG
7 miles N of Ormskirk on E side of A59
Open Apr–Oct: Sat–Wed 1–5. Thurs and other selected days in Aug
One of the finest sixteenth-century buildings in Lancashire. Home of the
Hesketh family, the Old Hall shows three phases of construction spanning 350
years. Originally a typical H-shaped house of Tudor times, only the central part
of this – the Great Hall – survives. This is a magnificent example of Tudor construction, richly carved and nobly proportioned, with a fine hammerbeam roof.
A three-storey brick building was erected at the north end of the east wing in
1662, and later the east wing itself was rebuilt using sixteenth-century timbers.
The east wing was then enlarged and refitted in an 1820s Tudor Gothic style by
the Liverpool architect John Foster. The house contains fine collections of six-
teenth- and seventeenth-century oak furniture, arms, armour and tapestries.

■220■ SPEKE HALL ☎ 0151 427 7231
The Walk, Speke, Liverpool, Merseyside L24 1XD
8 miles SE of Liverpool city centre, S of A561. Signposted
Open Apr–Oct: Tues–Sun and Bank Hol Mons 1–5.30; Nov–mid-Dec: Sat and Sun 1–4.30
Tucked between an industrial estate and the main runway of Liverpool's Speke
Airport is another great half-timbered manor. Speke Hall was started in 1490,
but most of the house is Elizabethan and the outside appearance has hardly
changed since then. Structurally, it is one of the least altered of Tudor houses,
with wooden panelling and elaborate plasterwork in a series of fairly small
rooms. But the furnishings and fittings are those of a Victorian family home –
an interesting and successful juxtaposition of Tudor and Victorian styles.

■221■ TATTON PARK ☎ 01625 534400
Knutsford, Cheshire WA16 6QN
5 miles from M6 junction 19 and M56 junction 8
Open Apr–Oct: check for times
Large Regency mansion with extravagantly decorated state rooms containing
collections of furniture, glass and paintings by Italian and Dutch masters. The
staircase hall has a screen of giant marble columns, and a domed skylight brings
natural light into the centre of the house. Sofas and chairs are in the style of
Robert Adam. The garden is set within extensive landscaped parkland and is one
of the finest and most important within the custody of the National Trust.

⛰ NORTH-EAST   MAP 7

■222■ ASKE HALL ☎ 01748 850391
Aske, Richmond, North Yorkshire DL10 5HJ
2 miles E of Richmond on Gilling West Road, B6274
Open: all year Sat and Sun. Phone for group bookings
Beautiful Georgian hall situated in Capability Brown parkland. Family seat of the
Dundas family for over 200 years, it boasts an impressive collection of eighteenth
century furniture, paintings and porcelain. Over the centuries the hall has undergone many changes, reflecting architectural trends of the time. Both the thirteenth-
century peel tower and remodelled Jacobean tower remain integral parts of the
house. The notable Yorkshire architect John Carr built a grand stableblock in
1764. It was converted into a family chapel in Victorian times, with an impressive

Italianate interior, and is still used today for services. A Georgian coach-house with clock tower houses the family's superb carriage. There are several follies in the grounds, including a Gothic-style temple designed by Daniel Garrett in 1745.

■223■ **AUCKLAND CASTLE**   ☎ 01388 601627
Bishop Auckland, Durham DL14 7NP
In Bishop Auckland
Open May–mid-July and Sept: Fri, Sun 2–5; mid-July–Aug: Sun–Fri 2–5; Bank Hols 2–5
Auckland Castle has been the home of the Bishops of Durham for the past 800 years. It has been extended every 200 years since the original banqueting hall was built in the twelfth century. The castle is approached through a magnificent Gothic gateway crowned by a turreted clock and weathervane dating from around 1760, adjoining which is the castellated gatehouse lodge, Elizabethan in appearance. The magnificent chapel, converted from a medieval aisled hall in the seventeenth century, has a beautifully ornamented ceiling.

■224■ **BENINGBROUGH HALL**   ☎ 01904 470666
Beningbrough, York, North Yorkshire YO30 1DD
8 miles NW of York signposted from A59 and A19
Open House Apr–Oct: Mon–Wed, Sat, Sun and Good Fri plus Fri July–Aug 12–5.30
(last admission 4.30). Garden same as House: 11–5.30
Beningbrough was completed in 1716, and its beautiful, symmetrical façade of fine rubbed red brick with stone quoins is little changed. It was built for the local squire, John Bourchier, by a York carpenter-architect, William Thornton, probably with the advice of the better-known Thomas Archer. Its dignified architecture is enriched by the quality of its decorative detail, particularly Thornton's elaborate woodcarving. The finest features are the Great Hall, which rises through two storeys , and the Great Staircase, which is built of oak, with wide parquetry treads and delicate balusters carved to imitate wrought iron. The hall, with its restrained plasterwork, elegant arches and fluted pilasters, is one of the most beautiful baroque interiors in England and contains furniture, oriental porcelain, and paintings.

■225■ **BOLLING HALL**   ☎ 01274 723057
Bowling Hall Road, Bradford, West Yorkshire BD4 7LP
1 mile from city centre off A650, follow signposts
Open all year: Wed–Fri 11–4, Sat 10–5, Sun 12–5, Bank Hol Mons 11–4
Classic West Yorkshire manor complete with galleried hall. The house dates mainly from the seventeenth-century but has medieval and eighteenth century sections. It has panelled rooms and plasterwork in original colours as well as heraldic glass and a rare Chippendale bed.

■226■ **BURTON AGNES HALL**   ☎ 01262 490324
Burton Agnes, Great Driffield, East Riding of Yorkshire YO25 4ND
On A166 between Great Driffield and Bridlington
Open Apr–Oct: daily 11–5
Fine example of a late-Elizabethan house with marvellous seventeenth-century carvings, still lived in by descendants of the family who built it in 1598. The beautifully proportioned hall has seen few alterations or additions in its history. Imposing gatehouse dates from 1610. Great Hall and Red Drawing-Room with Elizabethan carvings, plasterwork and panelling. Long Gallery fully restored in 1974. Beautiful state rooms full of carvings, lovely furniture and a fine collection of French and English Impressionist paintings.

■227■ BURTON CONSTABLE HALL ☎ 01964 562400

Nr Skirlaugh, East Riding of Yorkshire HU11 4LN
Off A165 Bridlington road from Hull
Open Easter–Oct: Sat–Thurs 1–5. Grounds 12–5
Great English country house. Surviving parts of the medieval manor house
include the north wing, its tower with projecting staircase turret, and possibly
also a southward extension. In the later 1560s Sir John Constable transformed
the house, adding a new range for the present Great Hall and a south wing
containing a kitchen, chapel and further lodgings. The sixteenth century saw
further alteration, including the south and west front. William Constable was
strongly tempted to demolish the house and rebuild. Instead he chose to mod-
ernise, sacrificing the Elizabethan great bay on the east front to make a grand
entrance door. The last major change was Sir Clifford's restoration of stone
mullioned windows in place of his predecessor's Georgian sashes on the west
front, and the building of a turret on top of the south tower.

■228■ CASTLE HOWARD ☎ 01653 648444

Castle Howard, York, North Yorkshire YO60 7DA
NE of York, off A64 near Malton
Open early Mar–mid-Oct: daily 11–4.30 (Grounds open at 10)
Stately palace designed by John Vanbrugh, a friend of the owner Charles
Howard, third Earl of Carlisle, in 1699. One of Britain's best-known and most
spectacular stately homes. Although building work began around 1700, the
construction took in total more than a hundred years. On completion, façades
decorated with coronets, ciphers and coats of arms and a beautiful masonry
dome, the first of its kind on a private residence in England, made Castle Howard
an impressive sight. No less dramatic is its interior, with its Grand Staircase, Great
Hall, beneath the dome, and Long Gallery. There is a china collection of over 300
pieces, including Crown Derby, Meissen and Chelsea. The Antique Passage has a
vaulted ceiling and is lined with statues and busts throughout its length.

■229■ CRAGSIDE ☎ 01669 620333

Cragside, Rothbury, Morpeth, Northumberland NE65 7PX

Fred's
FAVOURITE

E of Rothbury off B6341
Open House Apr–Oct: Tues–Sun and Bank Hol Mons 1–5.30
This dramatic Victorian country mansion, set in rugged countryside, is the
creation of the great Victorian inventor, engineer and gunmaker Sir William
(later Lord) Armstrong. At first an unexciting stone villa, the architect Richard
Norman Shaw continually added to it from 1870 to 1884 to create a building
large enough to be a family home and showy enough to impress visiting clients.
Shaw's old English style is demonstrated in a bewildering array of timber-framed
gables and tall chimney stacks and towers. Most of the living-rooms are sited to
receive superb views to the west. The house has retained most of its original
fittings, and the library survives as one of the best Victorian interiors still intact,
with stained glass made by William Morris & Co and designed by Rossetti. In
1880 this room became the first in the world to be lit by electricity powered by
a hydroelectric generator, which was invented by Sir William himself and which
can still be seen in the grounds today. The drawing-room, dominated by a huge
carved marble chimneypiece and inglenook, was the last great addition. In the
1880s, as well as electricity, the house had hot and cold running water, central
heating, fire alarms, phones and a passenger lift. Examples of Armstrong's ingenu-
ity in the field of hydraulics and engineering are all around the house and grounds.

■230■ EAST RIDDLESDEN HALL ☎ 01535 607075
Bradford Road, Keighley, West Yorkshire BD20 5EL
1 mile N of Keighley
Open Apr–Oct: Tues, Wed, Sun and Bank Hols (plus Mon July–Aug) 12–5, Sat 1–5
Charming seventeenth-century manor house with panelled rooms, fine plasterwork and mullioned windows. Mostly built around 1648 for James Murgatroyd,
a Halifax clothier. Both main façades are impressive, with mullioned windows,
gables, finials, and great porches with circular windows. The main part of the
house lies to the left of the northern entrance, with the banqueting hall to the
right. Beyond that is the classical façade of a wing that was added in 1692. The
house contains a good collection of Yorkshire oak furniture, pewter and textiles,
and the stone-flagged kitchen contains seventeenth- and eighteenth-century
furniture and domestic items. Also a seventeenth-century oak-framed barn.

■231■ FAIRFAX HOUSE ☎ 01904 655543
Castlegate, York, North Yorkshire YO1 9RN
In centre of York, near Clifford Tower
Open mid-Feb–Dec: Mon–Thurs and Sat 11–5, Sun 1.30–5 (last admission 4.30)
One of the finest town houses in England, this eighteenth-century house,
designed by John Carr of York, has been described as a 'class architectural
masterpiece of its age'. Superbly decorated plasterwork, wrought iron and
wood. The house contains fine examples of Georgian furniture, porcelain,
paintings and clocks that form the Terry collection. There is a special display of
a re-created meal dating from 1763 in the dining-room and kitchen.

■232■ HAREWOOD HOUSE ☎ 01132 886331
The Harewood Estate, Harewood, Leeds, West Yorkshire LS17 9LQ
7 miles from Leeds and Harrogate on A61
Open Apr–Oct: daily House 11–4.30, Bird Gardens 10–5; Grounds 10–6
Designed by John Carr of York and completed in 1772 with lavish interiors by
Robert Adam, Harewood House is an outstanding example of neoclassical architecture. Ceilings, friezes and chimneypieces throughout the house were designed
by Adam as part of an overall unified decorative scheme. Elegant gallery extending
over the whole west end of the house is one of his most magnificent achievements.
Thomas Chippendale, born a few miles away at Otley, was responsible for all the
furniture throughout the house. Art collections including works by Reynolds,
Hoppner and Gainsborough and contemporary art exhibitions. Capability Brown
gardens, complete with lake, surrounding the house feature a terrace overlooking
the lake added only in the nineteenth century.

■233■ NOSTELL PRIORY ☎ 01924 863892
Doncaster Road, Nostell, Wakefield, West Yorkshire WF4 1QE
On A638 Wakefield to Doncaster road
Open late Mar–Jun and early Sept–mid-Sept: Thurs–Sun 12–5; July–Aug: Wed–Sun 12–5
Mid-eighteenth-century mansion set in parkland, currently closed for refurbishment. Nostell Priory is an almost unchanged example of eighteenth-century
architecture and has superb decoration and furnishings. The main block was
designed by James Paine in around 1736, and Robert Adam added an additional wing and completed work on the interior in 1766. Fine rococo staircases,
dining-room and state bedchamber, all with magnificent plasterwork, and one
of the finest and most complete collections of Chippendale furniture in the
country. The house also contains many important paintings and beautiful

eighteenth-century wallpapers, a notable saloon and tapestry-room, and displays pictures and Chippendale furniture. Outside there are rose gardens and beautiful lakeside walks.

■234■ RIPLEY CASTLE ☎ 01423 770152
Estate Office, Ripley, Harrogate, North Yorkshire HG3 3AY
Off A61 3½ miles N of Harrogate
Open Jan–Mar and Nov–Dec: Tues, Thurs, Sat and Sun 10.30–3; Apr–Jun and Sept–Oct: Thurs–Sun 10.30–3; July–Aug: daily 10.30–3
Home to the Ingilby family since 1320, Ripley Castle's gatehouse was built to keep the Scots out in 1450, the old tower in 1555 and the rest of the castle that we see today in 1780. The Knight's Chamber contains a priest hole. Walled garden, lake and deer park in the grounds.

■235■ SEATON DELAVAL HALL ☎ 0191 237 1493
Estate Office, Whitley Bay, Northumberland NE26 4QR
½ mile from coast at Seaton Sluice
Open Jun–Sept: Wed, Sun and May and Aug Bank Hol Mons 2–6
Splendid English baroque house. Sir John Vanbrugh, the playwright turned architect, began the house in 1718 for Admiral George Delaval, but building work ceased in 1728 following the architect's death. The house consists of a central block between two arcaded and pedimented wings. In 1822 the central block was gutted by fire but was partially restored in 1862 and again in 1959. The east wing contains fine stables, and the grounds contain extensive gardens and statues. There is also a Norman church, a coach-house with an interesting collection of vehicles and an ice-house.

■236■ SHIBDEN HALL ☎ 01422 352246
Lister Road, Halifax, West Yorkshire HX3 6XG
Off A58 Halifax to Leeds road NE of Halifax
Open all year: Mon–Sat 10–5, Sun 12–5 (last admission 4.30 or earlier in winter)
Partly half-timbered house, built between the fifteenth and seventeenth centuries, standing in attractive park. Shibden Hall contains a good collection of period furniture. Seventeenth-century barn and outbuildings house the Folk Museum of West Yorkshire, which has a brewhouse, a dairy and a collection of agricultural implements and horse-drawn vehicles.

■237■ TREASURER'S HOUSE ☎ 01904 624247
Minster Yard, Chapter House Street, York, North Yorkshire YO1 7JL
In Minster Yard on N side of Minster, parking in Lord Mayor's Walk
Open Apr–Oct Nov: Sat–Thurs 10.30–5
Elegant seventeenth-century house standing within the tranquil surroundings of the Minster close. Medieval in origin, the house gets its name because successive treasurers of York Minster lived here from 1100 to 1547, but the bases of Roman columns in the cellars suggest that a house has occupied the site for almost 2,000 years. The present building dates mainly from the seventeenth and eighteenth centuries and, apart from the medieval character of the Great Hall and its staircase leading to a half-timbered gallery, the style of the house is Palladian and early Georgian. The garden front and centre range, dating from 1630, are the work of Thomas Young, while the Venetian windows and Dutch gables were added a century later when the house was divided up. All through the house, as we see it today, there is a rare quality of decorative detail, with

some outstanding examples of plasterwork, panelling and elaborate chimney-pieces. The house was rescued from years of neglect by wealthy local industrialist Frank Green, who carefully restored it between 1897 and 1914 and made it his home. It is now as he left it, with many fine pieces of furniture and notable collections of china, pottery and glass.

■238■ WALLINGTON HOUSE   ☎ 01670 774283
Cambo, Morpus, Northumberland NE61 4AP
S of Cambo on B6342, 6 miles NW of Belsay (A696)
Open House all year: Wed–Mon 1–5.30 (4.30 in Oct). Grounds all year: daily 10–dusk
Lying at the heart of a 13,000-acre estate in beautiful countryside, the original seventeenth-century house was extensively remodelled in the 1740s. The façade of the house is copied from Lindsey House in Lincoln's Inn Fields, London – one of the best-known English sources of the Palladian style of architecture – but what distinguishes Wallington is the superb quality of the decoration in its main rooms. Ornate Italian rococo plasterwork, panelling, furnishings and collections, especially of fine porcelain, all display eighteenth-century craftsmanship at its best.

■239■ WASHINGTON OLD HALL   ☎ 0191 416 6879
The Avenue, District 4, Washington, Tyne & Wear NE38 7LE
From A1 or A19 to A1231, signposted to Washington, District 4, Washington village
Open Apr–Oct: Sun–Wed 11–5 (last admission 4.30)
Fine example of an early-seventeenth-century manor, built using local, honey-coloured sandstone. Great Hall with furniture typical of the Jacobean period, kitchen with walls that survive from an earlier medieval building, and panelled room with exceptionally fine Jacobean panelling made from quartered oak. This splendid house also contains a fine collection of delftware, oil paintings and carved oak furniture. Gardens surrounding the hall contain many old English flowers and herbs used for both medicinal and culinary purposes.

Harewood House

🏰 SCOTLAND   MAP 8

■240■ ABBOTSFORD ☎ 01896 752043
Melrose, Borders TD6 9BQ
3 miles W of Melrose, off A7 and bypass, signposted
Open mid-Mar–Oct: Mon–Sat 10–5, Sun 2 (10 in Jun–Sept)
Sir Walter Scott's romantic mansion on the River Tweed remains much the
same as it was in his day. It was built in stages between 1812 and 1824, when
Scott had an existing farmhouse renovated and extended in the style of a
Scottish manor house to create what he described as 'a romance of stone and
mortar'. The job was given to the architect William Atkinson, who was responsible for the imaginative creation we see today, with its small oriels and battle-
ment-protected corner turrets. Much of it is copied from other buildings.
The entrance is similar to the main doorway of Linlithgow Palace, and the
library's elaborate wooden ceiling is a copy of that in Rosslyn Chapel. The house
is full of mementoes of Scott as well as a notable collection of weapons and
armour.

■241■ CULROSS PALACE ☎ 01383 880359
West Green House, Culross, Fife KY12 8JH
Off A985 12 miles W of Forth Road Bridge
Open Palace Apr–Sept: daily 11–5; Oct: Sat and Sun 11–5

Fred's **FAVOURITE**

Culross is the most complete example of a Scottish burgh of the seventeenth
and eighteenth centuries. Little white houses roofed with red pantiles line
narrow cobbled streets. Culross Palace, built for mine-owner, Sir George Bruce,
is a unique example of a merchant's house from the early seventeenth century.
The Hall has a plain vaulted ceiling and seventeenth-century paintings and
furnishings. The Painted Chamber contains original wood-panelled walls and
ceilings, decorated with sixteen scenes and rhyming couplets. Model seventeenth-century kitchen garden to the rear of the palace. The burgh's present
appearance is the result of continuing restoration by the National Trust for
Scotland over the last fifty years. The majority of the properties in the village
are lived in and can be viewed only from the outside, but the Palace, Town
House and the Study are all open to the public.

■242■ FALKLAND PALACE ☎ 01337 857397
Falkland, Cupar, Fife KY15 7BU
11 miles N of Kirkcaldy on A912
Open Palace and Gardens Apr–Oct: Mon–Sat 11–5.30,
Sun 1.30 –5.30 (last admission 4.30)

Fred's **FAVOURITE**

Country residence of the Stuart kings and queens. The palace was built between
1501 and 1541 by James IV and James V, replacing an earlier castle and palace
buildings dating from the twelfth century, traces of which can still be seen in
the grounds. The Renaissance palace of the Stuarts was damaged by fire while
occupied by Cromwell's troops and allowed to fall into ruin. It was rebuilt
and restored at the end of the nineteenth century by the third Marquess of
Bute, and much of what we see today, especially the fine carpentry and woodcarving, is the work of the craftsmen he employed. In his Victorian restoration
work, Lord Bute inserted a course of red sandstone to indicate where his reconstruction work began, leaving us with no doubt as to the identity of the original
masonry.

■243■ **FASQUE** ☎ 01561 340569
Fettercairn, Laurencekirk, Aberdeenshire AB30 1DN
1 mile N of Fettercairn on B974
Open May–Sept: daily 11–5.30. All-year admission for parties by arrangement
Home of the Gladstone family since 1829, Fasque has impressive state rooms, a
handsome sweeping staircase and extensive servants' quarters. The life and
work of the large household staff can be seen here, and there is an exhibition of
Prime Minister W. E. Gladstone's memorabilia. There is also a gamekeeper's hut
complete with mantrap and collections of farming machinery.

■244■ **FLOORS CASTLE** ☎ 01573 223333
Kelso, Roxburghshire TD5 7SF
Signposted from all directions near Kelso
Open Easter–Oct: daily 10.30–4.30 (last admission 4)
Resembling a French château, Floors Castle was transformed from an earlier
house into the fairy-tale castle we see today, which was described by Sir Walter
Scott as 'altogether a kingdom for Oberon and Titania to dwell in'. It is the
home of the tenth Duke of Roxburgh and it contains extensive collections of
French furniture, tapestries and paintings. The house was designed by William
Adam in 1721 and extended by W. H. Playfair over a century later. It has a
magnificent setting overlooking the River Tweed with the Cheviot Hills beyond.

■245■ **GEORGIAN HOUSE** ☎ 0131 226 3318
7 Charlotte Square, Edinburgh EH2 4DR
Signposted in Edinburgh city centre.
Open Apr (or Good Fri if earlier)–Oct: Mon–Sat 10–5, Sun 2–5 (last admission 4.30)
The Georgian House in Charlotte Square dates from 1796, when those who
could afford it began to escape from the cramped, squalid conditions of
Edinburgh's Old Town to settle in the fashionable New Town. The buildings in
the New Town are in neoclassical style, and the square was designed by Robert
Adam. Adam differentiates between the various uses of the floors through the
effective use of stone. Broached stonework was used for the servants' quarters
in the basement, rusticated stone base was used at the entrance level on the
ground floor, while polished ashlar stone was used on the living quarters of the
upper floors. No. 7 was acquired by the National Trust for Scotland, which converted the ground floor, first floor and basement into a Georgian show house,
displayed and arranged as it might have been when it was first occupied.

■246■ **GLADSTONE'S LAND** ☎ 0131 226 5856
477B The Lawnmarket, Edinburgh EH1 2NT
On Royal Mile
Open Apr (or Good Fri if earlier)–Oct: Mon–Sat 10–5, Sun 2–5 (last admission 4.30)
Typical example of seventeenth-century tenement building of Edinburgh's Old
Town. Gladstone's Land is the most important example of seventeenth-century
high-tenement housing. The cramped conditions of the overcrowded Old Town,
which grew up on the ridge between Edinburgh Castle and the Palace of
Holyroodhouse, determined the width of the lot on which the house was built,
which meant that extension was possible only in depth or upwards. Completed
in 1620, the six-storey building contains remarkable painted ceilings and was
the home of an Edinburgh merchant, Thomas Gledstane. On the ground floor
there is a reconstructed shop booth, and the first floor of the house has been
refurbished as a typical seventeenth-century Edinburgh home.

■247■ HILL HOUSE ☎ 01436 673900
Upper Colquhoun Street, Helensburgh, Dunbarton & Clydebank G84 9AJ
Off B832, between A82 and A814
Open April–Oct: daily 1.30–5.30 (last admission 5)
Early-twentieth-century work of the architect Charles Rennie Mackintosh skilfully
joins the old and the new in a union of two architectural opposites: traditional
Scottish values and modern international aspirations. Glasgow publisher Walter
Blackie commissioned not only the house and garden but much of the furniture
and all the interior fittings and decorative schemes. The overall effect is a unique
combination of traditional and modern forms with elegant, timeless rooms that
look as modern today as they did when the house was built in 1904, all contained
within a structure that echoes the style of Scottish baronial architecture.

■248■ HILL OF TARVIT MANSION HOUSE ☎ 01334 653127
Cupar, Fife KY15 5PB
Off A916, 2 miles S of Cupar
Open Good Fri and Easter Mon then May–early Oct: daily 1.30–5.30 (11 in Jun–Aug);
Oct: Sat and Sun 1.30–5.30
Interesting early-twentieth-century country house designed principally to be a
showcase for a collection of Flemish tapestries, Chinese porcelain and bronzes,
French and English furniture, European paintings and many other things that
had been acquired by a Dundee financier and jute manufacturer, Frederick
Bower Sharp. He commissioned Robert Lorimer, who was to become the leading
Scottish architect of his day, to carry out the work. The hall, with woodwork
inspired by eighteenth-century French provincial design, is an excellent example
of the sitting-room-hall that became popular at the turn of the twentieth century.
The dining-room is designed in a Palladian manner, with elaborate plasterwork.
Outside, the formal gardens were also designed by Lorimer. Within the grounds,
Scotstarvit Tower is a centuries-old keep. Missing from it is a magnificently
carved stone fireplace bearing the date 1627, which was removed from the
tower by Mr Sharp and installed in the smoking-room of his new house.

■249■ HOPETOUN HOUSE ☎ 0131 331 2451
South Queensferry, West Lothian EH30 9SL
2 miles W of Forth Road Bridge, 10 miles W of Edinburgh
Open Apr–Sept: daily 10–5.30; Oct: Sat and Sun 10–5.30
Great Adam mansion, home of the fourth Marquess of Linithgow. Hopetoun
House was built in 1699 to a design by William Bruce, but between 1721 and
1754 it was enlarged by William and Robert Adam. The reception rooms have
notable paintings, including works by Caneletto, Gainsborough and Raeburn,
and there are also fine examples of furniture and a collection of china.
Extensive grounds include deer parks with red and fallow deer.

■250■ HOUSE OF DUN ☎ 01674 810264
Montrose, Angus DD10 9LQ
On A935, 3 miles W of Montrose
Open May–early Oct: daily 1.30–5.30; Oct: Sat and Sun 1.30–5.30. Gardens and Grounds
all year: daily 9.30–dusk
Modest-sized Georgian country house designed and built by William Adam in
1730 for David Erskine, a judge of the Scottish Court of Session. Superb plasterwork by Joseph Enzer is a feature of the house, as are the paintings and
beautiful bed hangings and tapestries.

■251■ **LINLITHGOW PALACE** ☎ 01506 842896
Cook Gate, Linlithgow AH49 1SH
In Linlithgow off M9
Open Apr–Sept: daily 9.30–6.30; Oct–Mar: Mon–Sat 9.30–4.30, Sun 2–4.30
Magnificent ruin of a great royal palace. The oldest part of the castle is the hall block, with the original entrance leading under the hall into the courtyard. On one side of the entrance is a guard room with a dungeon beneath. On the first floor is the Great Hall, with a minstrels' gallery and an impressive Renaissance fireplace. On the side of the courtyard, opposite the hall block, were the king's private chambers. The present entrance, through a later block, has a small turreted gatehouse. The range opposite this entrance was rebuilt in the seventeenth century. The basement contains six chambers, and the first floor was occupied by a hall with two large fireplaces. There is also a fine carved fountain in the courtyard. Both James V and Mary Queen of Scots were born here.

■252■ **MELLERSTAIN HOUSE** ☎ 01573 410225
Gordon, Borders TD3 6LG
5 miles NE of Earlston off B6397, signposted
Open Easter–Sept: Sun–Fri 12.30–5 (last admission 4.30)
One of the great Adam houses of Scotland. Mellerstain was built in two stages: the two wings in 1725 by William Adam, and the large central block between 1770 and 1778 by his more famous son Robert. The library is regarded as one

of Robert Adam's most outstanding creations and contains one of his best-decorated ceilings in the original colours of 1773. Drawing-room, music room and small drawing-room are all excellent examples of Adam's skill and craftsmanship. The collection of paintings includes works by Van Dyck and Gainsborough, and there are pieces of period furniture. The Italian-style terrace garden was laid out in 1909 by Sir Reginald Blomfield and commands a view overlooking the lake to the Cheviot Hills.

■253■ PALACE OF HOLYROODHOUSE ☎ 0131 556 7371
The Canongate, Edinburgh EH8 8DX
At E end of Royal Mile, opposite Scottish Parliament
Open daily exc Good Friday, Christmas Day, Boxing Day and during Royal visits
Apr–Oct: 9.30–6; Nov–Mar 9.30–4.30 (check for times)
At the end of Edinburgh's Royal Mile stands the Palace of Holyroodhouse, Her Majesty the Queen's official residence in Scotland. Set against the spectacular backdrop of Arthur's Seat, Holyroodhouse evolved gradually from the Abbey of Holyrood, which was founded in 1128, into a medieval fortress and then into a baroque residence. Little remains of the original abbey except the ruined thirteenth-century nave of the church. The first palace was built by James IV, who extended the original abbey guesthouse. The oldest part of the palace that still exists today is James V's Tower, which has Mary Queen of Scots rooms on the second floor. The audience chamber where she debated with John Knox can also be seen. Most of the present building was erected between 1670 and 1679. The fine seventeenth-century state rooms contain works of art from the Royal Collection and are used by the Queen for State ceremonies.

■254■ SCONE PALACE ☎ 01738 552300
Perth, Perthshire & Kinross PH2 6BD
Just outside Perth on A93, Braemar road
Open Apr–late October: daily 9.30–4.45
Home of the Earl and Countess of Mansfield and the home of their ancestors for nearly 400 years. During this time Scone Palace has seen many changes, and what we see today is a house that was carefully Gothicised, adapted and enlarged by the architect William Atkinson in 1802. The Royal Gallery, 142 feet (43 metres) long, and magnificent state rooms are decorated with lavish furnishings, paintings and collections of porcelain and ivories.

■255■ TRAQUAIR HOUSE ☎ 01896 830323
Innerleithen, Borders EH44 6PW
On B709 off A72 at Innerleithen
Open mid-Apr–Oct: daily 12.30–5.30 (10.30 in Jun–Aug)
Scotland's oldest inhabited house, spanning over 1,000 years of history. Tower House has been altered and extended since the twelfth century. Numerous improvements were undertaken by successive lairds. John Stuart, whose portrait hangs in the dining-room, built an additional storey to the house in the seventeenth century and undertook the formidable task of diverting the River Tweed away from the house. The two wings extending from either side of the front of the house and the wrought-iron screen between them date from the early eighteenth century. There was originally an eighteenth-century domestic brewery producing beer for the house and estate workers. It was disused sometime after 1800, but the vessels and equipment remained untouched until it was rediscovered in 1965 and put into production once again.

🏰 NORTHERN IRELAND　　　　　　　　　　　　　　MAP 9

■256■ THE ARGORY ☎ 028 8778 4753
Derrycaw Road, Dungannon, Co. Tyrone BT71 6NA
4 miles NE of Dungannon
Open Easter–May: daily 2–6; Jun–Aug: Wed–Mon 2–6; Sept: Sat and Sun 2–6
Nineteenth-century house, built in the Greek revival style, which retains most of
its original contents. Designed by Dublin architects A. & J. Williams for barrister
Walter MacGeough and built between 1819 and 1824, it has imposing ashlar-faced
elevations in a restrained classical style. The centre of its two-storey seven-bay west
front breaks forward under a shallow pediment. It contains a porch with a door-
case framed by an elliptical arch and embellished with a squashed fanlight, glazed
side panels and a lion's mask. This leads into a hall with a theatrical cantilevered
staircase with brass banister supports, marbled walls and a cast-iron stove. There
is a stableyard with coach-house and carriages, a laundry and attractive gardens.

■257■ BELFAST CASTLE ☎ 028 9077 6925
Antrim Road, Belfast, Co. Antrim BT15 5GR
2½ miles from city centre. Follow signposts
Open all year: Mon–Sat 11–10, Sun 9–6　　　　　　　　　　　　　Belfast Castle

Grand castle in the Scottish baronial style with great square six-storey tower,
overlooks the city from a prominent site 400 feet (122 metres) above sea level.
Built in 1870 by the third Marquis of Donegal, it is most famous for its exterior
Italian Serpentine staircase, which connects the main reception rooms to the
garden terrace. The main staircase is beautifully carved in oak and has spacious
lobbies at both ground and first-floor levels. The main room, the Chichester Room,
with its polished light oak floor and chandeliers, runs the length of the building.

■258■ CASTLE COOLE ☎ 028 6632 2690
Enniskillen, Co. Fermanagh BT74 6JY
1 mile SE of Enniskillen on A4

Open Easter, May and Sept: Sat, Sun and Bank Hols: 1–6; June–Aug: Fri–Wed 1–6
Neoclassical house designed by James Wyatt. Family home of the Earls of
Belmore. Completed in 1798 after taking ten years to build. The interior of the
house was created by some of the leading craftsmen of the late eighteenth century, with chimneypieces carved by Westmacott, plasterwork created by Rose,
scagliola columns and pilasters created by Bartoli. Magnificent state rooms with
Regency furniture include the state bedroom, said to have been prepared for a
visit by George IV in 1821. Major stonework restoration recently completed.

■259■ CASTLE WARD ☎ 028 4488 1204
Castleward Estate, Strangford, Downpatrick, Co. Down BT30 7LS
7 miles NE of Downpatrick, 2 miles W of Strangford on A25
Open all year: Estate and Grounds dawn–dusk. House: check dates and times
An eccentric house built at one period (1762–70) but with two contrasting fronts:
a classical entrance façade on the west and a battlemented Gothic composition on
the east. The builder and his wife, Bernard Ward (later first Viscount Bangor) and
Lady Anne Magill, each favoured a different type of architecture. The division
between Gothic and classical goes right through the centre of the building, as it did
with their marriage (they were separated shortly after the house was completed).
The saloon, morning-room and Lady Anne's boudoir on the west side are all in
rococco Gothic style, while the hall, dining-room and Lord Bangor's library on the
east are in a more conventional Palladian vein. The domestic offices of the house,
including a fully equipped laundry, are carefully concealed in a sunken courtyard
to the north. Near the shore of Strangford Lough is the old peel tower, built by
Nicholas Ward in 1610. A formal canal called Temple Water is now a wildfowl
reserve, and above it there is a classical temple dating from about 1762.

■260■ FLORENCE COURT ☎ 028 6634 8249
Florence Court, Enniskillen, Co. Fermanagh BT92 1DB
8 miles SW of Enniskillen via A4 and A32
Open Easter: daily 1–6; Apr, May and Sept weekends and Bank Hols 1–6
Three-storey classical-style house. Built by the first Lord Mount Florence between
1756 and 1764 of rendered brick and embellished with superb rococo plasterwork by the Dublin stuccodore Robert West. The house is joined by long arcades
to small pavillions that were added in about 1770 by Davis Duckart. Nineteen
ninety-eight saw the return of many original paintings, furniture and artefacts
to the house – as a result of the Dowager Countess's donation to the National
Trust in her will. There are interesting servants' quarters grouped around cobbled courtyards, a water-powered sawmill, a walled garden and an ice house.

■261■ MOUNT STEWART HOUSE ☎ 028 4278 8387
Portaferry Road, Newtownards, Co. Down BT22 2AD
5 miles SE of Newtownards off A20
Open Apr and Oct: Sat and Sun 1–6; Easter and May–Sept: Wed–Mon 1–6
Eighteenth-century house with nineteenth-century additions. The original
house was rebuilt by the first and third Marquess of Londonderry. The present
west wing was built in 1804–5 to the designs of the architect George Dance.
The marquetry doors, dados and floors in the west wing were made by James
Ferguson, while the entrance portico and two-storey central hall were added
in the late 1830s by the celebrated Irish architect William Vitruvius Morrison.
Much of the interior was redecorated and furnished a century later by the wife
of the seventh Marquess, who also laid out the gardens surrounding the house.

CHAPTER

3

CHURCHES

As a steeplejack I always like working on church steeples and towers. I've just done the gold leaf and all that on two clock faces, and I'm presently working on the third tallest steeple in England. It's in Preston, and it's 311 feet (94.7 metres) high. When people see the enormous thickness of the walls at the base of a church tower, they have this strange idea that the steeple is almost solid, but it isn't. A steeple is very thin and very light. So why doesn't the top blow off in a gale? The answer to this is quite simple: a church steeple has a big nut and a great big long bolt that comes down on the inside for maybe 25 to 30 feet (8 to 9 metres); the nut is screwed on at the bottom, and that has the effect of clamping the capstone down to the top 20 feet (6 metres) of masonry. That's why the weather vane stays up there in a gale and doesn't end up in the cemetery.

The trouble is that, as the years go by, the rain gets in at the top of the steeple and runs down the rod. Then the rod starts to get rusty. Some church steeples have access to get at this rod so that you can paint it. The big steeple in Preston that I've got my ladders up has got this very thing. It has four cast-iron, Gothic arched opening lights, that have never opened for years, and they have that awful, ½-inch-thick (1.3-centimetre-thick), dark green glass in them. Part of the glass is broken, so that you can see the rod inside and you can see that it's in quite good condition. The top 30 feet (9 metres) of this steeple is only about 2 feet 6 inches (76 centimetres) across – really fine, just like a needle. It's so fine, in fact, that the top of the steeple rocks in the wind. Because of all the rocking, the head joints have cracked. Now, if this were a chimney stack, the obvious thing to do would be to put great big iron bands around it, like a set of corsets. There are some big steeples that have a lot of ironwork on them, but I think it would look rather unsightly on this one and I

Dunfermline Abbey

think I can get away with less drastic methods of keeping the thing up. First of all, though, I'm going to have to do an inspection, which entails dangling 300 feet (91 metres) up in the sky and leaning outwards on the end of a rope to look at the ornamental bits to see if there's anything ready for falling off.

The spire at Preston is a big one, but Britain's tallest spire, rising to a height of 404 feet (123 metres) is the one on Salisbury Cathedral. As a steeplejack, this is one I've always wanted to have a look at, and the BBC television series gave me the opportunity. When I got there, though, I found it a bit disappointing. I always thought it would look taller than it does. The present thing I'm mending in Preston is 100 feet (30 metres) shorter than the spire on Salisbury Cathedral but, because it goes to such a narrow needle point, the former looks taller.

In spite of my disappointment about the spire, Salisbury is still worth going to see, because, unlike nearly every other cathedral in the land, the whole building is of one style. It dates from 1220, when Bishop Richard Poore and his brilliant architect, Elias de Derham, decided to build a new Gothic-style cathedral to replace the Norman church at Old Sarum. Because they take so long to build, almost all other English cathedrals are a mixture of different architectural styles. Salisbury is all in the same style, because the main body of the cathedral was completed in a mere thirty-eight years. The huge cloister, which is the largest in England, and the magnificent chapterhouse were added in 1280. Then in 1313 the most spectacular addition was made. The tower was raised, and on top of it they built the slender, soaring spire we see today. Considering that the spire of Salisbury Cathedral is the tallest medieval structure in the world, it is amazing that it is still standing, with foundations only 4 feet (1.2 metres) deep. But I think it's because there's a thick bed of gravel underneath the cathedral and this supports the immense weight of the spire.

Not far from Salisbury we can see one of Britain's earliest churches. When the Saxons were converted to Christianity, churches as we know them started to appear. The church of St Laurence at Bradford-on-Avon in Wiltshire is one of the most complete surviving buildings that we have from the eighth century. It had been forgotten for more than 700 years and used at different times as a charnel house, a school, and as housing before being rediscovered in the nineteenth century. The interior and exterior are both sturdily built, and the whole church is beautifully plain and simple and remarkably well-preserved from such a long time ago.

The Middles Ages was the great age of cathedral-building and we've been left with some magnificent monuments to the skills of the medieval builders and stone-masons. One of the grandest of them all is York Minster – the largest medieval cathedral in the whole of northern Europe. It was in 1220 that the present building was begun, and it took 250 years to complete. The nave, which was begun in 1291, is the largest medieval hall and the widest Gothic nave in the whole of England. It has limestone pillars 100 feet (20 metres) high and, because they were worried by the potential weight of stone vaulting, the builders spanned the space with a ribbed vaulted roof made of wood.

The octagonal-shaped chapterhouse was begun in about 1260. It is unusual, given its size, in that it doesn't have a central column to support the roof vaulting. Around its walls are some of the minster's finest carvings, 80 per cent of which are original, dating from between 1270 and 1280. The Great East Window is one of the largest areas of stained glass in the world, with measurements that are similar to those of a tennis court. The glazier, John Thornton, came from Coventry,

A close-up view of Salisbury Cathedral's stonework

although he did eventually become a Freeman of York. Because of its vast area, the window is supported by extra stonework which forms an internal screen, and within this there are two walkways that go right across the face of the window.

In 1984 a fire destroyed the roof of the South Transept, so the skills of the minster's workforce were needed to restore it to its former glory. During the fire, the glass in the beautiful rose window in the South Transept cracked into 40,000 pieces, but because it had been recently cleaned and restored, the lead held and none of the glass was lost. As a result of the fire, the roof of the South Transept had to be completely rebuilt, and it was decided to use the traditional construction method. Oak ribs were used to form the shape of the roof, and these were locked into shape with bosses. As only six of the original bosses were sufficiently unscarred to be reused, sixty-eight new ones had to be designed and carved.

Then, of course, you come to the masonry on the outside of the minster, which is magnificent. The detail of it around the doors and the windows is beyond belief, marvellous. It has to be, without any shadow of a doubt, one continuous effort that will go on for ever just to keep the thing standing up. I bet they've been working on it every day since it was built. People say it's a pity that nobody has the skills to do this sort of work now, but around the back of the minster there's a good collection of craftsmen all beavering away. There's a young lady there who was making the most beautiful finial. I had a good chat with her and asked her how she went about starting it off and, as a result, if I were asked to make one now I would have a much better idea of how to go about it. She had been chiselling away at this one particular piece she was working on, for eleven weeks. Just think about it: every day for eleven weeks for one piece, and it was only about 2 feet (60 centimetres) tall. But think of that wonderful feeling of satisfaction when you get to the end, when you consider that you started with a pyramid-shaped lump of rock and transform it into a beautiful thing.

All our great medieval cathedrals like York Minster survived the Reformation and became Anglican cathedrals, but the monasteries suffered a very different fate. Yorkshire was a great centre of monasticism, and not far from York are the remains of some of our greatest medieval abbeys. Fountains Abbey dates from the twelfth century, but when, over 400 years later, Henry VIII demanded the closure of the abbey, the monks left behind what has now become the most complete Cistercian abbey remains in Britain. It was turned into the shell that we see today when its buildings were sold and its stone was used to build nearby Fountains Hall.

The Cistercian order has always been associated with the qualities of austerity and simplicity and these same values held good in Cistercian architecture – a severe, unadorned style that was reliant for its impact and effect on mass and proportion rather than on extravagant decoration and ornamentation. The ideals and aims of the order are reflected in the efficient design of its buildings. The remains of the west front of the abbey church that we see today at Fountains illustrate this perfectly. The most remarkable feature of the building is its scale, with a great uninterrupted vista from west to east, framed by the massive Norman pillars of the nave on either side. This is not how the church would have looked to a monk in the Middle Ages, though, when it was divided up by altars, chapels and screens.

From a doorway in the south aisle, steps lead into the cloister, which was the centre of monastic life. The principal room in the east range of the cloister is the chapterhouse, the administrative centre of the abbey. By the time it was completed in 1170, the Cistercians had relaxed their insistence on unadorned architecture, and some modest decoration was becoming acceptable. This is one of the few parts of the abbey that is ornamented with sculpture, and carved leaves and other simple designs can be seen on the corbels, which once supported the stone vaults of the roof.

Just over a hundred years after the Reformation and the Dissolution of the Monasteries, there rose in London a magnificent new church that didn't have any of the austerity of a medieval monastery like Fountains. St Paul's Cathedral, designed by Sir Christopher Wren, is something else. In its day it dominated the London skyline, but it's a shame that nowadays you can't really see it properly for all the modern buildings that have sprung up around it. A cathedral had stood on this site since the early years of the seventh century, and the original Saxon church had been destroyed by fire and rebuilt on a number of occasions. After the last disaster in 1087, the Normans constructed a massive church whose size and style reflected the importance of London, the capital of their newly conquered kingdom. The cathedral they built in grand and Gothic style was the largest church in England and the third largest in Europe. It had the tallest spire and steeple ever built in England, but the spire was made of wood and it was burned down on a number of occasions when lightning struck it. Then in 1666 came the greatest disaster of all when the Great Fire of London put it completely beyond restoration.

The man chosen to design and construct a new St Paul's was Christopher Wren. When the remains of the old cathedral had been demolished and the site cleared, work on the new cathedral could begin. Wren himself insisted on supervising the preliminary measurements. Throughout the thirty-five years of building work, he supervised and engaged the finest craftsmen, scrutinized and signed the accounts and visited the site each Saturday, presumably to prevent interference. He insisted that the work be carried out under conditions of some secrecy, with whole sections of his great design being kept under wraps as the building went up.

What Wren achieved during those thirty-five years is now one of our greatest national monuments; St Paul's Cathedral represents inspiration, beauty and craftsmanship on a grand scale. The architectural style of the church is English baroque. This was a style that was widely used in Europe during the seventeenth and early eighteenth centuries, but it was a daring and controversial choice for an English cathedral. The great west front, where the cathedral is entered, has two storeys of dignified classical columns flanked by twin towers.

When you enter you look down the nave towards the cathedral's crowning achievements – the dome. This is among the largest in the world, comparable with St Peter's in Rome. Eight piers support its 65,000-tonne weight, and eight arches spread the load. Above them is the Whispering Gallery, which gets its name because a whisper against the blank circular wall can be heard on the opposite side some 138 feet (42 metres) away. Above this are the Stone and the Golden Galleries. The dome is a brilliant piece of engineering, and it actually consists of three structures one within the other: an outer dome, an inner dome and a core that supports the lantern on top. When it was being built, Wren was hauled up in a basket two or three times a week to see how the work was progressing. The central pavement area underneath the dome is decorated in a compass design in coloured marble. On it are the words: 'Beneath lies buried the founder of this church and city, Christopher Wren. Reader if you seek his monument look around you'. Never was a truer word engraved in stone.

When I had the pleasure of visiting St Paul's, I went all the way to the top of the dome. When standing on the top, I could count no fewer than 200 tower cranes in that big city. But nothing that was being built was as impressive as St Paul's Cathedral and its dome. When you see it close to, there's a lot of evidence of repairs that were done in days gone by, but I was fortunate enough to be there to see some really impressive restoration work that was being done for the first time. It revealed some of Wren's engineering that keeps the dome standing. Inside the stonework is a great big wrought-iron chain that goes all around the perimeter of the dome, just at its base where it meets the main roof of the church. What this does is to take the strain of the outward pressure of the dome. The trouble is that over the years damp has started to seep through and corrode the metal, which has then expanded and started to crack the masonry. I was very pleased to see, though, that the gentlemen who are doing the restoration work are making a very good job of it, and I think Sir Christopher Wren himself would be highly delighted if he could see their work.

When you think how old St Paul's is, it really is a great credit to the man who designed it so well. For its age, it is a magnificent piece of engineering. One thing I noticed when I was there is that the architecture of St Paul's is almost identical to Bolton Town Hall. There are some great pillars on the outside and the balustrade around the top and the cornice moulding are almost identical. I think the guy who designed the town hall must have been down and had a good look at St Paul's to get some ideas. The Victorians used to copy everybody; they copied the Greeks and Romans and everything else that had come before them. They would copy all sorts of nice bits and pieces if they were good to look at.

But a church doesn't have to be big to be beautiful. On a recent job in Wales, we passed a magnificent marble church. St Margaret's Church at Bodelwyddan is known as the 'Marble Church' on account of all the different varieties of marble used in its interior construction. This finely ornate church is in the Decorated Gothic style, and there's an amazing richness of design in it. In the nave, the pillars have shafts of Belgian red marble, and the capitals are of richly carved stone. On the hammerbeam roof there's not a single screw or nail used in its construction; every junction of the timbers is secured by pegs. The chancel and the sanctuary steps and flooring are of Sicilian marble, and all in all there are fourteen varieties of different marble in the church. There are also some very fine examples of the craft of the woodcarver to be seen there.

The finely built tower and delicately carved and graceful spire of the Marble Church can be seen for miles in every direction. The spire rises to a height of 202 feet (61 metres), and its four traceried windows, bands of ornamental tracery, finely worked buttresses and the carved portraits at every corner of the four pinnacles or finials make this graceful spire unique. The whole spire stands on just eight stones, one on each corner, and it always amazes me how the man who designed it knew enough about the strength of the materials to calculate that the weight on those corners wouldn't crush the stones and result in the whole thing tumbling down. He was a man who knew the rock that it was built out of. Either that, or he was one hell of a gambler.

PLACES TO VISIT

⛪ SOUTH-WEST   **MAP 1**

■262■ BATH ABBEY   ☎ 01225 422462

Bath Abbey Office, 13 Kingston Buildings, Bath BA1 1LT
In centre of Bath, adjacent to Roman Baths
Open Easter–Oct daily: 9–6; Nov–Mar daily: 9–4:30. Sun between services

Recently cleaned and restored this fifteenth-century abbey is built on the site where Edgar was crowned first King of England in 973. The view of the west front is quite spectacular, with sculptured stone angels ascending and descending the abbey by ladder. The west window illustrates scenes and characters from the Old Testament, and the east window depicts fifty-six scenes from the New Testament. Perhaps the most impressive architectural sight is the fan-vaulted ceiling; this dates from the major restoration done in the 1860s. It is modelled on the original vault of the east end designed by the brothers William and Robert Vertue, master masons to King Henry VII.

■263■ BUCKFAST ABBEY   ☎ 01364 642519

Buckfastleigh, Devon TQ11 0EE
Off A38 Exeter–Plymouth road. Dart Bridge exit for Buckfast and Totnes
Open all year: daily 9–5.30 in summer, 10–4 in winter
Centrepiece of the abbey is the church containing splendid art treasures. The

church was rebuilt on its medieval foundations in the twentieth century. There are also three herb gardens (Physic, Sensory and Lavender)to visit.

■264■ CHURCH OF ST LAURENCE   ☎ 01225 865797
Church Street, Bradford-on-Avon, Wiltshire
In centre of Bradford-on-Avon
Open all year: daily 10–dusk, monthly services throughout the year
Dating from the early eighth century, the church is only 25 feet (7.6 metres) long, and it's all that survives of a Saxon monastery. The only decoration on the outside is the arcading, which was carved 200 years after the church was built, inspired by the churches of Charlemagne's great Holy Roman Empire. At the end of the tall stone nave there is a fragmented Saxon cross with flying angels.

■265■ CLEEVE ABBEY   ☎ 01984 640377
Abbey Road, Washford, Watchett, Somerset TA23 0PS
In Washford, ¼ mile S of A39. Signposted
Open all year: daily 10–6 (5 in Oct, 4 in Nov–Mar). Check for details
Founded in 1198 and dedicated to the Blessed Virgin. One of the few monastic sites with a complete set of cloister buildings. Highlights include the fifteenth-century timber roof in the refectory, with carved angels, the unique medieval wall-paintings, and the heraldic tile pavements (covered in winter).

■266■ GLASTONBURY ABBEY   ☎ 01458 832267
Abbey Gatehouse, Magdalene Street, Glastonbury, Somerset BA6 9EL
Off A39 between Glastonbury and Street
Opens all year: daily 9.30–6 (dusk if sooner, 9 in Jun–Aug, 10 in Dec–Feb)
Remains of one of the oldest religious foundations in Britain. Tradition maintains that the abbey ruins stand at the birthplace of Christianity in Britain, where Joseph of Arimathea brought the Holy Grail and founded a chapel in AD61. Present remains date from 1184, when the original abbey was rebuilt after it had been destroyed by fire. They include the Abbot's Kitchen, the only part of the domestic quarters of the monastery to survive almost intact.

■267■ SALISBURY CATHEDRAL   ☎ 01722 555100
The Close, Salisbury, Wiltshire SP1 2EF
Signposted locally
Open Sept–Apr: daily 8–6.30; May–Aug: daily 7.30–8.15pm. Restricted at evensong
Reaching a height of 404 feet (123 metres), the spire of Salisbury Cathedral is the tallest church spire in Britain and possibly the tallest surviving medieval structure in the world. In 1220 Bishop Richard Poore decided to build a new Gothic-style cathedral having been granted permission from the Pope to replace the old Norman cathedral at Old Sarum. Elias de Derham was appointed Clerk of the Works and unlike almost all other English cathedrals, which are a mixture of different architectural styles resulting from the many generations it took to build them, Salisbury has an architectural unity as the main body of the cathedral was completed in a mere thirty-eight years by armies of masons and labourers. The huge cloister built between 1240 and 1260 is the largest in England, and the chapterhouse, containing the Magna Carta was built later between 1263 and 1284. The most daring and astonishing addition was made between 1285 and 1315 when the tower was raised and on top of it they built the slender, soaring spire. In the Cathedral Close there is a splendid array of English architecture, including a fine medieval hall and work by Sir Christopher Wren.

■268■ WELLS, BISHOP'S PALACE ☎ 01749 678691
Wells, Somerset BA5 2PO
Adjoining cathedral, through medieval gateway from Market Place and over drawbridge
Open Apr–Oct and Bank Hols: Tues–Fri 10.30–6, Sun 2–6 (daily in Aug)
The palace comprises an exquisite grouping of perfectly preserved medieval
buildings, all in the same mellow, golden stone. It is set in 14 acres
(5 hectares) of gardens and water, containing the wells from which the city
takes its name. The central block of the palace, now known as the Henderson
Rooms, was built between 1230 and 1240 by Bishop Jocelin, and is flanked by
the Bishop's chapel and the fifteenth-century residential wing. On the south
side are ruins of a magnificent thirteenth-century Great Hall, which was
taken down in the sixteenth century. The walls, gatehouse and moat surrounding the palace were added by Bishop Ralph of Shrewsbury between
1329 and 1363.

■269■ WELLS CATHEDRAL ☎ 01749 674483
Cathedral Green, Wells, Somerset BA5 2UE
In centre of Wells
Open Apr–Sept: daily 7–7 (8.30 in July–Aug); Oct–Mar: daily 7–6.15
One of England's most beautiful cathedrals, the present building was started about
1180 and dedicated in 1239. The unity of its design gives the whole building a
harmonious style. Celebrated west front with more than 300 thirteenth-century
statues. Some fine fourteenth-century stained glass. The central tower was heightened in the early fourteenth century, and the western towers were added in the
late fourteenth and early fifteenth centuries. The inverted or 'scissor' arches in the
nave were a brilliant innovation, designed in 1338 when the weight of the
heightened tower caused problems.The octagonal chapterhouse, thirteenth–early
fourteenth century, has a magnificent vaulted roof supported by a single pillar.
Around and adjoining Cathedral Green are the handsome Old Deanery and several
former canonical houses, including the present Wells Museum, and Vicars' Close
(circa 1348), one of the most complete medieval street-scenes in Britain.

⟱ SOUTH-EAST   MAP 2

■270■ ABBEY CHURCH OF ST MARY & ST SEXBURGHA
☎ 01795 873185
Off High St, Minister-in-Sheppey, Shearness, Kent ME12 2HE
Off A249 Maidstone to Isle of Sheppey Rd, in centre of Minister-in-Sheppey
Open summer 10–12, 2–4; closed winter except for services and group bookings
Abbey Church of St Mary and St Sexburga, founded in 664, still has an original
Saxon window in the north aisle. In the seventh century one of the first nun-
neries in England was built on this site, and the church is now one of the oldest
places of Christian worship in England. Saxon stonework and a fine collection
of brasses that belonged to Sir Roger de Northwode. The abbey gatehouse next
to the church has been restored and houses a museum of local history.

■271■ ALL SAINTS CHURCH ☎ 01580 291454
High Street, Biddenden, Ashford, Kent TN27 8AH
On A262
Open Apr–Oct: Mon–Fri 10.30–4. Service each Sunday
Fine, well-preserved, medieval English country church. All Saints Church is in one

of the loveliest villages in the Weald of Kent, Biddenden. The church as it exists today is largely of Tunbridge Wells sandstone. The lightness and proportions of the interior are the most impressive elements of the church and can be best appreciated from beneath the great arch of the tower. The fine oak roof of the nave is typical of Kentish construction, and the north aisle retains two of its original windows from the decorated period of the thirteenth to fourteenth century. Also in same parish, St Michael's Church in Smarden is of architectural interest, too.

■272■ BATTLE ABBEY ☎ 01424 773792
1 High Street, Battle, East Sussex TN33 0AD
S on A21, then A2100 to Battle. Abbey is in village sqare in the centre of Battle
Open Apr–Sept: daily 10–6; Oct: daily 10–5; Nov–Mar exc Christmas: daily 10–4
Extensive remains of the abbey built soon after the Battle of Hastings by William the Conqueror to celebrate his victory and atone for the English dead. The abbey has many fine sights, including the great gatehouse, which has been described as one of the finest monastic gatehouses in England. The present structure largely dates from 1338 when the gatehouse was remodelled to provide a safer and more spectacular-looking entrance to the abbey. Fifteenth-century Great Hall with interior timbers replaced after fire in 1931. Novices' chamber with fine, high vaulting in the east range of the cloister. Medieval precinct wall, unusual for a monastery, might reflect the threat of French raids in the fourteenth century.

■273■ CANTERBURY CATHEDRAL ☎ 01227 762862
The Deane Chapter, Cathedral House, The Precincts, Canterbury, Kent CT1 2EH
M2 junction 7 then A2 or M20 junction 9 then A28 into city
Open Easter–Sept: Mon–Sat 9–7; Oct–Easter: Mon–Sat 9–5; Sun 12.30–2.30 and 4.30–5.30
The mother church of Anglican Christianity reflects the changing architectural styles of five centuries. The oldest parts are the remains of the church built by Lanfranc, the first Norman archbishop, between 1070 and 1089. This soon proved to be too small and St Anselm began to extend it in 1096. The next stage began after the cathedral had been destroyed by fire in 1174, leaving just the arches above the nave. Rebuilding began under the French master mason William of Sens, and his soaring pointed arches marked the introduction from France into England of the early Gothic style. At the end of the fourteenth century the Norman nave was pulled down and rebuilt in the High Gothic style we see today. Finally, in 1498 the tall Late Gothic central tower was erected over the crossing. It is the exterior of the cathedral that shows the building at its best. The central tower and its two low west towers, all in grey Caen stone, look impressive when viewed both from close quarters and from a distance. The interest in the interior lies mainly in details like some excellent stained glass and a profusion of elaborate tombs.

■274■ THE HOSPITAL OF ST CROSS ☎ 01962 878218
St Cross, Winchester, Hampshire SO23 9SD
A33 or M3 junction 10 into Winchester
Open Apr–Oct: Mon–Sat 9.30–5; Nov–Mar: 10.30–3.30. Closed Sun, Good Fri and 25 Dec
Britain's oldest existing charitable institution and one of the country's most beautiful groups of medieval buildings still in use. Founded in 1132 for the benefit of thirteen poor men and still functioning as an almshouse. In the Middle Ages bread and beer were given to passing travellers; this is still done today! There is a fine transitional Norman church; building was started in 1135 and was not completed until 1295 under Peter de Sancta Maria. The walls of

the church are over 3 feet (1 metre) thick, and the roof, which is now lead, was originally thatched. The medieval encaustic tiles, which can be seen at their best near the font, are very similar to those in Winchester Cathedral. Hospital buildings entered through the outer quadrangle include the Beaufort Tower, which guards the entrance to the inner quadrangle, the fourteenth-century Brethrens' Hall, with its beamed roof of Spanish chestnut, where brothers lived and fed for centuries, and, beyond the hall, an impressive kitchen with a fireplace dating from the fifteenth century.

■275■ **ST AUGUSTINE'S ABBEY** ☎ 01227 767345
Longport, Canterbury, Kent CT1 1TS
Longport, ½ mile E of Cathedral Close
Open April–Sept: daily 10–6; Oct: daily 10–5; Nov–Mar exc Christmas: daily 10–4
Remains of one of the earliest monastic sites in England. It was founded by St Augustine in 598, the year after he arrived in England from Rome, and it marks the birthplace of the reintroduction of Christianity in this country. Initially, the abbey was used to bury the kings of Kent and early archbishops of Canterbury, and St Augustine himself is buried at this site. The abbey became and took on the appearance of a standard Benedictine abbey after the Norman Conquest in the eleventh century. It continued in religious use until 1538 when it was suppressed by Henry VIII as part of the Dissolution of the Monasteries. Evidence of all these phases of the site's history can still be seen and an award-winning museum here displays all the artifacts from excavations. Along with the cathedral, the abbey is part of the Canterbury World Heritage Site.

■276■ **ST PAUL'S CATHEDRAL** ☎ 0207 236 4128
The Chapter House, St Paul's Churchyard, London EC4M 8AD
St Paul's or Blackfriars Underground

Fred's FAVOURITE

Open all year: Mon–Sat 8.30–4 and Sunday services. Check for times
St Paul's Cathedral, designed by Christopher Wren, has been described as the most powerful architectural statement ever made in the City of London. When entering from the west you are greeted by a quite magnificent view down the

St Paul's – these columns are just like the ones on Bolton Town Hall nave towards the cathedral's crowning achievements, the dome and the high altar. The architectural style of St Paul's is English baroque and, although widely used in Europe, it was still a controversial choice for an English cathedral. The dome is one of the largest in the world, comparable with St Peter's in Rome. Eight huge piers support, it and eight arches spread the load of the dome on to the piers. Above them is the famous Whispering Gallery. Beyond that are the Stone and Golden Galleries, from which there are superb views of London. The crypt is the largest in Europe. In it are tombs and memorials to some of the most famous figures in British history, including Wellington and Nelson.

■277■ **WESTMINSTER ABBEY** ☎ 0207 222 5152
Broad Sanctuary, London SW1P 3PA
St James's Park Underground
Open all year: Mon–Fri 9.30–4.45, Sat 9.30–2.45 (last admission 1 hour before closing).
Cloisters all year: daily 8–6
A masterpiece of Gothic architecture with the highest Gothic nave in England, Westminster Abbey is the church where most English monarchs have been crowned and buried. Saxon and Norman monasteries both stood on this site, but the present building, begun by Henry III in 1245, is largely Early English. After much rebuilding and additional work, the church, the Henry VII Lady Chapel and the two west towers were completed in 1740. Inside, the church is full of monuments, which make it England's chief memorial to its famous dead. In the Royal Chapels are the tombs of English rulers, while in the south transept, Poets' Corner is full of the graves and memorials of great writers. The monastic buildings include the cloisters and the thirteenth-century chapter-house, which has vaulting supported on a single pier.

■278■ **WINCHESTER CATHEDRAL** ☎ 01962 857200
The Close, Winchester, Hampshire SO23 9LS
M3 junction 9 then signposted in city centre
Open all year: daily 8.30–5.30
Founded in 1079 by Bishop William Walkelin, Winchester Cathedral is the longest medieval church in Europe, measuring 556 feet (169 metres). Between 1189 and 1204 the building was extended in the Early English style by Bishop Godfrey de Lucy, and between 1346 and 1366 Bishop Edington rebuilt the west front. He was also responsible for beginning the change of the nave from Norman to perpendicular. The twelfth-century font is made from black Tournai marble and is one of only seven in England. Jane Austen was buried here and there is a brass tablet and window for her. The cathedral also houses the twelfth-century illuminated Winchester Bible, medieval wall-paintings and pavements and six chantry chapels.

ᛃᚥᚳ EASTERN   MAP 3

■279■ **CASTLE ACRE PRIORY** ☎ 01760 755161
Castle Acre, Norfolk PE32 2XD
¼ mile W of Castle Acre, 5 miles N of Swaffham
Open Apr–Sept: daily 10–6; early Oct–mid-Oct daily 10–5; mid-Oct–Mar exc Christmas: Wed–Sun 10–4
Established in 1079 for a community of thirty-six monks and suppressed in 1537, Castle Acre Priory is the finest surviving Cluniac monastery in England. Together with the remains of the castle, built just after the Conquest, and the

walled town of Castle Acre, it makes up one of the best examples of Norman estate planning in the country. The surviving ruins of the priory, which include the church and the chapterhouse, were once covered in the elaborate, carved decoration that was typical of the Cluniac order. The elaborate decoration on the west front of the priory church is the best surviving example of this. Because it was still usable as a house, the prior's house survived the suppression of the monastery and is still very much as it would have been when it was remodelled in the fourteenth century to provide the prior with a house fitting to his social rank as a great landowner. Its layout is not dissimilar to that of a substantial medieval manor house and a herb garden has been created to grow culinary and medicinal herbs.

■280■ ELY CATHEDRAL ☎ 01353 667735
Chapter House, The College, Ely, Cambridgeshire CB7 4DL
Off A10, 15 miles N of Cambridge
Open summer: Mon–Sun 7–7; winter: Mon–Sat 7.30–6, Sun 7.30–5
Great Norman cathedral famous for its unique octagonal tower, which was added in the fourteenth century. Most of the original Norman work survives in the west front, the nave and the transepts. The present building was begun by Simeon, the first Norman abbot, in 1083. By 1109 the eastern part was complete, and the rest was finished by the end of the twelfth century. In 1322 the original Norman crossing tower collapsed and was replaced by the stone octagon. Eighty-two feet (25 metres) wide and supported by sixteen oak trunks, the octagon is the only structure of its kind in England, and it is as impressive from the inside as from outside. The long nave, with the massive piers of its twelve bays, is typically Norman in style, but the painted ceiling was a nineteenth-century addition. The fourteenth-century Lady Chapel, which once contained sculptured scenes from the life of the Virgin Mary that were destroyed during the Reformation, is a fine example of the Decorated style.

■281■ KING'S COLLEGE CHAPEL ☎ 01223 350411
King's Parade, Cambridge CB2 1SJ
In city centre
Open term time: Mon–Fri 9.30–3.30, Sat 9.30–3.15, Sun 1.15–2.15, 5–5.30; out-of-term time: Mon–Sat 9.30–4.30, Sun 10–5
Gothic masterpiece with breathtaking fan-vaulted ceiling and beautiful perpendicular tracery in the windows and on the walls. King's College Chapel, which was begun by Henry VI in 1146, is renowned for its twelve-bay interior. Eighty feet (24 metres) high and stretching nearly 300 feet (91 metres) it is one of the best examples of perpendicular architecture in England. The interior is rich with ornamentation, and the plan is bold and simple. All the windows are sixteenth century except for one at the west end, which is by Cayton and Bell. The chantries house an exhibition about the history of the buildings.

■282■ LINCOLN, THE MEDIEVAL BISHOP'S PALACE ☎ 01522 527468
Minster Yard, Lincoln, Lincolnshire LN2 1PU
On S side of Lincoln Cathedral
Open Apr–Oct: daily 10–6; Nov–Mar: Sat and Sun 10–4. Closed 24–26 Dec and 1 Jan
One of the most important medieval buildings in the country. The Bishop's Palace is over 800 years old and, although parts are in ruins, there is a lot of information on it due to surviving documentary records. The West Hall would have been one of the most magnificent buildings in the city of Lincoln during

the Middle Ages. Today, however, only the shell remains. The East Hall, with its vaulted barrel roof, dates from 1190 and is the earliest intact hall in Europe. To the south of the West Hall lie the remains of the great kitchen, below which was a vaulted undercroft or cellar. Traces of the vaulting can still be seen today. The Bishop's Palace also has one of Europe's most northerly vineyards.

■283■ LINCOLN CATHEDRAL ☎ 01522 544544
Lincoln LN2 1PX
In centre of Lincoln and signposted from all directions
Open May–mid-Sept: Mon–Sat 7.15am–8pm, Sun 7.15–6; mid-Sept–Apr: daily 7.15–6, Sun 7.15–5
Dominating the city from its hilltop position, Lincoln Cathedral is considered to be one of England's finest Gothic cathedrals. It has been a place of worship for over 900 years. The imposing twin-towered west front is a mixture of Romanesque and Gothic styles. The triple-aisled interior is impressive for its length and size, for the contrast between its honey-coloured limestone and dark Purbeck marble, and for the great sense of space. There is little to clutter the interior. There are some beautiful windows, but the most impressive sight inside the cathedral is the Angel Choir. The adjoining chapterhouse, which dates from the middle of the thirteenth century, is decagonal, with its vaulting supported by a central pier.

■284■ NORWICH CATHEDRAL ☎ 01603 764385 or 767617 (weekends)
62 The Close, Norwich, Norfolk NR1 4EH
In centre of Norwich, signposted from all directions
Open mid-May–mid-Sept: daily 7.30–7; mid-Sept–mid-May: daily 7.30–6
Gleaming white cathedral with a striking spire, which is the second tallest in England. Set in the largest close in England, Norwich Cathedral is a beautiful Norman building, which has probably preserved its Norman character better than any other building in the country. It was begun in 1096 and completed by 1146, but the spire collapsed in 1362 and was rebuilt in the Decorated style. The Norman style predominates in the aisles and the transepts and particularly in the nave, which has fourteen bays with massive columns. Because of the nave's comparative narrowness, it seems even longer than it actually is. The intact Romanesque arcading, which goes from floor level to clerestory, is very impressive. Norwich Cathedral was originally a Benedictine foundation, and it possesses the largest monastic cloisters in England. Built on two storeys, the passageways of the cloisters are full of architectural interest with embellishments in a range of styles from Decorated to perpendicular.

■285■ PETERBOROUGH CATHEDRAL ☎ 01733 343342
The Chapter Office, Little Priors Gate, 12a Minster Precincts, Peterborough, Cambridgeshire PE1 1XS
In centre of Peterborough

Fred's
FAVOURITE

Open all year: Mon–Sat 8.30–5.30, Sun 12–5.15
One of England's finest Norman buildings, begun in 1118. Magnificent west front of three soaring Gothic arches, added between 1200 and 1222, is one of the most unusual façades of the early-Gothic period. Three huge doorways , 81 feet (25 metres) high give the impression of forming a triumphal arch leading into the church. The three-aisled interior has retained its Norman appearance with massive rows of arches, arched galleries and triple windows. The beautiful painted ceiling dates from 1220. Magnificent examples of early rib vaulting can be seen in the aisles. This four-part rib vaulting is, after Durham, the earliest in

Peterborough Cathedral's beautiful vaulting

England. The cathedral is also home to perhaps the finest Norman apse in the country. In the north section of the choir is the tomb of Catherine of Aragon, and in the south section there is a plaque and some fine ironwork marking the site of the tomb of Mary Queen of Scots before she was moved to Westminster Abbey.

🏛 CENTRAL   MAP 4

■286■ BUILDWAS ABBEY ☎ 01952 433274
Buildwas, Telford, Nr Ironbridge, Shropshire TF8 7BW
On S bank of River Severn on A4169, 3 miles W of Ironbridge
Open April–Sept: daily 10–6; Oct: daily 10–5
Situated beside the River Severn, against a backdrop of wooded grounds, are the extensive remains of this Cistercian abbey. Buildwas was founded in 1135 by Roger de Clinton, Bishop of Coventry and Lichfield. Only the church and cloister are in the guardianship of English Heritage; other remains are on private property. The remains of the church consist of square-ended presbytery, a crossing with low central tower, north and south transepts and an aisled nave. Only the foundations of the cloister remain, but the chapterhouse medieval tiles, shows fine vaulting and decorated capitals.

■287■ COVENTRY CATHEDRAL ☎ 024 7622 7597
7 Priory Row, Coventry, West Midlands CV1 5ES
In centre of Coventry
Open Easter–Oct: daily 8.30–6; Nov–Easter: daily 9.30–5
Masterpiece of modern architecture. Twentieth-century cathedral in bold pink-grey sandstone, designed by Sir Basil Spence and built between 1956 and 1962, next to the ruins of its fourteenth-century predecessor, which was destroyed in a Second World War bombing raid. After the air raid in November 1940, the Reverend Arthur Wales took three of the medieval nails from the ruined smouldering roof timbers and wired them together into the shape of a cross. The cross

of nails has since become a sign of reconciliation and has been taken right across the world. Of the old cathedral, only parts of the external walls, together with the slender 295-feet (90-metre) high Gothic spire survived. These remains are linked to the modern cathedral by a tall canopied porch. The west screen, designed by John Hutton, shows new life rising from disaster and is a link between the old and the new cathedrals. Above the alter hangs Graham Sutherland's huge tapestry in glowing colours showing Christ In Glory.

■288■ GLOUCESTER CATHEDRAL ☎ 01452 528095
The Chapter Office, 17 College Green, Gloucester, Gloucestershire GL1 2LR
In centre of Gloucester, signposted off College St and Westgate St
Open all year: daily 7.30–6.15
Magnificent medieval abbey church begun under the instruction of William the Conqueror in 1089 to replace an earlier Anglo-Saxon monastery. Originally it was called St Peter's Abbey, and it was not until after Henry VIII's Dissolution of the monasteries that, in 1541, it became Gloucester Cathedral. Uniform Gothic exterior contrasts with the Norman interior, with its massive cylindrical pillars, and hugh rounded arches in the nave. In the transepts and choir the tall, elegant lines of the fourteenth-century perpendicular style are part of the remodelling that took place after King Edward II's burial in 1327. The east window, dating from the mid-fourteenth century, is the largest stained-glass window in Britain. In the cloister there is a magnificent example of late fourteenth-century fan vaulting, considered to be some of the finest and earliest in the country.

■289■ HAILES ABBEY ☎ 01242 602398
Nr Winchcombe, Gloucestershire GL54 5PB
2 miles NE of Winchcombe off B4632
Open Apr–Sept: daily 10–6; Oct: daily 10–5; Nov–Mar exc Christmas: Sat and Sun 10–4. Closed 1–2 in winter
Cistercian abbey built by Richard, Earl of Cornwall, in the thirteenth century in gratitude for surviving a perilous sea journey. Demolished after the Dissolution of the monasteries, Hailes Abbey was excavated in the late nineteenth century, and the ruins now stand peacefully in secluded Cotswolds wooded pastureland.

■290■ HEREFORD CATHEDRAL ☎ 01432 359880
Cathedral Office, 5 College Cloisters, Cathedral Close, Hereford, Herefordshire HR1 2NG
In centre of Hereford
Cathedral open all year: Mon–Sat 7.30–6.15, Sun 7.30–4. Mappa Mundi Exhibition open summer: Mon–Sat 10–4.15, Sun 11–3.15; winter: Mon–Sun 1–3.15
Beautiful medieval cathedral whose structure and contents have gradually evolved over its long history. Much of what we see today dates from Victorian times. By the beginning of the nineteenth century the building had been badly neglected, and the quire floor, the pew ends, parts of the high altar, and the replica Norman arch and its carvings all date from Victorian restoration. The south transept, built between 1080 and 1130, is the best place to see what the cathedral must have looked like when it was first built. The nave was first built in about 1100 but was changed extensively about 250 years later when the large windows replaced much smaller ones. The cathedral is full of wonderful artefacts dating from the thirteenth century, including the well-known Mappa Mundi. The windows in the west wall of the north transept, which also date from this time, are believed to be among the largest expanses of church glass in the country.

■291■ **LICHFIELD CATHEDRAL** ☎ 01543 306100
The Chapter House, 19a The Close, Lichfield, Staffordshire WS13 7LD
In centre of Lichfield
Open all year: daily 7.45–6

Fred's **FAVOURITE**

Eight-hundred-year-old Gothic cathedral, distinctive for its three spires,
known as the 'Ladies of the Vale'. Inside there is a fine display of both medieval
and modern craftsmanship, including extensive carving in wood and stone,
three wall-paintings dating from 1400, outstanding sixteenth-century glass from
Belgium, now in the Lady Chapel, and much fine nineteenth-century stained
glass. Tilework is another of the cathedral's treasures:the floor of the library
above the chapterhouse still has its original thirteenth-century tiles, while the
choir and presbytery have a fine Victorian tiled floor by Minton.

■292■ **WENLOCK PRIORY** ☎ 01952 727466
Wenlock Priory, Much Wenlock, Shropshire TF13 6HS
A458 from Shrewsbury into Much Wenlock, signposted
Open daily: Apr–Sept 10–6; Oct 10–5; Nov–Mar Wed–Sun 10–4 (closed 1–2)
Founded in 680, a place of pilgrimage and frequently visited by Henry III, today
the ruins of the large Cluniac priory are in an attractive garden setting with
topiary. There are substantial remains of the early-thirteenth-century church
and the Norman chapterhouse. The ruins show that this was one of the biggest
(over 350 feet/107 metres long) and finest monastic churches in the country.
The south transept is the most impressive part of the ruins at over 70 feet
(21 metres) high. Much of the elaborate arcading and detailed stone carving,
typical of Cluniac buildings, can still be seen on the interior walls of the chapterhouse. The remains of a late-Norman Lavatorium – a separate building for
washing – can also be seen. Accurate replicas have replaced its carved panels.

■293■ **WORCESTER CATHEDRAL** ☎ 01905 28854
10A College Green, Worcester, Worcestershire WR1 2LH
In centre of Worcester
Open all year: daily 7.30–6
Worcester Cathedral, with its 202-foot (61.5-metre) tower, stands majestically
on the banks of the River Severn. Built of red sandstone, it was begun in 1084,
but the exterior was altered considerably by A. E. Perkins and Sir Gilbert Scott
in the nineteenth century during restoration work. Inside, the crypt is a classic
example of Norman architecture; it was built in 1084 by St Wulstan. There are
cloisters and a chapterhouse, which is the oldest circular example of its type in
the country, and examples of architectural styles from many periods.

🏛 **WALES**   **MAP 5**

■294■ **BANGOR CATHEDRAL** ☎ 01248 353983
High Street, Bangor, Gwynedd LL57 1NY
In city centre
Open all year: Sun–Fri 7.30–6, Sat 10–1.30
Largely a Victorian creation of the nineteenth-century architect Sir Gilbert Scott,
who was brought in to restore the medieval cathedral which stood here.
Founded in 525 by St Deiniol, Bangor Cathedral occupies the site of one of the
earliest monastic settlements in Britain. In 546 Deiniol was consecrated bishop
and his church became a cathedral. The building was begun in 1120 and

completed by 1139. A great deal of damage was sustained during the Welsh wars and it was not until late fifteenth century that rebuilding took place. During the English Civil Wars the cathedral was damaged again, then in the nineteenth century Sir Gilbert Scott came to supervise the massive restoration of the central tower and the crossing. There's an exhibition on the Anian Pontifical (thirteenth-century service book for bishops, set to music) and a twelfth-century tomb.

■295■ ST ASAPH CATHEDRAL ☎ 01745 583597
St Asaph, Denbighshire SA70 7DN
Off A55 towards centre of St Asaph
Open all year: daily 7.30–6.30

St Asaph Cathedral

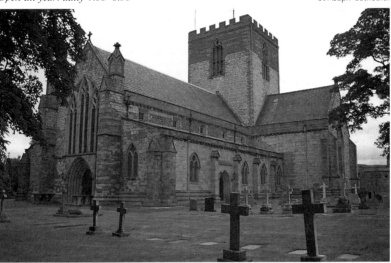

Britain's smallest ancient cathedral stands on a hill by the side of the River Elwy. Founded in 560 by St Kentigern (better known as St Mungo). There is a Kentigern Window in the north aisle and a carving on the choir ceiling of the salmon and the ring that are associated with him. The present building is mainly from the late thirteenth century and early fourteenth century and has a mixture of architectural styles, dating from the thirteenth to the nineteenth century. The arches and pillars are an unusual feature as they have no capitals. Also look out for the medieval stone carvings and the clerestory windows from 1403. On the carved stalls of the presbytery (from 1483) is a man's face thought to be that of the master carver. The cathedral also has a copy of the 1588 William Morgan Welsh Bible which the Prince of Wales took his oath on in 1969.

■296■ ST DAVID'S CATHEDRAL ☎ 01437 720199
The Close, St David's, Pembrokeshire SA62 6PE
In centre of St David's
Open all year: Mon–Sat 8–6; Sun 1.30–5.30
Set on a remote peninsula and built in a hollow to escape the attentions of marauders from the sea, St David's is one of Britain's earliest cathedrals. The cathedral is mainly late Norman with some rebuilding from the thirteenth century, when the tower collapsed, and from the fourteenth century. Triple-aisled Norman interior, with a beautiful ceiling of Irish oak added in the late fifteenth

century. The cathedral's entrance is through a ruined gateway and down a steep flight of stone steps known locally as the 39 Articles. On the north side of the cathedral are the ruins of St Mary's College, founded in 1365, and to the west is the Bishop's Palace, which has fine arcading and an impressive Great Hall.

■297■ ST MARGARET'S, THE MARBLE CHURCH ☎ 01745 583034
The Village, Bodelwyddan, Denbighshire LL18 5UR
On A55 between St Asaph and Abergele, signed off the motorway
Open: daily winter 8.30–5 and summer 8.30–8

Fred's
FAVOURITE

St Margaret's is popularly known as the 'Marble Church' due to the vast amount and variety of marble used in its interior construction. Altogether there are fourteen different types used. John Gibson designed the church, and building began in 1856. St Margaret's took four years to build and is considered to be Gibson's principal work. The tower and delicately carved 202-feet (61-metre) spire can be seen for miles around. The church possesses some of the finest examples of English woodcarving from the nineteenth century: take particular note of the lectern and the pulpit; and a stained glass window by Burn-Jones who worked with William Morris.

🏛 NORTH-WEST   MAP 6

■298■ CHESTER CATHEDRAL ☎ 01244 324756
12 Abbey Square, Chester, Cheshire CH1 2HU
In centre of Chester, opposite town hall on Werburgh St
Open all year: daily 7.30–6.30, Sunday morning services
Originally a Benedictine monastry founded in 1092 which was disolved in 1539 to become the cathedral of the new diocese of Chester, today the site is an unusually well-preserved example of a medieval monastic complex, with a cathedral displaying all the main periods of Gothic architecture. Inside, the outstanding feature is the quire, with its beautifully tiled floor and meticulously carved wooden stalls. The stalls were originally constructed in around 1380 from Baltic oak, and above every individually carved stall is an intricate canopy. These canopies are made up of hundreds of individually carved pieces of wood, jointed up and held together by small pegs. The adjoining monastic buildings are among the best preserved in England, and the thirteenth-century refectory is still in use today.

■299■ FURNESS ABBEY ☎ 01229 823420
Barrow-in-Furness, Cumbria LH13 0TJ
1½ miles N of Barrow-in-Furness on minor road off A590
Open Apr–Sept: daily 10–6; Oct–Mar exc Christmas: Wed–Sun 10–4. Closed 1–2 in winter
Extensive red-sandstone ruins of abbey founded in 1127 by the future King Stephen. In its day Furness was the second richest Cistercian monastery in England. The main approach is from the north, and the early-Gothic design of the abbey church is best appreciated in the north transept. Remains of chapterhouse can also be seen. In the fifteenth century the church was remodelled, and you can see where many of the windows were replaced or enlarged.

■300■ LIVERPOOL CATHEDRAL ☎ 0151 709 6271
Liverpool, Merseyside L1 7AZ
In centre of Liverpool
Open all year: daily 9–6. Tower July–Sept: Mon–Sat 11–3; Refectory: daily 10–4

Largest Anglican cathedral in Britain and one of the largest in the world,
Liverpool's Anglican cathedral can accommodate a congregation of 2,500.
Building began in 1904, when Edward VII laid the foundation stone. It is probably the last Gothic-style cathedral to be built in Britain, but its architect, Sir
Giles Gilbert Scott, also employed modern techniques and material for its construction. Liverpool Cathedral has the highest and heaviest ringing peal of bells
in the world, the heaviest bell, Great George, weighing nearly fifteen tonnes.
The west window, by Carl Edwards, is a spectacular sight, and the high altar is
quite breathtaking. The whole cathedral is best approached from Rodney Street
to appreciate the massive proportions of the building.

■301■ **LIVERPOOL METROPOLITAN CATHEDRAL OF CHRIST
THE KING** ☎ 0151 709 9222
Cathedral House, Mount Pleasant, Liverpool, Merseyside L3 5TQ
About 5 minutes' walk from Lime Street Station, near the Aldephi Hotel
Open all year: daily 8–6
In 1960 architects from all over the world were invited to design a cathedral
for Liverpool which could be built within five years and would cost no more
than £1 million for the shell. Frederick Gibberd's design was chosen from 300
entries, and building began in 1962, with the opening ceremony held on 14
May 1967. This ultramodern cathedral is startlingly different in both design and
layout. The 2,000-tonne tower stands out boldly, letting coloured light seep in
by day and shining it out by night. The cathedral contains much less decoration
than its older brothers and certainly makes an interesting comparison with its
neighbour, the huge Anglican cathedral.

🏛 NORTH-EAST   MAP 6

■302■ **BEVERLEY MINSTER** ☎ 01482 868540
Minster Yard North, Beverley, East Yorkshire HU17 ODP
In centre of Beverley
Open summer: daily 9–7; autumn and spring: daily 9–5; winter: daily 9–4
Beverley Minster has its origins in a monastery founded in around 700. The
present church is the fourth on the site. Its construction has taken place over
three centuries – hence the three styles of Gothic architecture: the east end
(1220–60, early English), the Nave (1308–49, Decorated) and the west end, with
its twin towers (1390–1400, perpendicular). It also houses superb early-sixteenth-century choir stalls containing a collection of 68 misericord seats. From
the last couple of centuries notable alterations include the Snetzler organ, the
nineteenth-century statues and woodwork and the round nave altar, from 1970.

■303■ **BOLTON ABBEY** ☎ 01756 710533 or 710238
The Priory of St Mary and St Cuthbert, Skipton, North Yorkshire BD23 6AL
On B6160 off A59 Harrogate to Skipton road
Open summer: daily 8–6 (4 on Fri); winter: daily 8–4 (dusk if sooner). Tours available
This twelfth-century Augustinian priory is now part working parish church and
part ruin. They stand in beautiful riverside setting on the River Wharfe estate of
the Duke and Duchess of Devonshire. The priory's original nave was lengthened
and conserved as the parish church. The original choir and transepts, which are
still joined to it, are ruins. There are eleven paintings on the east wall of the
church, which represent the life of Christ.

■304■ **DURHAM CATHEDRAL** ☎ 0191 386 4266
The Chapter Office, The College, Durham, Durham DH1 3EH
From Durham centre a short uphill walk;City minibus to Palace Green in front of cathedral
Open May–Aug: daily 9–8; Sept–Apr: daily 9–6, 7.30am for services
Durham Cathedral, England's greatest masterpiece of early-Norman architecture, started in 1093 as a shrine to St Cuthbert, is an awe-inspiring sight, particularly when viewed from the banks of the River Wear. The rib vaulting of the massive ceiling, supported on huge piers and columns, is the earliest of its kind in Europe and was considered a construction miracle of its day. The character of the building on the whole is Romanesque, but the pointed transverse arches of the nave show a Gothic approach. Much detail was removed from the walls when they were pared down during eighteenth-century restoration. Sir Gilbert Scott restored the current choir screen in 1870–7. The Galilee Chapel, with its graceful columns and arches is a late Romanesque-Norman masterpiece. The adjoining monastic buildings include early-fifteenth-century cloisters, monks' dormitory and an octagonal kitchen with fine vaulting, which was in use until 1940 and is now the cathedral bookshop.

■305■ **FOUNTAINS ABBEY** ☎ 01765 608888
Fountains Abbey and Studley Royal, Studley Park, Ripon, North Yorkshire HG4 3DY
4 miles W of Ripon off B6265 to Pateley Bridge. Signposted from A1
Open Jan–Mar: daily 10–5; Apr–Sept: daily 10–7; Oct–Dec: daily 10–5. Last admission 1 hour before closing. Closed Fri Nov–Jan and 24–25 Dec
Fountains Abbey is the most complete Cistercian abbey remains in Britain. Excellent views of the whole west front of the abbey from the main approach. The shell of the abbey's church is remarkable for its scale, with a great uninterrupted vista from west to east framed by the massive Norman pillars of the nave on either side. Well-preserved cloister and west range with magnificent vaulted roof. The ruins provide a dramatic focal point for the Studley Royal landscape gardens, which were created by John and William Aislabie in the eighteenth century. They include formal water gardens, ornamental temples, follies and magnificent views. They are bordered by a lake and acres of deer park. There is also an Elizabethan mansion (lived in for over 400 years), of which two of the rooms may be viewed. In contrast to the abbey remains, St Mary's Church, which is in the deer park beyond the garden, is an example of high Victorian Gothic designed by the architect William Burges.

■306■ **HEXHAM ABBEY** ☎ 01434 602031
Beaumont Street, Hexham, Northumberland NE46 3NB
Off A69 W of Newcastle, in Hexham
Open Oct–Apr: daily 9–5; May–Sept: daily 9–7. Visits to crypt: daily at 11 and 3.30. Closed Good Friday
Hexham Abbey is bigger than many cathedrals and is one of the great achievements of the early-English style. The crypt from the first church to be built on this site about 674 by St Wilfred still remains and is said to be the best surviving Saxon crypt in the country. Also remaining are the Saxon apse and some parts of the nave. In 1114 an Augustinian priory was founded, and the choir and long transepts were built by the canons of the time. The night stair from the dormitory can still be seen in the south transept. In 1296 the Scots destroyed the nave, and it was not until 1907 that Temple Moore rebuilt it. The church contains rich furnishings and decoration from several periods.

■307■ KIRKSTALL ABBEY ☎ 01132 637861
Abbey Walk, Abbey Road, Kirkstall, Leeds, West Yorkshire LS5 3EH
Off A65 3–4 m W of Leeds city centre
Open all year: daily dawn–dusk
Built of millstone grit, Kirkstall Abbey is England's most complete Cistercian abbey. So much of it remains that it is easy to visualize how the place would have looked in its time. It was founded in 1152 by the monks who had come from Fountains Abbey (see entry 305) and first tried to establish themselves at Barnoldswick. Kirkstall Abbey is very similar to Fountains and is of the typical Cistercian plan. For its time the abbey has a very simple exterior which is dominated by the crossing tower, of which the lower parts are original.

■308■ LINDISFARNE PRIORY ☎ 01289 389200
Lindisfarne Priory, Holy Island Berwick-upon-Tweed TD15 2RX
On Holy Island, reached at low tides across causeway
Open Apr–Sept: daily 10–6; Oct: daily 10–5; Nov–Mar: daily 10–4. Closed 24–26 Dec and 1 Jan
Lindisfarne, founded by St Aidan in 635 and later also known as Holy Island of Lindisfarne, was the site of one of the most important centres of Christianity in Anglo-Saxon England. It became a treasure house of jewels and manuscripts and was easy prey for the first Viking raiders at the end of the eighth century. The monks fled, and the dramatic ruins we see today on the island are partly the remains of the Norman church priory (completed in c.1190) and partly the medieval priory that was there from the time of the return of the monks in the twelfth century until the Dissolution of the Monasteries in 1537.

■309■ RIEVAULX ABBEY ☎ 01439 798228
Rievaulx, York YO6 5LB
2 miles W of Helmsley on minor road off B1257
Open Apr–June: daily 10–6; July–Aug: daily 9.30–7; Sept: daily 10–6; Oct: daily 10–5; Nov–Mar: daily 10–4. Closed 24–26 Dec and 1 Jan
Standing in a beautiful valley, Rievaulx was the first Cistercian monastery in the north of England. St Bernard of Clairvaux founded it in 1132, when he came here with twelve monks. Although it began modestly it became one of the wealthiest monasteries of medieval England. Most of the presbytery and the eastern part of the abbey church still stand to almost full height. A wealthy family protected the abbey throughout the Middle Ages, and the eastern part of the church was elaborately rebuilt in the 1220s for the canonization of the author and preacher Aelred.

■310■ RIPON CATHEDRAL ☎ 01765 603462
Ripon, North Yorkshire HG4 1QT
In centre of Ripon
Open daily: 8–6.30
Built originally by St Wilfred in 672 as one of England's first stone churches, the crypt has survived nearly intact throughout the last 1300 years and lies preserved at the heart of the cathedral we see today. Construction of this began in around 1080 and continued until around 1300. The present choir, north and south transepts and the exceptional early English west front all date from this period. The nave and the central tower date from a period of rebuilding which began in 1485. Eight hundred years of craftsmanship in wood and stone can be seen within the nave and the choir, and there is a stained-glass window that

dates from medieval times. Look out for the misericords – beautifully carved shelved seating designed for old and infirm priests so that they could still appear to be standing during worship.

■311■ ST ANDREWS CHURCH ☎ 01670 775360
Bolam, Morpeth, Northumberland NE61
A696 to Belsay, then follow signposts for Bolam
Open all year: daily 9–7
Village church with Saxon tower which dates from 960. When the Normans came to Bolam they rebuilt the east end of the church, putting in a new quire and sanctuary and a fine chancel arch on which the remains of many carved heads can be seen. The church has been well maintained down the ages and has been used for at least a thousand years of worship.

■312■ THE SAXON CHURCH, ESCOMB ☎ 01388 662265/602861
Escomb, Nr Bishop Auckland, Durham DL14 7ST
1½ miles W of Bishop Auckland
Open summer: daily 9–8; winter: daily 9–4. Keys available during daylight hours from 22 Saxon Green
Simple, tiny church of enormous antiquity and primitive simplicity. The Saxon church at Escomb is one of Britain's earliest surviving churches, built largely from Roman stones foraged from the nearby abandoned Roman fort of Binchester. No one knows for certain who built the church, when it was built, or why it was built in this particular location. However, various architectural features suggest the date of construction to be between 670 and 690, and it is generally agreed from the general shape and style of the building that it could not have been constructed later than the end of the seventh century. From the outside, the outline of the building is sombre and severe. Inside, the supports for the chancel arch have distinctive 'Escomb style – long and short' stonework. The arch itself is believed to have been reassembled from a Roman archway. Windows are splayed to let in the maximum amount of light while keeping out some of the wind and rain. The main crossbeams in the roof have been dated by dendrochronology (the counting of tree rings) and found to have been felled betwen 1450 and 1470.

■313■ YORK MINSTER ☎ 01904 557216
The Visitors' Dept, St Williams College, 5 College St, York, North Yorkshire YO1 7JF

Fred's
FAVOURITE

In centre of York
Open summer Mon–Sat 9–8.30, Sun 1–6; winter Mon–Sat 109–6, Sun 1–6
York Minster, the chief church in the Northern Province of the Church of England, has offered worship for over 1,300 years. The minster is the largest Gothic cathedral in northern Europe. Work on the present building started in 1220 and took over 250 years to complete. The minster is a place of superlatives. The nave was begun in 1291 and is the widest Gothic nave and largest medieval hall in England. The Great East Window is one of the largest areas of medieval stained glass in the world. The octagonal-shaped Chapter House, begun in about 1260, has some of the minster's finest carvings. The South Transept, with a beautiful rose window, has a recently restored roof and vaulting following a fire in 1984. Remains of York's Roman legionary fortress, Viking gravestones and parts of the Norman foundations can be seen alongside the twentieth-century engineering that was needed to support the

York Minster

building in the foundations and treasury. The crypt has an interesting mixture of Norman architecture, medieval carvings and modern works of art. Climb the 275 spiral steps of the massive central tower for superb views of York and the surrounding countryside. On clear days you can see for over 35 miles (55 kilometres).

⛭ SCOTLAND   MAP 8

■314■ ARBROATH ABBEY ☎ 01241 878756
Arbroath, Angus DD11 1EG
In Arbroath centre on A92
Open Apr–Sept: daily 9.30–6.30; Oct–Mar: Mon–Sat 9.30–4.30, Sun 2–4.30
Tironensian monastery founded by King William the Lion in 1178 and intended as his own burial place. The abbey and its surrounding buildings were enclosed by a large wall, which had four well-defended gatehouses. Substantial ruins remain, including parts of the abbey church, the gatehouse range and the abbot's house.

■315■ DRYBURGH ABBEY ☎ 01835 822381

Dryburgh, St Boswells, Roxburghshire, Borders TD6 0RG

8 miles SE of Melrose on B6404, 3½ miles from St Boswells, signposted from St Boswells
Open Apr–Sept: daily 9.30–6.30; Oct–Mar: Mon–Sat 9.30–4.30, Sun 2–4.30

Attractive and tranquil monastic ruin. Hugo de Morville, Lord of Lauderdale, and his wife Beatrix founded the abbey some time before 1150 for Premon-stratensian monks. Throughout the fourteenth century it was repeatedly plundered by the English and was finally destroyed in 1545. In spite of this, the High Gothic ruins of Dryburgh are remarkably complete. They include the beautiful west doorway, the rose window at the western end of the refectory and the chapterhouse. Sir Walter Scott is buried in the north transept and Field Marshall Haig lies here, too.

■316■ DUNFERMLINE ABBEY ☎ 01383 739026

St Margaret's Street, Dunfermline, Fife

Off A994 in Dunfermline
Open Apr–Sept: daily 9.30–6.30; Oct–Mar: Mon–Sat 9.30–4.30 (last admission ½ hour before closing). Closed Thur pm and Fri in winter and Sun am

Remains of a great Benedictine abbey founded by Queen Margaret in the eleventh century. Underneath the superb nave, built in the twelfth century in the Romanesque style, are the foundations of her church. Substantial parts of the abbey buildings still remain, particularly the vast refectory. Next to the abbey is the ruin of the Royal Palace, which was rebuilt from the guesthouse of the monastery in the sixteenth century for James VI.

■317■ GLASGOW CATHEDRAL ☎ 0141 552 6891

Cathedral Square, Glasgow G4 0QZ

In centre of Glasgow
Open Apr–Sept: daily 9.30–6.30; Oct–Mar: Mon–Fri 9.30–4.30, Sun 2–4.30. Closed 25 and 26 Dec and 1–3 Jan

The only Scottish mainland medieval cathedral to have survived the Reformation complete and Scotland's finest Gothic building. The cathedral we see today was begun in the fourteenth century and finished early in the fifteenth and has the appearance of a unified whole. Notable features include the elaborate fan vaulting around St Kentigern's (St Mungo's) tomb in the crypt, a rare fifteenth-century stone screen in the choir and the unfinished Blackadder Aisle.

■318■ JEDBURGH ABBEY ☎ 01835 863925

4 Abbey Bridgend, Jedburgh, Borders TD8 6JQ

In Jedburgh on A68
Open Apr–Sept: daily 9.30–6.30; Oct–Mar: Mon–Sat 9.30–4.30, Sun 2–4.30

Founded in 1138 by David I for Augustinian canons, Jedburgh Abbey is one of the four great abbeys built in the Scottish Borders in the Middle Ages. The church, mostly in the Romanesque and early-Gothic styles, is remarkably complete. Its best features are two arches, the arcades in the nave and the west façade, with a magnificent rose window. Around a fragrant cloister garden lie the remains of the canons' domestic buildings. There is also a display of finds from recent excavations of the cloister buildings.

■319■ MELROSE ABBEY ☎ 01896 822562

Abbey Street, Melrose, Borders TD6 9LG

A68 and turn off at Melrose, into Market Square
Open Apr–Sept: daily 9.30–6.30; Oct–Mar: Mon–Sat 9.30–4.30, Sun 2–4.30

The most magnificent of the four Scottish Borders abbeys (the other three being Dryburgh, Jedburgh and Kelso), the ruins that can be seen today are mostly those of the fifteenth-century abbey. Built in red sandstone, the original abbey was founded in the twelfth century by David I for the Cistercians, but it was often devastated and plundered by English armies. In spite of all these ravages, the remains are still very impressive, with elaborate masonry and beautiful detail in the capitals and sculptures, which include a fourteenth-century continental-style Virgin and Child, the Coronation of the Virgin and many dragons, flowers, gargoyles and plants. In the Commendator's House is a large collection of objects found during excavation.

■320■ ST ANDREW'S CATHEDRAL   ☎ 01334 472563
The Pends, St Andrews, Fife KY16 9QU
In centre of St Andrews on A91
Open Apr–Sept: daily 9.30–6.30; Oct–Mar: Mon–Sat 9.30–4.30, Sun 2–4.30
Remains of the largest cathedral in Scotland and of the associated domestic ranges of the priory. The precinct walls are particularly well kept and most impressive. Within the precinct St Rule's Tower, built in the early twelfth century, is part of the first church of the Augustinian canons at St Andrews.

■321■ SWEETHEART ABBEY   ☎ 01387 850397
New Abbey, Dumfries & Galloway DG2 8BU
In New Abbey on A710 7 miles S of Dumfries
Open Apr–Sept: daily 9.30–6.30; Oct–Mar: Mon–Sat 9.30–4.30, Sun 2–4.30
Beautiful ruins of a Cistercian abbey founded in 1273 by Lady Devorguilla of Galloway in memory of her husband. The most impressive feature today is the remains of the precinct walls, which enclose 30 acres (12 hectares).

Jedburgh Abbey

CHAPTER

4

PUBLIC, COMMERCIAL AND INDUSTRIAL BUILDINGS

When I was a kid all the beautiful chimneys in Bolton had wonderful names. This is because in the olden days when a bunch of men came together, as directors, to build a spinning mill one of the first things they did was to christen it. Then, when they'd built it they'd put the name on the chimney in white tiles. When I was a little lad, Bolton was full of them. They all had names like the Dove, the Ocean and the Swan, and they all had beautiful tops, great flared fancy overhanging ones. Sadly, the Swan is the only one of them that is left now.

But as all the chimneys in Bolton have disappeared, and as my life has progressed on to my twilight years, as you might say, I'm pleased to say I've been able to build a chimney myself in my back garden. It's nearly finished, and I'm going to have a topping out-ceremony like they did in the olden days. There are many tales about the finishing off of great buildings and chimneys, and they always had a topping-out ceremony. So I'm going to get my old gramophone and a crate of Guinness and I'm going to take them to the top and have my own music and a pint on top of the chimney that I have built in my own back garden.

Most traces of Bolton's industrial past have gone, but there are still a number of very impressive buildings around the country that were built for trade and industry. The Merchant Adventurers' Hall in York is Britain's finest surviving medieval guildhall. It was built in the 1350s for the powerful Merchant Adventurers' Company, and they used the hall to transact their business affairs, meet together socially, look after the poor and pray. No other medieval guildhall in Europe, which is still under the ownership of the company that built it, has survived with its business room, hospital and chapel intact. The whole thing looks very good because the lower part of the hall

Liverpool's most famous landmark, the Royal Liver Building

is constructed mainly of bricks, while the upper part of the hall is timber-framed. To build this top bit, each section was first put together on the ground, then it was dismantled after the timbers had been marked. In this way the carpenters could easily find the right timber when they reassembled the section upright in its position on the building. The Great Hall, where the merchants did their trading, is built as a double nave because no timbers of English oak could be found that were long enough to form the great tie-beams needed to stretch all the way from one side to the other. The sash windows that we see now aren't original, though. They were inserted in the 1740s; before this the windows had been smaller and higher up.

For hundreds of years cloth was our most important trade and the village of Lacock in Wiltshire was an important trading centre from the thirteenth to the eighteeenth century. Many Lacock villagers lived by weaving and, by the fourteenth century, cloth was being made there and sold far and wide, even exported from Bristol. The village was on the old main road from London to Bristol. Today the village has cottages, inns, a lockup jail and shops dating from the thirteenth to the nineteenth century as well as a medieval tithe barn, a fifteenth-century church and a Victorian workhouse.

In medieval times only local materials could be used to build the houses, so the earliest ones were all built of timber, plaster, thatch and stone. Bricks, brick tiles and slates came much later. Stone can be used in lumps as it comes out of the ground or it can be carved to give a smooth surface. If you see a house built of shaped stone, this is a clue that money had been spent on buying a stonemason's time and skill. Houses of both kinds can still be found in Lacock. Although many of the cottages and houses have been altered since medieval times, some of them still have features dating back that far, and Lacock is as good a place as anywhere to get a feel of what a medieval trading centre would have been like.

As Britain is an island, much of our trade has to be carried out by sea, so shipbuilding was always one of our most important industries. The Historic Dockyard at Chatham is the most complete naval shipyard in the world dating from Georgian and early-Victorian times. Most of the buildings were erected during the eighteenth century to provide facilities to support the building, repair and maintenance of the ships of the Royal Navy in the age of sail. Between 1700 and the end of the Napoleonic Wars in 1815, Chatham Dockyard built and launched 125 ships. Repairs and maintenance of other ships were also carried out, providing additional work for the typically 1,700 men who worked in the dockyard at any one time during this period. The shipwrights were the yard's most important artisans, and their skill lay at the heart of the shipbuilding and ship-repairing process. In the years before the Industrial Revolution the Royal Dockyard was the largest manufacturing site in the world. Hundreds of people from over twenty-six different trades were employed here – all working to produce a single object: the warship of the age of sail.

The first dry docks at Chatham were shallow trenches dug in the river bank and lined with timber. These trenches relied on gravity for drainage and hinged gates to keep the water out. Between 1820 and 1860 they were deepened and rebuilt in stone. Together with the dry docks, the covered slips formed the industrial heart of the dock-

The covered slips, Chatham

yard. The majority of shipbuilding was concentrated in this area and, although some ships were built in the dry docks, most were constructed on slipways that sloped down into the river. The first slips were built during the seventeenth century. Shortly after the end of the Napoleonic Wars, they were renewed in stone and covers were built over those that were used for shipbuilding to help prevent ships rotting before they were launched. Ships' masts were made and repaired in the timber-framed mast houses, which were built largely from reused warship timbers. The Commissioner's House, built in 1704 to house the resident commissioner, his family and servants, is the oldest naval building to survive intact in Britain, and it has changed very little since it was first built.

Britain's finest example of a commercial dock from the age of sail is Liverpool's Albert Dock. Opened by Prince Albert in 1846 as

The Albert Dock, Liverpool

England's gateway to the New World, the Albert Dock symbolizes Liverpool's nineteenth-century greatness as a port of world importance. Built to accommodate the biggest sailing ships of the day, the warehouses and quaysides once overflowed with produce from all corners of the earth. However, by the end of the century, steam had replaced sail and the dock's days were numbered. Today it has the largest group of Grade I listed buildings in Britain.

When it was built, the five blocks of five-storey warehouses provided a staggering amount of floor space surrounding a quadrangle of water the size of London's Trafalgar Square. Work started on it in November 1841 and hundreds of navvies toiled night and day to dig out the docks and build the walls that would provide good secure fireproof warehouses for the rising tonnage of valuable cargo that was passing through. This included cotton for the booming Lancashire mills.

The man responsible for the design and construction of the dock was Jesse Hartley, Chief Engineer to the Port of Liverpool from 1824 to 1860. He doubled the dock space and improved many of the cargo-handling facilities to make Liverpool the most efficient port of its time. The Albert Dock was his masterpiece, and its warehouses are one of the supreme examples of our industrial architecture. The dock was designed for sailing ships carrying up to a hundred tonnes of cargo, but as the nineteenth century went on, more and more valuable cargoes started to be moved by larger steam ships. This meant fewer cargoes were received direct by the dock; instead they came by barge or road from the larger, more modern docks that had been built to accommodate the steam ships.

Liverpool's success and prosperity in the nineteenth and early-twentieth centuries left a rich legacy of magnificent buildings. St George's Hall was hailed as a symbol of the city's greatness when it was opened in 1854. It is one of the finest neoclassical civic buildings in Europe, built between 1841 and 1854 to the design of Harvey Lonsdale Elms, whose brief was to provide a concert hall and law courts in one building. It is a remarkable achievement for so young an architect (he was twenty-seven) who hadn't even visited Greece or Italy. Particularly impressive is the eastern façade opposite Lime Street Station, with sixteen Corinthian columns flanked by two wings of square pilasters with carved panels between. While the inspiration for the exterior of the hall can be seen as Greece, the interior is Rome, with a Great Hall whose long sides are each divided into five bays by sets of six granite columns which give a great sense of grandeur.

If St George's Hall is a symbol of the city's Victorian civic pride, the building that has come to symbolise the city itself is the Royal Liver Building. This architectural monument on the Pier Head of the River Mersey was built for the Royal Liver Company between 1908 and 1911 to house its rapidly expanding life assurance business. The construction of the building involved a revolutionary building technique known as the Hennebique principle, named after its inventor. The technique used a self-contained ferro-concrete frame with a network of columns and steel beams to carry the weight of the outer and inner walls and floors. The outer walls were designed to act merely as weather screens comprising thin panels of concrete clothed with a curtain of granite.

But another insurance building, built less than eighty years after the Liver Building and even more revolutionary in its design and construction, shows how much architecture and styles of building changed during the course of the twentieth century. Lloyd's was around at the time that the Albert Dock was built, providing insurance for the ships that sailed from there. Today, the Lloyd's Building has become a major architectural landmark in the City of London, representing as it does the modern face of a commercial building. Its 300-foot (91-metre) silver and glass structure makes a startling impact and epitomizes architect Richard Rodgers's concern with total flexibility and technological advance. But will it be a Grade I listed building in a hundred years time?

I must say I didn't really like the building when I first saw it, but when I got the chance to have a closer look it appeared very impressive and all so very well put together. The reinforced concrete vertical columns and the beams across are almost like Victorian engineering. There are lots of things about it that you could compare with the way in which things were done in the olden days. The roof right up at the top is almost like the Crystal Palace – same shape and same sort of window configuration. Then, of course, there are the great diagonals at each end that give the building stability. The quality of the design, the workmanship and the materials throughout, is superb.

One wonderful thing about the whole lot is that on arrival on the top floor you are in this unbelievable world of make-believe; a futuristic world of computers, offices, stainless steel, glass and light. Then they open a door and you step into a beautiful Adam dining room with superb plastering and antique Georgian furniture and a 35-foot-long (10-metre-long) table that evidently has around it every now and then all the important people of Lloyd's. I couldn't believe that in this amazing, futuristic building they had this strange room upstairs on the top deck – like a time machine where you step back into the Georgian era.

The room at the top of the Lloyd's Building wouldn't have looked out of place in Bath, the city that Robert Adam helped to create. Bath owes its architectural style to an industry that is much older than we think – the tourist industry. From the early eighteenth century onwards the old Roman city underwent a meteoric rise to become the most fashionable and popular leisure resort in Georgian England. Today, the city is full of architectural masterpieces. Bath was almost completely rebuilt in the eighteenth century and it became famous for its early town planning, with graceful buildings set in beautiful terraces and crescents.

It was a Yorkshireman, John Wood, whose vision helped to change the face of Bath. In 1725 he devised a grand plan to develop the city with central circuses for sport, royal forums for assemblies and a variety of elegant squares. When his scheme was rejected by the council because it was too ambitious, Wood, and later his son, John Wood the younger, set about building as much of it as they could privately, covering Bath in a succession of fine Palladian mansions. Queen's Square, which took him six years to build, is a perfect example of his idea of a planned layout, with all the houses in it built to the same proportions and of the same stone. His greatest project, the Circus, has thirty houses built on a curve around a paved square. His inspiration for it was the Colosseum in Rome, but he died before he finished it and it was left to his son to complete his work. Like his father, the young John Wood was deeply influenced by the classical style of ancient Greece and Imperial Rome.

Admiring the beautiful architecture in Bath

His greatest work, the Royal Crescent, has been described as the finest crescent in Europe.

The style that father and son created became so popular that other architects soon flocked to Bath to adopt the Palladian style and to use the rich golden stone that the Woods had used for all of their buildings. Pulteney Bridge was designed by Robert Adam in the style of the Ponte Vecchio in Florence. Bath continued as a popular resort for the rest of the century but, by the nineteenth century, the world of fashion has passed it by, leaving behind a city that is one of our most magnificent monuments to this great age of Georgian elegance.

PLACES TO VISIT

🏛 SOUTH-WEST   MAP 1

■322■ ASSEMBLY ROOMS   ☎ 01225 477789
Bennett Street, Bath, Bath & NE Somerset BA1 2HQ
Signposted in Bath centre, off the 'circus'
Open all year: daily 10–5. Phone in advance as rooms are used for private functions
Fine Georgian building designed by John Wood the younger. U-shaped building
with the main entrance on the west side under a single-storey Doric portico.
Centre of Bath's thriving eighteenth-century social scene for polite society,
pioneered by 'Beau' Nash. Each room had a purpose: for dancing, playing cards
or drinking tea. Elegant decoration in the ballroom with beautiful chandeliers in
all rooms by William Parker. At the west end of the tea room is a colonnade of six
columns and ten pilasters. The Octagon, containing four marble chimneypieces,
was used for playing cards, and due to its popularity an additional card-room was
added in 1777. The Assembly Rooms also houses the Museum of Costume.

■323■ BRADFORD-ON-AVON TITHE BARN   ☎ 01179 750700
Bradford-on-Avon, Wiltshire BA15
Just S of town centre off B3109
Open all year: daily 10.30–4. Closed 24–26 Dec
Medieval barn with slate roof and wooden-beamed interior. A 'tithe' means a
'tenth'. Householders paid a tenth of their agricultural produce, such as grain or
cattle, each year for the upkeep of the clergy or as a tax. The barns were used
to store the tithes. The roof is made of local stone slate and is formed with arch-
braced trusses and three windbraces on each side. The barn is divided into fourteen bays, and porches project from the fifth and tenth bays on each side. The
restored granary is now a shop, while the dovecote on the farmhouse wall recalls
a time when pigeons were a welcome source of meat in winter.

■324■ COLDHARBOUR MILL WORKING WOOL MUSEUM
☎ 01884 840960
Uffculme, Cullompton, Devon EX15 3EE
2 miles from M5 junction 27, off B3181. Follow signs to Willand then brown signs
Open mid-Mar–Oct: daily 10.30–5 (last tour 4); Nov–mid-Mar: Mon–Fri 10.30–5
Two-hundred-year-old working woollen mill in the Culm Valley in the heart of
rural Devon. The mill saw the biggest change in 1865 when steam power
arrived. You can see the old waterwheel, which was still used for the night shift
until 1978. There is also a fully working 1910 Pollit and Wigzell drop valve horizontal cross compound steam engine and an 1867 beam engine. Engines are in
steam every bank holiday Sunday and Monday. In the mill they have been
spinning wool and worsted yarn for over 200 years and the old machinery is still
in action. There is also a giant twenty-panel New World tapestry which tells the
story of the English colonisation of the Americas between 1583 and 1642.

■325■ GEEVOR TIN MINE   ☎ 01736 788662
Pendeen, Penzance, Cornwall TR19 7EW
By B3306 St Just to Zennor Rd
Open Full Site Mar–Oct: Sun–Fri 10.30–5.30; Museum and Shop Nov–Feb: Mon–Fri 10–4

Cornish tin mine preserved very much as it was when the last shift finished in 1991. Victory Shaft, with working winding engine, was used for hoisting both men and ore. The site includes a museum with a 3-D model of the underground workings, compressor, winder house and an underground tour of the adit mine.

■326■ OLD POST OFFICE ☎ 01840 770024
Fore Street, Tintagel, Cornwall PL34 0DB
Follow A39 then take B3263 to Tintagel and go to centre of village
Open Apr–Sept: daily 11–5.30; Oct: daily 11–4 (last admission ¼ hour before closing)
Delightful, small fourteenth-century manor house which is well furnished with local oak pieces. In the nineteenth century it was used as the letter receiving office for the district, and it is now restored to that period and function. It is built of local brown slate, which has long since weathered to an even grey, and an occasional piece of granite. Granite was also used for the heavy arch over the entrance doorway and local green stone for the window surrounds. The walls are between 30 and 39 inches (75 and 100 centimetres) thick, but despite their massive construction have had to be buttressed at the back to support the immense weight of the roof slates, which came from the nearby cliff quarry. The plan is typical of many late-medieval manor houses, with the central single-storey hall open to the roof, flanked by smaller service rooms and a kitchen (now the parlour) with bedroom above. In spite of its small scale the house is surprisingly spacious and its garden is also open to visitors.

■327■ ROMAN BATHS AND PUMP ROOM ☎ 01225 477785
Pump Room, Abbey Church Yard, Bath, Bath & NE Somerset BA1 1LZ
In Bath city centre next to Abbey, 10 minutes' walk from bus and rail stations
Open Apr–Sept: daily 9–6 (9.30pm in Aug); Oct–Mar exc Christmas: daily 9.30–5

The Roman Baths

Substantial remains of the temple and complex of baths built at the centre of the Roman city of Aquae Sulis between the first and the fourth centuries. The remains are some 20 feet (6 metres) below the present street level, and they give a vivid impression of life nearly 2,000 years ago. The baths, built next to Britain's only hot spring, served the sick and pilgrims visiting the adjacent temple of Sulis Minerva. The spring was a sacred site lying within the courtyard of the temple. Votive offerings and temple treasures discovered during the excavations of the spring can be seen in the museum display. The most impressive sight, the Great Bath, is now roofless and, although its pillars, terrace and statues of famous Romans are nineteenth century, the bath itself and the surrounding pavement are original and are well preserved. Today the temple courtyard is beneath the pump room. This building became a popular meeting place in the eighteenth century, when Bath became the leading resort for fashionable society.

■328■ SALLY LUNN'S ☎ 01225 461634
4 North Parade Passage, Bath, Bath & NE Somerset BA1 1NX
In Bath city centre next to Abbey
Open all year: Mon–Sat 10–6, Sun and 1 Jan 1–6

Teatime at Sally Lunn's

Tudor building that can be traced back to Roman times. It is the oldest house in Bath and became a popular meeting place in the eighteenth century. In the cellars, a fascinating museum reveals the findings of recent excavations. Here, too, is the original kitchen, with its faggot oven, Georgian cooking range and collection of baking utensils. The restaurant still serves the famous Sally Lunn bun, believed to have been named after its first maker, who came to live in Bath in 1680.

■329■ TOTNES GUILDHALL ☎ 01803 862147
Ramparts Walk, Totnes, Devon TQ9 5QH
In centre of Totnes behind St Mary's Church
Open Easter–Oct: Mon–Fri 10.30–1 and 2–4.30
The pillared building we see today dates from the sixteenth century when, on
30 June 1553, the Priory of St Mary, which had been founded in 1088, became
a guildhall. The foundation and some of the walls that you can see date from
1088, and the Purbeck marble floor is from 1553, when the slabs were laid over
the original priory floor. The stair-treads of the original staircase can still be seen
in the walls. In 1624 the guildhall was converted into a courthouse, and in the
prison administrative area there are still the original iron strappings and bars
around the window surround. On display in the Mayor's Parlour is a piece of
chestnut timber from the original roof.

⛪ SOUTH   MAP 2

■330■ BANQUETING HOUSE ☎ 0207 930 4179
Whitehall, London SW1A 2ER
Westminster Underground
Open all year: Mon–Sat 10–5. Closed Bank Hol Mons. May close at short notice for
government functions. Check for details
Designed by Inigo Jones in classical style for James I, the Banqueting House
is the only remaining complete building of Whitehall Palace, which was the
principal residence of the sovereign during the seventeenth century until it was
destroyed by fire in 1689. The magnificent nine-panelled painted ceiling by the
Flemish artist Peter Paul Rubens depicts the divine right of kings. It was commissioned by Charles I in 1635 to celebrate the life and wise government of his
father, James I. The Banqueting House was also the scene of the execution of
Charles I in 1649.

■331■ ELSTOW MOOT HALL ☎ 01234 266889
Church End, Elstow, Bedfordshire MK42 9XT
Just off A6 S of Bedford, signed with brown heritage signs
Open Apr–Oct: Tue–Sat and Bank Hols 2–5
Well-preserved half-timbered moot hall standing on traditional English village
green. Meaning 'meeting place', a moot hall was a medieval market house.
The one at Elstow was built in the late fourteenth and fifteenth century. Owned
by the abbey, it was originally known as the Green House. Its walls would have
been wattle and daub rather than the present-day brickwork. The Bunyan
Room end of the building was added 100 years after the original construction.
Downstairs, the moot hall was used for the storage of market stalls and six
small shops rented out by the nuns during markets. In the upstairs room Manor
Courts were held, to settle trading disputes and to hand out local justice.

■332■ GEORGE INN ☎ 0207 407 2056
77 Borough High Street, Southwark, London SE1 1NH
On E side of Borough High Street near London Bridge Station. London Bridge
Underground
Open: licensing hours
Have a drink at the only remaining galleried inn in London. The George is a
famous seventeenth-century coaching-inn which is mentioned by Charles

Dickens in *Little Dorrit*. It is the last survivor of the ancient inns that once lined Southwark High Street, providing refreshment for playgoers from the Bankside theatres and coach passengers on their way to and from London.

The oldest part of the George has a brick exterior, a fashionable material in the second half of the seventeenth century and far less of a fire risk than half-timbering. The English bond of brickwork and the style of the large window on the first floor are also typical of the period. The segmental arches to the other windows on this floor suggest that they were replaced in the eighteenth century. The much smaller windows on the second floor are typical of those for less important rooms from the seventeenth century to the nineteenth centuries. The dormer windows in the attic are Victorian, but replaced smaller, original ones.

■333■ THE GUILDHALL ☎ 0207 606 3030
off Gresham Street, London EC2P 2EJ
Bank, Mansion House, Moorgate or St Paul's Underground
Open all year: daily 10–5. Sometimes closed for official functions. Check for details
Impressive example of medieval civic architecture. Built between 1411 and 1430, the crypt, porch and medieval walls all emerged unscathed from both the Great Fire of London and the Blitz. The crypt is the largest medieval crypt in London, and the western part is thought to date from the thirteenth century and was probably the undercroft of an earlier guildhall. The Great Hall is used as the setting for ceremonial and civic events, and in places the stonework still bears faint traces of paint and gilding, indicating that they were once brightly decorated. Restoration after the Blitz was completed to the designs of Sir Giles Gilbert Scott in 1954. In 1973 the west end of the guildhall yard was remodelled and the west crypt restored and in 1974 the west wing was completed.

■334■ HOP FARM COUNTRY PARK ☎ 01622 872068
Beltring, Paddock Wood, Kent TN12 6PY
On A228 at Paddock Wood
Open summer: daily 10–5; winter: daily 10–4. Closed 25 and 26 Dec
The world's largest collection of original Victorian oast houses set in the heart of the Kent countryside. Thirty-two white-coned oast houses and galleried barns all built in the nineteenth century, the heyday of the hopping industry. The harvested hops were dried in the oast houses by placing the hops on horsehair blankets over the drying-room floor. Exhibitions tell the story of the hop industry. Dray rides round the park are pulled by shire horses.

■335■ KEW BRIDGE STEAM MUSEUM ☎ 0208 568 4757
Green Dragon Lane, Brentford, Middlesex TW8 0EN
100 yards from N side of Kew Bridge, next to Victorian tower
Open all year: daily 11–5. Engines in steam at weekends and Bank Hol Mons
Nineteenth-century pumping station that supplied water to West London. An impressive collection of Grade I and Grade II* listed buildings, including the original engine rooms and boiler houses and also some of the outbuildings. Even though it was a purpose-built and purely functional building, care was taken to make it aesthetically pleasing. The main entrance lobby looks similar to the vestibule of a grand town house, with the window casement finished off in fine Georgian style. The dominant feature of the site is the splendid brick tower dating from 1867. Often confused for a chimney, the standpipe tower acts as a safety device to ensure pressure in the water mains. A listed building, the tower is 197 feet (60 metres) high and was restored in 1990. Within the building

there is a very impressive collection of water-pumping machinery, including the Grand Junction 90, a huge, working Cornish beam engine that pumped water to West London.

■336■ THE KING'S HEAD ☎ 01296 334590
King's Head Passage, Market Square, Aylesbury, Buckinghamshire HP20 2RW
NW corner of Market Square in town centre
Open all year daily: Mon–Sat 9–5, plus Fri–Sat 6–10
Magnificent old coaching inn. Founded in 1386, the King's Head has a medieval gateway leading into a cobbled courtyard. The inn has fine mullioned windows and fifteenth-century stained glass.

■337■ LLOYD'S BUILDING
1 Lime Street, London EC3M 7HA
Monument or Liverpool Street Underground
Exterior viewing only (tours for architectural groups of eight–twenty, phone 01245 609425)
Startling, futuristic silver steel and glass structure built in 1986 to house the world-famous insurance underwriters. Designed by Richard Rogers and described by one observer as a 'mechanical cathedral' the building has become an icon of modern architecture. Its basic form, which embodies Rogers's concern with total flexibility and technological advance, is that of a large atrium, surmounted by a steel and glass arched roof, surrounded by galleries. One of the most controversial aspects of the design is that, in order to create the maximum amount of space and flexiblity for those working in the building, all the services including lifts, lavatories and tubes to carry electric wiring, plumbing and drainage, are fixed to the outside of the building.

■338■ LONG CRENDON COURTHOUSE ☎ 01494 528051
Long Crendon, Aylesbury, Buckinghamshire HP18 9AN
In Long Crendon, 2 miles N of Thame via B4011
Open Upper Floor only Apr–Sept: Wed 2–6, Sat, Sun and Bank Hol Mons 11–6
Long, low two-storey courthouse dating from the fourteenth or fifteenth century. The building is constructed of timber framing, red brick, and wattle and daub. The foundations are of stone, and the roof is of plain hand-made red tiles. The building is constructed in five bays, with the ground floor rearranged to form modern accommodation. The upper storey is made up of one large room of four bays, with the fifth partitioned off to make a small room. The projecting upper storey has arched braces to the timber framing and is supported on an alignment of stout joists. The gables at either end of the building have simple timber-framing. The lord of the manor held court here from the early fifteenth century to Victorian times. After that the building was used as a poorhouse and a school before falling into decay. Restoration work was carried out on the building early this century by the National Trust.

■339■ MIDDLE TEMPLE ☎ 0207 427 4800
Middle Temple Lane, off The Strand or Tudor St, London EC4Y 9AT
Temple or Blackfriars Underground
Open all year: Mon–Fri 10–12 and 3–4 if available. Closed Bank Hols. Check for details
One of the four great Inns of Court that originated in the thirteenth century. Fine example of Tudor architecture built during the reign of Queen Elizabeth I and completed in around 1570. Gatehouse dates from 1648. The restored hall, dating from 1562, has a double hammerbeam roof and fine stained-glass

windows. The 29-foot (8.8-metre) long table was made from a single oak from Windsor Forest.

■340■ **PALACE OF WESTMINSTER** ☎ 0207 219 3000
House of Commons, Parliament Square, Westminster, London SW1A 2PW
Westminster Underground
Visitors wishing to watch proceedings should obtain tickets from their MP eight weeks in advance, or join the queue outside St Stephen's entrance. For guided parties to tour Palace and Westminster Hall ask local MP. Visits can only be made when the House is sitting – usually Mon, Tue, Thur am and Fri pm after 3.30. Phone 0207 219 4272 for information
Principal residence of the kings of England from the middle of the eleventh century until 1512. Westminster Hall, built in the reign of William Rufus, still stands today after 900 years of use. The magnificent hammerbeam roof was designed in the reign of Richard II to replace the original roof, which was supported by a line of posts down either side. The fire of 1834 destroyed all except Westminster Hall, the crypt of St Stephen's Chapel, the adjacent cloisters and the Jewel Tower. The present Houses of Parliament were built over the next thirty years by Sir Charles Barry and his assistant, Augustus Welby Pugin. Pugin was responsible for adding innumerable Gothic detail to Barry's symmetrical style of late perpendicular. Barry beautifully incorporated Westminster Hall and the remains of St Stephen's into his new building. The House of Commons Chamber was destroyed during the Second World War and was rebuilt by Sir Giles Gilbert Scott, who took care to preserve all the essential features of Barry's building.

■341■ **ROYAL ALBERT HALL** ☎ 0207 589 8212
Kensington Gore, London SW7 2AP
South Kensington or High Street Kensington Underground
Box office open 9–9
Magnificent oval concert hall, planned by Queen Victoria's husband, Prince Albert, who was inspired by Roman amphitheatres he had seen in Europe. Completed in 1871, a terracotta frieze outside illustrates man's progress in the arts. Albert's concept was originally for an immense ovoid auditorium that would house 30,000 people. This was rationalized due to financial restraints, and today the auditorium seats just over 5,000. Nevertheless, at the time of its completion it was regarded as an extraordinarily daring construction, and its distinctive architecture is a lasting memorial to Victorian engineering skills.

■342■ **ROYAL OBSERVATORY GREENWICH** ☎ 0208 312 6565
National Maritime Museum, Park Row, Greenwich, London SE10 9NF
Frequent trains from Charing Cross and London Bridge Station
Open all year: daily 10–5 (last admission 4.30)
Commissioned by Charles II and designed by Christopher Wren, the Royal Observatory was created for the use of John Flamsteed when he was appointed the first Astronomer Royal. As Charles II was very short of funds, second-hand materials were used to build the observatory. Brick and stone were brought along the River Thames from an old Tudor fort at Tilbury that was being repaired. In spite of these limitations, Wren still managed to create the beautiful Octagon Room, as well as living quarters for the Astronomer Royal underneath. It stands at zero meridian longitude and is the original home of Greenwich Mean Time, with the Meridian Line dividing east from west running through the courtyard. It now houses an extensive collection of historical time-keeping, astronomical and navigational instruments.

■343■ SHAKESPEARE'S GLOBE ☎ 0207 902 1500
21 New Globe Walk, Bankside, London SE1 9DT
London Bridge or Mansion House Underground
Open May–Sept: Mon 9–5, Tue–Sun 9–12; Oct–Apr: daily 10–5.30. Performances May–Sept
Reconstruction of Shakespeare's Globe Theatre (completed in 1997) is just
200 yards (183 metres) from the site of the original, the foundations of which
were found in 1989 under a Georgian terrace. The Globe is reconstructed using
original materials and building techniques in order to make the theatre as
authentic as possible. The thatched roof is made of Norfolk reed, the timber
frame of green oak and the walls of lime plaster.

■344■ THE VICTORIA AND ALBERT MUSEUM ☎ 0207 938 8500
Cromwell Road, South Kensington, London SW7 2RL
South Kensington Underground
Open all year: Mon–Sun 10–5.45 plus Wed 6.30–9.30
Fine Victorian building with grand façade and main entrance. Designed by Sir
Aston Webb, the foundation stone was laid by Queen Victoria in 1899. It started
as the South Kensington Museum and grew, with new buildings erected when
needed. Many of these buildings, with their iron frames and glass roofs, were
intended to be semi-permanent exhibition halls, but all have survived and com-
prise one of the finest groups of Victorian buildings in Britain. With its 7 miles
(11 kilometres) of galleries, it forms the world's largest decorative arts museum.

■345■ WHITCHURCH SILK MILL ☎ 01256 892065
28 Winchester Street, Whitchurch, Hampshire RG28 7AL
Halfway between Winchester and Newbury, off A34 near centre of Whitchurch. Signposted
Open all year exc Christmas: Tue–Sun and Bank Hol Mons 10.30–5
A Grade II* listed building and the oldest surviving silk-weaving water mill in
Britain. Built at the turn of the nineteenth century on the River Test, originally
as a two-storey fulling mill. In 1815 the floor levels were altered so that a middle
floor could be inserted, and the cupola and clock were also added. Since then
very few alterations have been made to the building, and the outer skin of red
bricks over thick chalk walls is fully preserved. The original cast-iron window
frames also remain, many with the crown glass of the time still fitted. The windows were made as large as possible to let in the maximum amount of natural
light. The front elevation is surmounted by a handsome pediment, while the
slate-tiled roof, which was restored in 1987, is crowned by the elegant wooden
cupola, typical of this period. The mill has been associated with the silk industry
since the 1820s. For most of the nineteenth century all the work was done by
hand, but machinery was installed in the 1880s to make the operation water-
powered. Silk is still produced at the mill today, using some of this original winding, warping and weaving machinery from the late nineteenth century.

■346■ WORLD NAVAL BASE ☎ 01634 823800
The Historic Dockyard, Chatham, Kent ME4 4TZ

Fred's
FAVOURITE

Signposted from M2 junctions 1 and 3 and M20 junction 6
Open Apr–Oct: daily 10–6 (last admission 4); Nov, Feb and Mar:
Wed, Sat and Sun 10–4 (last admission 3)
Most complete Georgian dockyard in the world, where twenty-six different trades
were employed on-site to produce sailing ships for the Royal Navy. Impressive
collection of buildings includes the Mast Houses, Wheelwrights' Shop, Foundry,
Sawmill and Sail Lofts. The magnificent Ropery building is a quarter of a mile

Chatham dockyard

(0.4 kilometre) long and is where the 20 miles (32 kilometres) of rope needed for each sailing ship was made. It is still in commercial operation today. The massive covered slips are where the main work on the ships was done, and the timber-framed No. 3 Slip is particularly impressive, with its linked truss roof. The Commissioner's House, built in 1704, is the oldest naval building to survive intact in Britain and has been altered little since it was built. There are displays and exhibitions throughout the site, including the Wooden Walls gallery that re-creates the story of the construction of the ship *Valiant* through the eyes of an apprentice.

🏛 EASTERN   MAP 3

■347■ FITZWILLIAM MUSEUM ☎ 01223 332900
Trumpington Street, Cambridge, Cambridgeshire CB2 1RB
In centre of Cambridge
Open all year: Tue–Sat: 10–5, Sun and Bank Hols 2.15–5. Closed Christmas period
Beautiful neoclassical building in Portland stone built between 1837 and 1847. The Fitzwilliam Museum is the masterpiece of its creator, the architect George Basevi who designed it for the collections that Lord Fitzwilliam left to the university in 1816. The building was finished in 1875 by E. M. Barry, who designed the magnificent entrance hall. The museum is worth going to see for the building itself, but it also has excellent collections of English pottery and china, Greek, Roman and Egyptian antiquities, armour and illuminated manu-scripts in the lower galleries. The upper galleries contain major collections of British and European paintings, including works by Turner, Hogarth and Gainsborough as well as the Impressionists and Dutch Old Masters.

■348■ LONG SHOP STEAM MUSEUM ☎ 01728 832189
Main Street, Leiston, Suffolk IP16 4ES
B119 off A12, to town centre
Open Apr–Oct: Mon–Sat 10–5, Sun 11–5

Grade II listed building, once known locally as the 'Cathedral', believed to be the first flow-line production assembly plant in the world. Completed in 1853, the building is 85 feet (26 metres) long by 41 feet (12.5 metres) wide and 43 feet (13 metres) high. It was conceived by Richard Garrett III as a means of assembling the Garrett range of portable steam engines on a production-line basis. Engines were constructed in the centre aisle, moving along on their wheels as assemblies and machined parts were fed in from the benches and machines on either side and from the wide galleries above. Machines were driven from continuous lengths of shafting by lay shafts, pulleys and belts. In their turn the main shafts were driven by a horizontal steam engine outside the west end of the wall. The Long Shop houses a collection of Garrett engines, and the adjoining museum concentrates on 200 years of local, social and industrial history.

■349■ THE OLD MERCHANT'S HOUSE & ROW 111 HOUSE
☎ 01493 857900
South Quay, Great Yarmouth, Norfolk NR30 2RQ
½ mile inland from beach, signposted from South Quay
Open Apr–Sept: daily 10–1 and 2–6; Oct: daily 10–1 and 2–5 (last admission 1 hour before closing)
Two seventeenth-century Row Houses, a type of building unique to Great Yarmouth. The architecture of these houses is characteristic of the extensive rebuilding of the Rows in the early seventeenth century when, through its international maritime activities, Great Yarmouth reached the height of its prosperity. In their style and design can be seen influences from the western seaboard of Europe and from the New World, both of which had close trading links with the town. The changing fortunes of the inhabitants of Great Yarmouth since the seventeenth century are reflected in the internal modifications of the houses, from eighteenth-century gentrification to late-nineteenth-century subdivisions to provide for multiple occupancy.

■350■ ST JOHN'S COLLEGE ☎ 01223 338600
St John Street, Cambridge, Cambridgeshire CB2 1TP
In centre of Cambridge
Phone for opening times and access details. Guided tours can be arranged through the Tourist Information Centre (01223 322640)
Founded in 1511 by Lady Margaret Beaufort, the mother of Henry VII, to replace several earlier colleges. St John's includes three courts, dining-hall and library. A richly ornamented gateway leads into the First Court, an excellent example of Tudor architecture. The chapel, added in the nineteenth century, is the work of Sir George Gilbert Scott. The dining-hall of 1519, known simply as 'the hall', was enlarged in 1826. It contains fine panelling and a hammerbeam roof. The Second Court, built by Ralph Symons, has attractive plum-red brickwork. Within it, the Combination Room is one of the finest panelled galleries in England, with a rich plastered ceiling. From the Third Court, which contains the Old Library, the Bridge of Sighs leads over the River Cam to the Gothic New Court.

■351■ THE THEATRE ROYAL ☎ 01284 755127
Westgate Street, Bury St Edmunds, Suffolk IP33 1QR
In centre of Bury St Edmunds
Open all year: Mon–Sat exc Bank Hols 10.30–3.30
Elegant early-nineteenth-century theatre, which was opened by its proprietor

and architect, William Wilkins in 1819. The classical façade is disciplined by a proportioned framework of interlocking squares and triangles which determine the position of every important feature in the theatre as a whole. Today the auditorium holds 350, but in 1819 it would have housed around 800. The elegant design of sweeping curves is constructed of wood and plaster, and the Upper Circle is supported on slender columns of cast iron. The stage roof is actually lower than that of the auditorium, a not uncommon feature in Georgian playhouses where stage machinery was rarely very complex. (Fly towers were introduced as the machinery became more ambitious in the course of the nineteenth century.) The Theatre Royal continues to be used.

■352■ TRINITY COLLEGE ☎ see below
Trinity Street, Cambridge, Cambridgeshire CB2 1TQ
In centre of Cambridge
Phone for opening times and access details. Guided tours can be arranged through the Tourist Information Centre (01223 322640)
Established in 1546 by Henry VIII to replace several earlier colleges. Turreted, brick Great Gatehouse leads into magnificent Great Court, with a fountain in the centre. Laid out in around 1600, it is the largest courtyard in Cambridge. The west side is dominated by the Great Hall, built by Thomas Neville in the perpendicular style. Other buildings include the sixteenth-century chapel, the quaint little King's Hostel, the Queen's Gate and King Edward III's Tower. A passage leads to Neville's Court and Christopher Wren's library of 1695. Faced with the problem of damp from the river damaging the books, Wren built the library on the first floor and left the ground floor as an open arcade. The oak bookcases have impressive limewood carving by Grinling Gibbons.

🏛 CENTRAL   MAP 4

■353■ BLACK COUNTRY LIVING MUSEUM ☎ 0121 557 9643
Tipton Road, Dudley, West Midlands DY1 4SQ
On A4037, 10 miles from Birmingham city centre, and signposted from M5 junction 2
Open Mar–Oct: daily 10–5; Nov–Feb: Wed–Sun 10–4
A 26-acre open-air museum relating to the social and industrial history of the Black Country. The museum has a vast collection of houses and buildings, many of which have been moved here brick by brick from their original sites around the Black Country. They include a Victorian schoolroom and a pair of cast-iron houses, built after the First World War had left a shortage of skilled workers and constructed by bolting cast-iron plates together. The village centre contains a variety of shops, including a chemist's, haberdashery and hardware store as well as an early-nineteenth-century pub, the Bottle and Glass Inn. The impressive industrial buildings include a chainmaker's, nailmaker's and a rolling mill.

■354■ CHRIST CHURCH ☎ 01865 276499
St Aldate's, Oxford, Oxfordshire OX1 1DP
Enter via Meadow Gate
Open Cathedral summer: Mon–Sat 9–6, Sun 11.30–6; winter: daily 9–4.30. Hall all year: daily 9.30–12 and 2–5.30. Meadows all year: daily 7–dusk
Founded in 1525 by Cardinal Wolsey, Christ Church is set around the largest quadrangle in Oxford, Tom Quad. Entry is by way of the sixteenth-century Great Gate. Tom Tower, added by Christopher Wren in 1681, contains the huge

bell, weighing over 7 tonnes, known as Great Tom. The chapel acquired the status of a cathedral in 1546 and is now one of the smallest in Britain. The staircase at the south-west corner of the quad has a fine fan-vaulted roof. It leads up to the Great Hall, which has a hammerbeam roof with intricate carvings. The library on the south side of the quad has ornate plasterwork ceilings and fine woodwork.

■355■ CROMFORD MILL ☎ 01629 824297

The Arkwright Society, Mill Road, Cromford, Derbyshire DE4 3RQ
Turn off A6 Derby to Matlock road at junction with B5012 and follow brown signs
Open all year: daily 9–5
Site of the world's first water-powered cotton-spinning mill, Cromford Mill was built in 1771 by Richard Arkwright and partners and ceased production in 1846. The site includes the first mill, a mill/warehouse opposite and an L-shaped building that was linked to the send mill at first-floor level. Arkwright established the pattern of early mill-building with the plain, long, thin rectangular design 30 feet (9 metres) wide. Lavatory columns, stairwells and offices were attached to the main building so as not to take up floor space, evidence of which can be seen at the main gates, where the buildings are essentially rectangular with semicircular extensions keyed in at the top housing the stairwell and offices. In the L-shaped building there is a lavatory column and a stairwell where the two wings of the building meet. At the western end of the site lies Grace Cottage, which is thought to have been a gatekeeper's house. The red-brick building next to it is likely to have been the counting house, while Rock House, where Arkwright lived, stands on the hill overlooking the site, giving him an excellent view of his workers.

■356■ IRONBRIDGE GORGE MUSEUM TRUST ☎ 01952 433522

The Wharfage, Ironbridge, Telford,
Shropshire TF8 7AW
Signposted from M54, junction 4
Open all year: daily 10–5, Sun and Bank Hol
Mons 10–6. Check for times
Nine museums spread over 6 square miles
(15.5 square kilometres) along the banks of
the River Severn close to Abraham Darby's
first iron bridge. Blists Hill Victorian Town
is a re-created town with shops, cottages, a
pub, an ironworks, a pit and other industrial premises, which show life at the turn
of the century. Coalport China Museum
houses a collection of Coalport china with
displays on how it was produced; at Coal-
brookdale, the Museum of Iron recounts
how iron was first smelted with coke in
1709; and at Ironbridge, the visitors' centre
provides an introduction to the history of
the valley. Crafts and skills are demonstrated (carpenter, cobbler, foundry, leather-
work, tinsmith, potter, glazier) and all work
is on sale. The Jackfield Tile Museum is
based around two decorative tileworks.

Bottle ovens, the Coalport China Museum

■**357**■ **MERTON COLLEGE** ☎ 01865 276310
Merton Street, Oxford, Oxfordshire OX1 4JD
In centre of Oxford, just off High St
Open all year: Chapel and Quadrangle: Mon–Fri 2–4 and Sat and Sun 10–4. Guided
tours available from Oxford Guide of Guides (01865 726871)
Dating from 1264, it's the oldest college in Oxford. The Front Quad contains the
Hall, which was rebuilt in the nineteenth century but still retains the original
thirteenth-century ironwork on the door. The Treasury, with its pitched stone
roof, is on the west side and leads through to the Mob Quad and the chapel.
The choir of the chapel dates from 1227, and the windows retain much of the
original glass. The large ante-chapel and tower were added in the fifteenth century. The medieval library building, also situated in Mob Quad, is the oldest still
in use in England and contains many historical books.

■**358**■ **SWALCLIFFE BARN** ☎ 01295 788278
Swalcliffe, Banbury, Oxfordshire OX15
6 miles W of Banbury on B4035
Open Easter–Oct: Sun and Bank Hol Mons 2–5
Fifteenth-century half-cruck barn built by New College Oxford. Measuring
128 feet by 22 feet 9 inches (39 metres by 6.9 metres) internally, with walls
3 feet (0.9 metres) thick, it was built almost entirely of local limestone. The
mortar used was a mixture of lime and stone dust with very little sand in it.
Almost every stone bears the deep grooves of the stonemasons' tools. Only on
the finer masonry around the doorway and windows was any attempt made to
remove the grooves. The barn houses some of the county's collection of agricultural vehicles from the turn of the twentieth century and an historical exhibition.

⛰ WALES   MAP 5

■**359**■ **BLAENAVON IRON WORKS** ☎ 01495 752036
Blaenavon, Torfaen NP4 6JH
From A4042 to Pontypool take A4043. Follow signs for Big Pit and Blaenavon Iron Works
Open May–Sept: Mon–Sat 11–5, Sun 2–5
Remains of eighteenth-century ironworks. Stack Square gives us a rare picture
of what working-class housing was like at the time of the Industrial Revolution.
A path from the houses leads up under the arch of the balance tower to the
high-level furnace top area. The remains of the furnaces stand in a line along
what was originally a shallow stream valley. At the end of this is the impressive-
looking water balance tower of 1839, which was used to carry heavy materials
between the high-level furnace top and the low-level furnace yard. Other
prominent features include cast houses (where the molten iron was tapped into
sand pig beds in the floor), furnaces and calcining kilns. One of the furnaces
(No. 2) still retains its stone casing and roofed cast house.

■**360**■ **FFESTINIOG POWER STATION** ☎ 01766 830465
Ffestiniog Visitors' Centre, Tanygrisiau, Blaenau Ffestiniog, Gwynedd LL41 3TP
Off A496 SW of Blaenau Ffestiniog
Open Easter week and mid-July–mid-Aug: daily 10.30–4.30; Aug–Sep: Sun–Fri
10.30–4.30; Oct: Mon–Fri 10.30–4.30
Construction began in 1957 and Ffestiniog power station was opened in 1963 as
the first hydroelectric-pumped storage scheme. It is capable of generating

360MW of electricity from zero output within 60 seconds. This is enough to supply North Wales with all its electricity for several hours. After the excavation of 142,000 tonnes of rock, the four underground areas were created in a huge chamber. What you see above ground is only a third of the plant, the rest is set deep in the Moelwyn mountains. The extent and mass of this engineering achievement is quite remarkable.

■361■ LLECHWEDD SLATE CAVERNS ☎ 01766 830306
Blaenau Ffesteniog, Gwynedd LL41 3NB
Beside A470 just N of Blaenau Ffestiniog
Open Mar–Sept: daily 10–5.15; Oct–Feb: daily 10–4.15
Nineteenth-century slate mine and Victorian village. At the mine are two underground tours. The miners' tramway carries visitors into areas where early mining conditions have been re-created. The deep mine is reached by an incline railway, Britain's steepest underground passenger railway, with a gradient of 1:8. Once you have made the descent in the specially made car there is an amazing 25 miles (40 kilometres) of man-made tunnels that connect the massive caverns of Llechwedd. There is also an on-site village which has been restored and includes shops, a bank and miners' pub.

■362■ WELSH SLATE MUSEUM ☎ 01766 830306
Gilfach Ddu, Padarn Country Park, Llanberis, Gwynedd LL55 4TY
Follow signs for Llanberis from A55 and A5
Open Easter–Oct: daily 10–5; Nov–Easter: Sun–Fri 10–4
Perfectly preserved quarry workshop with one of the world's largest working waterwheels set among the towering slate quarries of Llanberis. The Dinorwig Slate Quarry Company closed its doors for business in 1969. But now you can visit the site of the carved slopes of the 'mountain that roofed the world' as a working museum. Most of the machinery on this site was originally driven by the 50-foot (15-metre) waterwheel – which is still in working order. The quarry workshop continues to be operational, while the forge produces specialized tools and gifts. There is also a narrow-gauge steam locomotive and loco shed on-site. The newest additions to the museum are four houses that have been transported literally brick by brick from 30 miles (48 kilometres) away in Tanygrisiau. The houses each represent a key period in the history of the slate industry.

⚒ NORTH-WEST   MAP 6

■363■ ALBERT DOCK ☎ 0151 708 8838
Mersey Tourism, Atlantic Pavilion, Albert Dock, Liverpool, Merseyside L3 4AE
Signposted from all major routes into city
Exterior viewing at any time. For details of museums and attractions contact Mersey Tourism. Museum open daily 10–6
Largest Grade I listed building in Britain. Opened by Prince Albert in 1846, it symbolises Liverpool's importance as a nineteenth-century port. Built on the Mersey shore, the five blocks of five-storey warehouses provided 1¼ million square feet (116,125 square metres) of floor space surrounding a quadrangle of water. Jesse Hartley, Chief Engineer to the port from 1824 to 1860, was responsible for the design and construction, and his unique experiment in warehouse building meant that the cargoes of the largest sailing ships of the

day could be unloaded speedily by cranes on to the quays of the warehouses. The advent of the large steam ships saw the decline of the dock in the late nineteenth and early twentieth century, but the warehouses continued to be used for bonded storage until the dock's closure in 1972. The dock now houses shops, cafés and museums, including the Tate Gallery and Merseyside Maritime Museum.

■364■ THE ROYAL LIVER BUILDING ☎ 0151 236 2748
Pier Head, Liverpool, Merseyside L3 1HT
Follow signs for Albert Dock
Guided tours for individuals and groups from Apr–Sept. Must be booked in advance (by telephone)
Early-twentieth-century insurance building on Liverpool's Pier Head with Liver Birds on top which have come to symbolise the city. Built by the Royal Liver Friendly Society, now Royal Liver Assurance, between 1908 and 1911 to house its rapidly expanding life assurance business. The construction involved a revolutionary building technique known, after the inventor, as the Hennebique Principle.

■365■ ST GEORGE'S HALL ☎ 0151 707 2391
William Brown Street, Liverpool, Merseyside L1 1JJ
Opposite Lime Street Station
Open mid-July–Aug: daily 11–4. Town Hall open 2 weeks during May: Mon–Sat 11–4. Phone for details
Fine neoclassical civic building, hailed in the nineteenth century as a symbol of Liverpool's success and civic pride. It was built between 1841 and 1854 to the design of a young architect, Harvey Lonsdale Elmes, who had to combine concert hall and law court facilities in one building. The eastern façade was conceived as the ceremonial entrance, and its colonnade of sixteen Corinthian columns is flanked by two wings of square pilasters with carved panels between. The magnificent Great Hall is 169 feet (51.5 metres) long, with six granite columns along each side and an encaustic tile floor, the design of which consists of three large circles, and is estimated to have used over 30,000 tiles. The two main law courts, the Crown Court and the Civil Court, are in the north and south ends of the Great Hall respectively, while the small concert room is on the first floor and contains a beautiful early-Victorian interior designed by Charles Cockerell.

🏛 NORTH-EAST   MAP 7

■366■ GEORGIAN THEATRE ROYAL AND MUSEUM ☎ 01748 823021
Victoria Road, Richmond, North Yorkshire DL10 4DW
In centre of Richmond
Guided tours of the theatre and museum all year: Mon–Sat 10.30–3.45,
group tours by arrangement only on Sun

Fred's **FAVOURITE**

Most authentic eighteenth-century theatre in existence. Built in 1788 by an actor/manager, Samuel Butler, its unique feature is that it has the Georgian proscenium with two side doors surmounted by balconies. The proscenium with its doors and balconies intervening between the stage proper and the audience enabled actors to enter either through the scenery on to the main stage or by the proscenium doors on to the forestage. The museum houses a collection of original playbills related to the theatre, together with the oldest and largest complete set of Georgian scenery in Britain.

■367■ **MERCHANT ADVENTURERS' HALL**   ☎ 01904 654818
Fossgate, York, North Yorkshire YO1 9XD
Signposted in city centre. Main entrance from Piccadilly
Open all year: Mon–Sat 9.30–5; Easter–Sept: Sun 12–4
Britain's finest surviving medieval guild hall, built in the late fourteenth century. The Great Hall was built as a double nave because no long enough timbers of English oak could be found to form the great tie-beams stretching all the way from one side to the other. The plain wooden panelling is Tudor, and the governor's stall is an import from the Assize Court in York Castle. The Committee Room was formed in a corner of the hall in Regency times and now houses a display of items used by the guild over the centuries. The hall is still in the ownership of the same guild, although it is no longer a trading association.

■368■ **PIECE HALL**   ☎ 01422 358087
Museums and Arts Division, Piece Hall, Halifax, West Yorkshire HX1 1RE
Signposted in Halifax centre, entrances from Horton Street, Westgate and Wool Shop
Open all year: daily 10–5. Shops 9–5. Phone for times

Piece Hall

Impressive Georgian hall built for local wool merchants to sell 'pieces' of homespun cloth – hence the name. Piece Hall is based around a large cobbled courtyard enclosed on all four sides by three storeys of regular open galleries consisting of a basement arcade, a middle gallery of rusticated piers and an upper colonnade of Tuscan columns. One of the most interesting features is the south entrance. The cast-iron gates, weighing several tonnes, were made in Glasgow in 1871 and replaced the original oak gates. The intricate designs on the gates contain many clues to local history. The merchants' rooms are now occupied by a variety of shops.

■369■ SALTAIRE ☎ Tourist Office 01274 774993
Saltaire, Nr Shipley, West Yorkshire
Just off A650 between Bradford and Keighley, follow signs to The 1853 Gallery

Saltaire

Built between 1851 and 1876, Sir Titus Salt's model village comprises 22 streets, 775 houses, 45 almshouses and occupies an area of 25 acres (10 hectares). Salt was a successful mill owner and by 1853, when his grand scheme for a mill and a village beside the River Aire near Shipley was taking shape, he already had six mills in Bradford. Having been brought up in a Congregational family, a church featured prominently in Salt's plans. It was started in 1858 and opened in 1859. There were no pubs within the confines of the village, and the Club and Institute were erected to cater for the moral and physical welfare of the community. There were reading-rooms, a library, a lecture theatre and a school of art. All survive and can still be seen. In the mill itself is the 1853 Gallery devoted to works by David Hockney.

▟▙ SCOTLAND   MAP 8

■370■ NEW LANARK WORLD HERITAGE VILLAGE ☎ 01555 661345
New Lanark Mills, Lanark, North Lanarkshire MLll 9DB
1 mile S of Lanark, signposted from all major routes
Open all year: daily 11–5
Classic industrial architecture set against a backdrop of river and woodlands. Built in the late eighteenth century, this cotton mill village has survived little changed from the period of the early Industrial Revolution, when it became renowned as a model village under the management of the social pioneer Robert Owen. The first mill was constructed in 1785 and three others soon

followed. The workers were housed in the rows of tall tenement buildings. This design was unusual for a rural area but solved the problem of a limited amount of flat land to build on. The houses were built in the style known as 'random rubble', in which the locally quarried sandstone was not cut into regular blocks; instead, the natural shapes of the stones were used at random. Around the doors, windows and corners, a light-coloured dressed sandstone was used. New Lanark is a living community which is today home to around 200 people. The visitors' centre has displays of working textile machinery, and other exhibitions include restored mill workers' homes, a period village store and Robert Owen's house.

■371■ **SCOTTISH MINING MUSEUM** ☎ 0131 663 7519
Lady Victoria Colliery, Newtongrange, Dalkeith, Midlothian EH22 4QN
On A7 at Newtongrange, 10 miles south of Edinburgh
Open Feb–Nov: daily 10–5
Founded in 1984, the museum is based at the Lady Victoria Colliery in Newtongrange. The entire colliery complex is listed Grade A and is recognized as the best surviving example in Europe of a pre-1914 colliery. Constructed on a grandiose scale and dominating the surrounding countryside, the entire colliery complex is still largely as it was first conceived in the 1890s. The giant winding machine, a scheduled Ancient Monument, is the largest steam engine to survive in Scotland.

■372■ **SUMMERLEE** ☎ 01236 431261
Heritage Park, West Canal St, Coatbridge, North Lanarkshire ML5 1QD
M8 junction 8 eastbound, A8 westbound, signposted off motorway
Open all year: daily 10–5. Closed 25–26 Dec and 1–2 Jan
Museum of social and industrial history based around the remains of the Summerlee Ironworks of the 1830s. Exhibition hall displays working machinery and reconstructed workshops, such as a brass foundry and tinsmith's. Outside, there is a reconstructed coal mine and engine house, with the 1810 beam engine from Farme Colliery, and reconstructed miners' rows dating from the 1840s. There is also a working tram on site.

⛏ NORTHERN IRELAND   MAP 9

■373■ **PATTERSONS SPADE MILL** ☎ 028 9443 3619
751 Antrim Road, Templepatrick, Co. Antrim
M2 junction 4. Mill is near Templepatrick off A6 to Antrim
Open Apr, May and Sept: Sat, Sun and bank hols 2–6; June–Aug: Wed–Mon 2–6
The last surviving water-driven spade mill in Ireland. Spades were made here until 1990, and now the mill has been completely restored by the National Trust and is back in production employing two spademakers. The complete process of spademaking is demonstrated and there is a water-powered turbine.

■374■ **WELLBROOK BEETLING MILL** ☎ 028 8675 1735/1715
Wellbrook Beetling Mill, Cookstown, Co. Tyrone
3 miles W of Cookstown on A505
Open Apr, May, June and Sept: Sat, Sun and bank hols 2–6; July and Aug: Wed–Mon 2–6
Beetling was the final stage in the production process of Irish linen. This water-powered hammer mill has its original machinery still in working order.

CHAPTER

MONUMENTS AND TOWERS

Thirty years ago I bought the detached cottage that I live in (originally a gatehouse) from the Earl of Bradford. It was never really big enough for me and I needed more space, so, just as all the castles and wonderful buildings we have been to see have all been extended by the men who lived in them, I decided that I would build an extension. Basically all the men who owned these places were all just like me: DIY men. Even kings were DIY men with all the messing about they did with their castles and palaces.

There had been extensions done on my house in the days of the Earl of Bradford, but the original bits of the house had got some nice stone mouldings and Gothic arched windows with moulding around their edges. The work that had been done for the earl had been done very crudely and whoever did it hadn't extended the ornamentation into the stonework. So I decided that I would cut twelve blocks of stone to the thickness of the moulding and then put some ornamentation on the front of it. When I was doing the extension to the house, I put this ornamental stonework that I'd made on to the front but, when I'd finished, it all looked very clean and didn't match at all. So I just got a paintbrush and a tin can and mixed some soil out of the garden with mud and water and painted it all over the new mouldings and let the rain wash it off. Now you can hardly tell the difference; it looks almost the same as the other stuff.

It is something they could have tried on the Scott Monument in Edinburgh. They have done a lot of restoration work on it recently, repairing stonework that had broken away. It's beautiful stonework, but the problem is that all the new stuff they've done when they were restoring it has been left perfectly white. It's exactly the same stone that the thing is built out of, but it will never, ever go to the same colour as the original stone because there will never be that

The Scott Monument, Edinburgh

amount of coal smoke in Edinburgh again. I think I would have secured the services of someone like me, on the end of a big piece of rope with a tin of matt black paint, and I would have painted all the new stonework to make it blend in with the old in the way that I have done with the mouldings on my house. I am certainly in agreement with them on one thing, though, in that they haven't cleaned the monument. A lot of that shot-blasting and cleaning that is done now, apart from making things look like brand-new biscuits, can also be harmful to the stone itself.

Having said all that, the monument is a wonderful creation, all done by a joiner by the name of George Meikle Kemp. It's one of a handful of landmarks around the world instantly recognized as being associated with a particular city, and the top of it makes a very good viewpoint for the castle.

Sir Walter Scott was the greatest writer of his day, and it's not surprising that when he died a committee was set up to consider the erection of a monument. It was decided to hold a competition for its design with prizes of fifty guineas for the three plans that were most worthy of consideration. Of the fifty-four entries that came in from eminent architects of the time, the design chosen was by George Meikle Kemp, a joiner from Midlothian who had a fancy for Gothic architecture. Mr Kemp had a bit of a flair for the pencil and beautiful architecture. He'd studied lots of buildings around Scotland, then spent a lot of time in London, looking at buildings. I think he went abroad as well. Anyway, he was a very observant man for monuments, and when he came back he entered the competition and submitted his drawings under a false name, so that the architects of Edinburgh would not know that it was a mere carpenter who was sending them in. But his were the drawings that were selected, and he duly started work on the monument.

But disaster struck when the monument was halfway up. He went to see the main contractor and is said to have had a wee dram too many, and he fell into the canal on his way home and drowned. After Kemp's death, his brother-in-law, William Bonner, took over the supervision of the work and the height of the tower was increased from 176 feet (53.6 metres) to 200 feet and 6 inches (61.1 metres). When the capstone was placed on the pinnacle by Kemp's young son Thomas, the monument was complete except for the statue of Sir Walter. Even then the problems continued, and they had difficulty in getting the block of marble from Italy to Edinburgh. At Livorno the crane broke and the block, weighing 30 tonnes, fell into the sea, then at Leith they had no lifting gear to get it on to the wagon for its journey to Edinburgh, so the statue was two years late. If only they'd had a traction engine.

London has many great monuments, but there are two structures in particular that have become monumental symbols of the city. Tower Bridge and Big Ben are known and recognized all over the world. It's the clock tower on the Palace of Westminster that is commonly known as Big Ben, but even this is not strictly correct. Big Ben is actually the name of the hour bell within the tower, but that doesn't stop everybody referring to the tower itself as Big Ben. The construction of the tower, completed in 1858, was helped by the ingenious device of an inner lifting platform powered by a steam engine. This meant that all the building materials could be hoisted up to the appropriate level without the need for any exterior scaffolding.

Big Ben is without a shadow of a doubt a magnificent piece of cast iron and stonework with some nice ornamental wrought iron. I suppose there are lots of people in England who would like to get up there and have a look around. I once had the privilege to surmount the steps of the clock itself, and it was really interesting. The actual mechanism of the clock was made by a naval man, and it is almost identical to a grandfather clock with its great weights; the only difference now is that instead of being wound by hand the weights are wound by an electric winding mechanism.

To stand under Big Ben at 12 o'clock as it chimes is quite an experience. Maybe that's why I'm deaf. The hammer must weigh about 3 to 4 hundredweight (150 to 200 kilograms) and it makes a fantastic bong. Three hundred and thirty-four steps lead to the belfry, with a further fifty-nine to the lantern above, and there's no lift. I found out the hard way when I had to walk all the way up. I wonder why it is, though, that walking up these spiral staircases in towers and castles and cathedral domes is so much harder than climbing straight up the ladders on a chimney.

Anyone, looking at that other great symbol of London, Tower Bridge, would think that it's like a drawbridge going up and down. But down below, in the foundations, there are great curved boxes full of iron that counterbalance the weight of the roadway, so not that much power is needed to actually open it up. Much of the original machinery for working the bridge is still in place and can be seen in the engine rooms. The clever thing about it is that both sides of the roadway were actually constructed in a vertical position, and it must have been an exciting day when they first lowered them down to see whether they met in the middle or whether there would be a big gap.

For many people the most famous tower in the country is the one that generations of holidaymakers have looked out for as they travelled across the flat Lancashire coastal plain on their way to Blackpool. The excitement of that first sight of Blackpool Tower always meant that the holiday had really begun. This proud Victorian landmark, which has recently been restored, was opened in 1894. It was built in imitation of the Eiffel Tower, which had been opened in Paris in 1889, and it soon became a popular attraction, helping to turn Blackpool into Britain's busiest seaside resort.

But my favourite tower is one I first found out about as a small boy when I read in a history book about a man who built a magnificent chimney with what looked like a Victorian solid-silver salt cellar on top of it. Wainhouse Tower dominates the Calder Valley to the west of Halifax, and I well remember as a lad of about fifteen going over Blackstone Edge on a Lambretta scooter to go and look at it. It is probable that John Edward Wainhouse, who built this ornate folly in the late nineteenth century, worked in his uncle's Washer Lane Dyeworks, because it was on his uncle's death in 1856 that he inherited these premises along with various other properties and land.

The Washer Lane Dyeworks were fairly typical of the day, causing a lot of pollution through smoke emission, and it is because of this nuisance that we are now blessed with Wainhouse's unique tower. For many generations it was believed that the tower was built by Wainhouse to spite a wealthy neighbour, Sir Henry Edwards, but, although Sir Henry did have some part to play in the story, this is not entirely true. What can be clearly determined is that the tower was originally designed as a chimney to serve the Washer Lane Dyeworks.

Wainhouse came up with the idea of building a chimney about 350 yards (320 metres) up the hillside from the dyeworks linked by an underground flue or tunnel leading to the chimney. This was quite a common practice at that time, and it is thought that Wainhouse asked his architect, Isaac Booth, to design and build for him a mill chimney that would be aesthetically pleasing. Booth designed a fairly conventional circular mill chimney with a brick flue, but the chimney was surrounded by a square-based octagonal-shaped stone casing with a spiral staircase between the casing and the chimney. The stairs led up to four pedimented balcony features. Nobody seems to know for certain why there had to be a staircase, but it seems probable that it was put there to meet the whims of an eccentric man rather than to serve any practical purpose. After all, who would have stood on a balcony with smoke belching out from the flue of the chimney?

What the balcony did, however, was to highlight a deepening feud between Wainhouse and Sir Henry. Sir Henry Edwards was an extrovert and boastful man who claimed that from no house on the hills around his Pye Nest estate could a view be obtained of his private grounds. Wainhouse said that he would change all that by having an observatory built at the top of his mill chimney. Wainhouse himself supervised the work, and the finished article is a masterpiece of the stonemason's craft. Each stone was cut to fit like a jigsaw and, although cement mortar was used, it is likely that many of the stones are dowelled together, probably with copper pins.

We will never really know why Wainhouse chose to spend £15,000, which was a lot of money in those days, to install a spiral staircase and a fabulous balcony at the top of this great big chimney stack. We are all left to wonder why, but it is interesting that no attempt was ever made to connect the chimney to the dyeworks, even if it had been practicable. Does this give us a real clue to the inner thoughts of Wainhouse from the day when he originally conceived his folly?

Wainhouse Tower might be my favourite monument, but I don't think there's any shadow of doubt that Britain's most impressive monument is also its most ancient. Stonehenge is the most important prehistoric monument in the whole of Britain. It is unique; there's nothing like it anywhere in the world. The huge engineering project began with the transportation of the stones. The biggest of these, the sarsen stones, each weighed over 25 tonnes; they came from the Marlborough Downs, 20 miles (32 kilometres) to the north, and they must have been dragged all the way overland on massive sledges and rollers. To pull the heaviest stone, weighing about 50 tonnes, up one of the hills on the route would have needed about 500 people, with an extra 100 at least to lay the rollers in front of the sledge and keep it from wandering sideways.

The extraordinary design and construction of Stonehenge shows a number of refinements that can't be found anywhere else among prehistoric monuments in Europe. First, all the stones have been squared and dressed to shape by pounding their surfaces with heavy stone hammers before they were erected. Secondly, the lintels are held in place on the uprights by mortice and tenon joints worked in solid stone, and the lintels in the circle are locked end to end by vertical tongue and groove joints. Thirdly, the sides of the lintels are shaped to the curve of the circle. The jointing of the stones was probably copied from woodworking methods, given the size and weight of the stones and the primitive means available for moving, shaping and erecting them.

The grand collection of ancient stones we see today is the much ruined final phase of the prehistoric temple that was in use some 3,600 years ago. They remind me of a big row of rotten teeth in a way and one of them has a filling of concrete because it was so badly eroded. At one time the circle was complete, but to me it looks as though the bits that fell down have been carted away or stolen and used for other purposes. But when you look at the ones that remain it is rather intriguing to wonder how they managed to do mortice and tenon joints to fit them together so long ago. It is quite remarkable, really, when you consider that they had no metal tools and it was all done by banging the stones with other stones. It must have taken for ever to reduce the tops of the stones to get them all in line or to get them level to put the lintels across the top.

I suppose the mode of erection is pretty self-explanatory. Number one, you lay the stone horizontally on the ground. It would then be rolled into position on the timbers that it had been dragged on. Next, they would dig the hole and then apparently on the far side of the hole they would put a row of timbers, so that as the thing tipped up it didn't bash in the far side of the hole. To raise the stones into position they would have started off with crowbars, levering them up to an angle of about 45 degrees. Then they would have attached ropes and had literally hundreds of men pulling on the other side. It has been estimated that as many as 600 men would have been needed for this operation. And when you look at the stones you've got to remember that what you see isn't the full stone. I think they must go down in the ground for the equivalent of about a third of the height you see sticking up above, which makes them pretty formidable lumps of rock.

The whole thing was really a massive engineering project, and what men they must have been to be able to do this all that time ago, when there were no steam engines and the only motive power they had was human muscles aided by the simplest devices such as ropes, levers and rollers. Stonehenge represents one of the most remarkable and astonishing achievements of all prehistoric people in Europe.

Stonehenge

PLACES TO VISIT

⚒ SOUTH-WEST   MAP 1

■375■ AVEBURY STONE CIRCLE
Calne, Wiltshire
1 mile N of A4 on A4361
Open: any reasonable time
Largest prehistoric stone circle in Britain dating from around 2000 BC.
Encompassing part of the village of Avebury, it is enclosed by a ditch and external bank. It originally consisted of an outer circle with four main entrances,
and two smaller inner circles. Most of the surviving stones, the largest weighing
around 60 tonnes, are on the west side of the circle. An avenue of stones,
known as West Kennet Avenue, runs away in a curve to another stone circle,
probably dating from 5000 BC, known as the Sanctuary. This consists of two
concentric circles of stones and six of timber uprights indicated by concrete posts.

■376■ CARN EUNY ANCIENT VILLAGE
Sancreed, Penzance, Cornwall
1 mile SW of Sancreed off A30
Open: any reasonable time
Archaeological remains of Iron Age village. More than ten houses have been
excavated, three of which are large enclosures, while the others are smaller,
mostly oval enclosures. The best preserved of the large enclosures is House I,
where there is evidence of two rooms, as well as the remains of a later wall of
larger stones built inside the house wall. One of the most interesting features of
the site is the fully excavated 'fogou' or underground structure, which consists
of a long curved passage with eleven capstones in their original position and a
round corbelled chamber, roofed with four capstones. The purpose of the fogou
is unknown: it might have been a cellar for storage or a place of worship.

■377■ CHYSAUSTER ANCIENT VILLAGE   ☎ 0831 757934
Newmill, Penzance, Cornwall
4 miles N of Penzance signposted off B3311
Open Apr–Sept: daily 10–6; Oct: 10–5
Remains of ancient stone-walled village constructed during the Roman period.
The site consists of eight courtyard houses aligned in pairs to form one of the
oldest village streets in Britain. Each house has a main entrance which leads
through to the courtyard; opposite the entrance is a roughly circular room, and
on the right is a long narrow room. This general plan is repeated, with minor
variations, in every house, suggesting that each room had its own special use.
There is a 'fogou', or underground structure, common to these ancient villages.

■378■ STONEHENGE   ☎ 01980 624715
Amesbury, Salisbury, Wiltshire SP4 7DE
2 miles W of Amesbury at junctions of A303 and A344/A360
Open all year: daily exc 24–26 Dec and 1 Jan. Times vary,
depending on time of year, so phone to check

Fred's
FAVOURITE

Britain's oldest and most important prehistoric monument stands impressive
and mysterious in the rolling landscape of Salisbury Plain. Stonehenge, the

most famous monument of prehistoric Europe, is a circular setting of massive standing stones. It was built in three main stages between 2800BC and 1300BC and the monument we see today is the much-ruined final phase. It includes the famous trilithons, pairs of huge upright stones with a third laid across their tops and held in place by mortice and tenon joints. At present Stonehenge can be viewed only from a distance.

🏛 SOUTH-EAST   MAP 2

■379■ ALBERT MEMORIAL   ☎ 0207 298 2117
The Albert Memorial Road, Kensington Gardens, London SW7 5ET
South Kensington or Kensington High Street Underground
Open: any reasonable time
Elaborate monument standing opposite the Royal Albert Hall. When it was opened in 1872 it was thought of as one of the greatest sculptural achievments of the Victorian era. Built by Sir George Gilbert Scott, the memorial has a marble frieze depicting poets, architects, artists and composers. Ornate pinnacles and a cross adorn the huge neo-Gothic spire. The figure of Albert, husband of Queen Victoria, reading a catalogue from the Great Exhibition of 1851, sits on an underground pyramid of 868 brick arches, and has above it a lofty Gothic canopy supported by granite columns. English Heritage undertook a massive restoration programme between 1994 and 1998. The gilding of bronze sculpture and ornament, which was removed during the First World War, was renewed. Lost details in the statuary and mosaics were replaced to preserve their meaning.

■380■ BIG BEN
Bridge Street, London SW1
Westminster Underground
External viewing only
Westminster's clock tower or 'Big Ben' as it is affectionately known throughout the world, stands at 316 feet (96 metres) high and 40 feet (12 metres) square. Altogether there are 393 steps to the top, 334 to the belfry, then another 59 to the lantern above. In 1858 the tower was finished, its construction helped along by an inner lifting platform (powered by a steam engine) to raise building materials within the tower itself. This meant there was no need for exterior scaffolding. There are four quarter-hour bells and one hour bell, and it is the hour bell which is called 'Big Ben'. The clock's time is checked three times a week and is accurate to within one second.

Fred's **FAVOURITE**

Big Ben

■381■ BIGNOR ROMAN VILLA ☎ 01798 869259
Bignor, Pulborough, West Sussex RH20 1PH
6 miles N of Arundel, signposted from A29 and A285
Open Mar–May and Oct: Tues–Sun and Bank Hol Mons 10–5;. June–Sept: daily 10–6
Discovered in 1811, the archaeological remains of one of the largest Roman villas in Britain cover nearly 5 acres (2 hectares). The site contains some of the finest Roman mosaics in Britain, including 'Venus and the Gladiators', 'The Head of Medusa' and the surviving part of the geometric mosaic in the north portico measuring 78 feet (24 metres) long. The rocks from southern England provided an excellent source of colours for the mosaics: limestone or chalk was used for white and Purbeck marble for blue and grey.

■382■ THE CENOTAPH
Whitehall, London SW1
Westminster or Charing Cross Underground
External viewing only
The Cenotaph, meaning 'Empty Tomb', commemorates the dead of both world wars. They are symbolised by the flags and emblems of the army, air force and royal and merchant navies. Built from Portland stone, it was completed in 1920 by Sir Edwin Lutyens and stands in the middle of Whitehall.

■383■ CROFTON ROMAN VILLA ☎ 01689 873826 (Bromley Museum)
Orpington, Kent
Off Crofton Road in Orpington, opposite station
Open all year: Wed–Fri and Bank Hol Mons 10–1 and 2–5, Sun 2–5 (last admission 4.30)
Well-preserved remains of a Roman villa. The villa was established in around AD140–170 and initially consisted of about five rooms. The villa was altered several times during the following 260 years of occupation. The remains of ten rooms can be seen today, now within a modern cover building. Two rooms contain the remains of their opus signinum (concrete) floors and three have evidence of tessellated (tiled) floor. Details of the underfloor central heating or hypocaust can also be seen, featuring both channelled and pillared systems.

■384■ DYMCHURCH MARTELLO TOWER ☎ 01732 778000
Dymchurch, Kent
Access from High Street, not seafront
Open Bank Hol Mons and May–mid-July: Sat and Sun 2–5.30; mid-July–Aug: daily 2–5.30; Sept: Sat and Sun 2–5.30. Check other dates
One of the many artillery towers that formed part of a chain of strongholds intended to resist invasion by Napoleon. It is entered through a doorway halfway up the tower which led to the separated living quarters for the officers and men. On this floor there was also a small store and a trapdoor that led down to larger storerooms and a magazine, which would be at ground level.

■385■ LONDON EYE ☎ 0207 487 0294
South Bank, London
Waterloo Underground
Open Nov–Mar: 10–6; Apr–Oct: 9–late evening
Newly built for the millennium and sweeping the skyline at 135 feet (41 metres), London Eye is the world's largest observation wheel. Its central hub and spindle are connected to outer and inner rims by fine cable spokes. The eighty spokes consist of a total of 3.7 miles (6 kilometres) of cables. The hub

and the spindle that hold the wheel structure are, at 75 feet (23 metres) tall, around the size of a church spire, and weigh in at 330 tonnes. The thirty-two high-tech passenger capsules positioned on the outside of the wheel structure can carry up to 15,000 visitors a day, and passengers can see over 25 miles (40 kilometres) in each direction.

■386■ **LULLINGSTONE ROMAN VILLA** ☎ 01322 863467

Lullingstone Lane, Eynsford, Kent DA4 0JA
Just SW of Eynsford off A225
Open Apr–Sept: daily 10–6; Oct: daily 10–5; Nov–Mar: daily 10–4
Archaeological remains of one of the seven known Roman villas in the Darent Valley. Initially it was constructed of timber and daub, but in the second century AD the villa was rebuilt in flint and tile. In the fourth century the villa was enlarged with the addition of heated rooms, baths and a semicircular dining-room. The villa has been well preserved, and the layout of the twenty-five rooms can be clearly seen along with fine mosaics and wall-paintings. Finds from the excavations are also on display, including marble busts and a bronze flagon.

■387■ **MILLENNIUM DOME** ☎ 0870 603 2000

Greenwich, London
North Greenwich Underground
Single-sessions days: 10–6.30; double-session days: 10am–10.30pm. Phone for details

The Millennium Dome, Greenwich

The monument for the millennium celebrations is the largest structure of its kind in the world. Covering 20 acres (8 hectares), the dome was designed by the Richard Rogers Partnership. It consists of a network of cable netting suspended from twelve masts, covered by a canopy of PTFE-coated fibreglass. It is the largest roof in the world, covering a million square feet (100,000 square metres). Construction began on 23 June 1997 when the first 8,000 concrete piles were driven into the site. The masts, which stand 3288 feet (100 metres) above the ground, were erected in October 1997. The cable netting, consisting of a grid of seventy-two paired radial cables and seven circumference rings, was then added. The main dome structure was completed on 22 June 1998, a year after construction began.

■388■ THE MONUMENT ☎ 0207 403 3761
Monument Street, London EC3R 8AH
Monument Underground
Open all year: Mon–Fri 10–6, Sat and Sun 2–5
Built between 1671 and 1677 by Sir Christopher Wren to commemorate the
Great Fire of 1666. The Monument is constructed of Portland stone. Standing at
a height of 202 feet (61.5 metres), which is its distance from the source of the
fire, it was, at the time of its building, the tallest monument in the world. The
flaming gilt bronze urn at the summit was the idea of Robert Knowles, a friend
of Wren. The carved base depicts the sense of optimism that existed, as the fire
had swept away the medieval timber buildings, offering the opportunity to
replace them in brick, in a style that would be ideally suited to a new commercial era.

■389■ NELSON'S COLUMN AND TRAFALGAR SQUARE
Charing Cross Underground
External viewing only
The square was built in honour of Admiral Nelson after his victory in 1805 at
the Battle of Trafalgar. John Nash designed the square in the 1830s on a site
that was originally the mews for royal hawks, then royal stables. The centrepiece is Nelson's Column at 170 feet (52 metres) high, which supports an
18-foot (5.5-metre) statue of Nelson. The four bronze lions round the foot of
the column were designed by Landseer and added in 1868. The fountains by
Lutyens were added in 1939.

■390■ ROCKBOURNE ROMAN VILLA ☎ 01725 518541
The Roman Villa, Rockbourne, Fordingbridge, Hampshire SP6 3PG
3 miles NW of Fordingbridge off B3078
Open Apr–Oct: Mon–Fri 12–6, Sat, Sun and Bank Hol Mons 10.30–6; July and Aug:
daily 10.30–6
Remains of forty-room Roman villa with fine mosaics. Rockbourne was discovered in 1942 by a farmer, but the main excavation work began in 1956 and
continued until 1974. Most of the remains have been filled back in to prevent
more deterioration, but the better of the mosaic pavements have been restored
and walls are marked out by stone chippings and gravel. Over seventy rooms
were identified, but they are not all from the same time period, and only about
forty would have been used.

■391■ THE ROMAN PAINTED HOUSE ☎ 01304 203279
New Street, Dover, Kent
In Dover town centre
Open Apr–Sept: Tues–Sun 10–5
One of the best-preserved Roman house remains in Britain. Built in around
AD200, the Roman Painted House formed part of a large mansion, or official
hotel, for travellers crossing the Channel. It stood outside the great naval fort
of Classis Britannica, but in AD270 it was demolished by the Roman army
during the construction of a larger fort. Three of the main rooms were then
buried, substantially intact, under its ramparts. The burial resulted in the sur-
vival of over 400 square feet (37 square metres) of painted plaster. Under a
lower dado, many coloured panels framed by fluted columns can be seen. The
walls in four rooms survive to a height of 4 to 6 feet (1.2 to 1.8 metres) and
the hard red concrete floors cover a substantially complete central heating

system. Displays tell the story of the discovery of the house and the development of Roman Dover.

■392■ STATUE OF EROS
Piccadilly Circus, London W1
External viewing only
Unveiled in 1893, this famous statue is one of the symbols of London. It was originally called the Shaftesbury Monument because it was erected as a memorial to the philanthropist Lord Shaftesbury. The actual figure rises above a fountain, which is made of bronze, but Eros is made of aluminium, at that time a rare and novel material. The sculptor was Alfred Gilbert RA, who used the fountain idea as an excuse for incorporating a variety of fish and crustaceous life in the design.

■393■ WELLINGTON ARCH
Hyde Park Corner, London SW1
Hyde Park Underground
External viewing only
Vast archway designed by Decimus Burton and originally erected near the Duke of Wellington's home at Apsley House in 1828 but then moved to the top of Constitution Hill in 1883. The sculpture by Adrian Jones was added some time later, in 1912.

🏛 EASTERN — MAP 3

■394■ CLOCK TOWER, ST ALBANS ☎ 01727 853301
Market Place, St Albans, Hertforshire
In St Albans High Street
Open Good Fri–mid-Sept: Sat, Sun and Bank Hol Mons 10.30–5
Early-fifteenth-century curfew tower, built between 1403 and 1412. One of the only two medieval clock towers in the country. Its bell, which strikes the hour, is older than the tower itself.

■395■ COW TOWER ☎ 0500 626116
On riverside in centre of Norwich. Access from near cathedral
Open: any reasonable time
Fourteenth-century tower with impressive medieval brickwork, believed to be one of the earliest blockhouses to be built. Blockhouses housed a small artillery garrison and were normally located to defend a river or harbour entrance. Twenty-seven blockhouses have survived, most of them built in the sixteenth century by Henry VIII. Standing on the bank of the River Wensum, this three-storey tower is built with a core of mortared flint rubble, faced internally and externally with brick. The first and second floors each have seven splayed openings that would have been used for firing small guns. Larger guns would have been mounted on the roof platform and fired through the nine rectangular embrasures in the parapet.

■396■ ENGLAND'S SECRET NUCLEAR BUNKER ☎ 01277 364883
Kelvedon Hall Lane, Brentwood, Essex CM14 5TL
Off A128 NW of Brentwood at Kelvedon Hatch, signposted
Open Mar–Oct: daily, 10–4 (5 on Sat, Sun and Bank Hols); Nov–Feb: Thur–Sun 10–4

From the outside this rural bungalow appears to be just that; inside you experience the Cold War. If nuclear war had broken out, this is where central government and military commanders would have run the country from. The hideaway, which is inside a hill, is encased in reinforced concrete 10 feet (3 metres) thick and is 100 feet (30 metres) underground. What is inside is remarkable: a BBC studio, water supply, electricity generator and a scientists' room. Amazingly, the whole thing was built in complete secrecy from the local villagers.

■397■ **ESSEX SECRET BUNKER** ☎ 01206 392271
Crown Building, Mistley, Essex CO11 1HS
At centre of Mistley. Take B1352 from Manningtree: road passes the gate
Open Apr–Sept: daily 10.30–5 (6 in Aug); Oct–Mar exc Christmas and New Year: Sat and Sun 10.30–4.30
Built in 1951 and operational until 1993, Essex Secret Bunker would have controlled the whole county in the event of nuclear war. Everything is in complete working order; visit the radio room, communications centre, telephone exchange, dormitory and many more rooms. Audio-visual material and sound effects accompany your journey to make the whole experience even more authentic. This vast and complex structure was kept top secret for over forty-five years.

■398■ **ROMAN THEATRE OF VERULAMIUM** ☎ 01727 835035
Gorhambury Drive, St Michaels, St Albans, Hertfordshire AL3 6AH
Signposted off A4147
Open all year: daily 10–5 (4 in winter)
Semicircular theatre constructed in around AD160. It is 180 feet (55 metres) across and could hold 1,600 spectators. It was used for religious processions, ceremonies and plays. The theatre was unearthed during excavation work undertaken between 1930 and 1940 along with the remains of a fortress and a mosaic floor with a hypocaust heating system. Other finds are displayed in the adjoining Verulamium Museum.

🏛 CENTRAL   MAP 4

■399■ **BROADWAY TOWER** ☎ 01386 852390
Broadway, Worcestershire WR12 7LB
1 mile E of Broadway off A44
Open Mar–Oct: daily 10.30–5 (dusk if sooner); Nov–Mar: Sat and Sun 11–3.
Confirm by phone
Built as a folly by the Earl of Coventry in 1799 on an ancient beacon, one of the highest points of the Cotswolds, at over 1,000 feet (305 metres) above sea-level, and one of England's outstanding viewpoints. The climb to the top by way of a spiral staircase is rewarded with a view that includes as many as twelve counties. The tower was much admired by Victorian artist and craftsman William Morris, who spent his holidays here.

■400■ **CHEDWORTH ROMAN VILLA** ☎ 01242 890256
Yanworth, Cheltenham, Gloucestershire GL54 3LJ
3 miles NW of Fossebridge off A429
Open May–Sept: Tues–Sun, Bank Hol Mons 10–5; Oct–Nov and Mar–Apr: Wed–Sun 11–4
Remains of a Roman villa occupied between second and fourth centuries. Over thirty 'rooms' have been identified, including two sets of baths. A number of

mosaics have been well preserved, and the hypocaust heating system is well displayed. Local finds are displayed in the museum.

■401■ RUSHTON TRIANGULAR LODGE   ☎ 01536 710761

Rushton, Kettering, Northamptonshire NN14 1RP

Fred's
FAVOURITE

1 mile W of Rushton on unclassified road, 3 miles from Desborough
on A6 from Kettering
Open Apr–Sept: daily 10–6; Oct: daily 10–5

Ornate, three storeyed, three-sided building in the shape of an equilateral triangle. The design of the Triangular Lodge is symbolic of the Holy Trinity. The three storeys of the building have three windows on each floor of each of its three sides. It was begun in July 1594 and completed in September 1597 by Roman Catholic Sir Thomas Tresham. He devised the plan for the building while in prison for his religious beliefs. The interior is much less ornate than the exterior. Each floor has one large hexagonal room, leaving small triangular spaces in each corner. Two of the corners were for storage, one for the staircase. Also of interest are the windows, different on each floor, and the various inscriptions around the building.

■402■ THE UFFINGTON WHITE HORSE

Uffington, Oxfordshire

South of B4507
Open: any reasonable time

Cut out of the turf on the upper slopes of Uffington Castle near the Ridgeway, the White Horse is 374 feet (114 metres) long and is thought to represent a Celtic god or tribal symbol. For centuries, however, local people have maintained that it is a portrait of the dragon slain by St George. First recorded in the twelfth century, it was believed to have been carved by Saxons celebrating King Alfred's victory over the Danes in AD871. Best viewed from a distance, as it is almost impossible to make sense of the figure while standing on the hill into which it has been carved.

⛰ WALES   MAP 5

■403■ CAERLEON – THE ROMAN FORTRESS OF ISCA

☎ 01633 422656

High Street, Caerleon, Newport NP6 1AE

On B4236
Open Mar–Sept: daily 9.30–6.30; Oct–Mar: Mon–Sat 9.30–4 (last admission 1 hour before closing)

Site of the Roman fortress of Isca, built in around AD75, which housed the 6,000 men of the second Augustian Legion. Excavations include the amphitheatre, barracks and bathhouse. The amphitheatre, once used for gladiatorial events, was designed to hold 6,000 spectators and is the only fully excavated example in Britain. The foundations of the barracks and parts of the ramparts can be seen, along with the remains of the cookhouse, latrines and baths. The baths were excavated in 1970 and represent the most complete example of a Roman legionary bath building in Britain. There's also a museum of objects found.

■404■ PORTMEIRION   ☎ 01766 770228

Penrhyndeudraeth, Gwynedd LL48 6ET

Off A487 W of Penrhyndeudraeth
Open Gardens and Shops all year: daily 9.30–5.30 (10 for Shops, last admission 4.30)

Fantasy Italianate village with pastel-shaded cottages and cobbled squares, a castle, bell tower and town hall created by Sir Clough Williams Ellis. The focus of the village is the waterfront hotel, rebuilt from the original house in 1925. The village contains a wide variety of architectural styles, including the Jacobean town hall and the Victorian-Gothic Castell Deudraeth. Ellis continued to make additions to the village throughout his lifetime, including the Villa Winch and Piazza in 1966 and the Georgian Cliff House in 1968. He deemed his creation complete in 1972 and lived to enjoy it for a further six years.

🏛 NORTH-WEST   MAP 6

■405■ BLACKPOOL NORTH PIER   ☎ 01253 621452
The Promenade, Blackpool
On promenade
Open: any reasonable time
The oldest of Blackpool's three piers was opened to the public on 23 May 1893. It had cost £11,500 to build, and the price of admission was one penny. Designed by Eugenius Birch, North Pier is also Blackpool's longest, with its cast-iron columns stretching 1,410 feet (430 metres) into the sea. Surprisingly, it has many of its original Victorian features despite two fires. Recent improvements have been made on a Victorian theme with glazed conservatories and a carousel.

■406■ BLACKPOOL TOWER   ☎ 01253 622242
The Promenade, Blackpool, Lancashire FY1 4BJ

Fred's
FAVOURITE

On promenade
Open Easter–early Nov: daily 10–6
Proud Victorian landmark recently restored to its original glory, Blackpool Tower took three years to build and was opened in May 1894. It was built in imitation of the Eiffel Tower, which had been opened in Paris in 1889. Designed by R. J. G Reade and Maxwell & Tuke, it took 2,493 tonnes of steel and 93 tonnes of cast iron to build it. It rises to a height at the top of the flagstaff of 518 feet 9 inches (158.1 metres) with an observation platform 480 feet (146.3 metres) above the base. Inside the tower are many attractions, including a fine listed ballroom with a fantastically ornate ceiling.

Blackpool Tower

■407■ KING CHARLES TOWER, CHESTER   ☎ 01244 402008
City Walls, Chester, Cheshire
Signposted from city walls
External viewing only

The tower stands on the site of the north-east angle tower of the Roman fortress. Its present name comes from the local legend that King Charles I saw from the top of the tower the final stages of his army's defeat by the Parliamentarians at the Battle of Rowton Moor in September 1645. In earlier times it had been called Newton's or the Phoenix Tower. The phoenix is the emblem of the painters', glaziers', embroiderers' and stationers' company, a medieval guild that used the tower as a meeting house. A phoenix and the date 1613 are carved above the door of the tower chamber.

🏛 NORTH-EAST · MAP 7

■408■ THE ANGEL OF THE NORTH
Gateshead, Tyne & Wear
Take A1(M) exit for A167 (Gateshead South). Take A167 exit at roundabout, parking on left
External viewing only
Sculpture symbolising the regeneration of the North-East and celebrating its engineering skills. The Angel stands 65 feet (20 metres) high, and its wings span a massive 177 feet (54 metres). Designed by Antony Gormley, the 208-tonne figure is built of steel, containing copper that forms a patina on the surface and mellows with age. The hollow figure is supported by concrete foundations 72 feet (22 metres) deep that anchor it to the solid rock beneath.

■409■ WAINHOUSE TOWER ☎ 01422 368725
Kings Cross, Halifax, West Yorkshire
From centre of Halifax to Savile Park, then down Wakefield Gate
Open: Easter weekend, Bank Hol Mons and selected days throughout the year.
Phone for details

Fred's **FAVOURITE**

Ornate, 235-foot (72-metre) high tower that dominates the Calder Valley to the west of Halifax. Wainhouse Tower was originally conceived and designed as a chimney to serve John Edward Wainhouse's Washer Lane Dyeworks. The chimney was surrounded by a square-based, octagonal-shaped stone casing with a spiral staircase of over 400 steps between the two. The stairs lead to four pedimented balcony features. It is estimated that over 9,000 tonnes of material were used to build this elaborate folly, and Wainhouse himself supervised the construction. Each stone was quarried and dressed locally and cut to fit rather like the pieces of a jigsaw. The building was completed on 9 September 1875, and by that time it had already become clear that it would never be used as a chimney.

🏛 SCOTLAND · MAP 8

■410■ CALANAIS STANDING STONES ☎ 01851 621422
Callanish, Isle of Lewis PA86 9DY
12 miles W of Stornaway off A859
Open summer: daily 10–7; winter: daily 10–4. Visitors' Centre closed Sun
A circle of thirteen stones with a small chambered tomb inside. Believed to have been built around 3000BC, an avenue of nineteen stones leads northwards from the stone circle. Other avenues of stones also lead off to the east, west and south.

■411■ GLENFINNAN MONUMENT ☎ 01397 722250
NTS Information Centre, Glenfinnan, Highland PH37 4LT
On A830, 18 miles W of Fort William
Open Apr (or Good Fri)–Oct: daily 10–5 (6 in mid-May–Aug)
Erected in 1815 by Alexander Macdonald of Glenalade in tribute to the clansmen
who fought and died for the Jacobite cause. Prince Charles Edward Stuart's
standard was raised near here in 1745, marking the inspirational start to a
campaign that ended at the Battle of Culloden the following year. A sandstone
statue of a Highlander surmounts a 60-foot (18-metre) rubble column which
has a corbelled and crenellated wallhead. The monument is surrounded by a
coped, octagonal rubble wall with three later pedimented sections containing
inscriptions in Gaelic, English and Latin on large cast-iron plaques. The story of
the Jacobite campaign is told in the visitors' centre.

■412■ JARLSHOF PREHISTORIC AND NORSE SETTLEMENT
☎ 01950 460112
At Sumburgh Head, on A970 about 22 miles S of Lerwick, Shetland
Open Apr–Sept: daily 9.30–6.30
Remarkable archaeological site with important remains of a complex of ancient
homestead spanning over 3,000 years of history. The earliest remains date from
the Stone Age. The Bronze Age village, where the main excavations are, contains the house of a bronze smith who worked at Jarlshof in around 800BC.
Above this is an Iron Age broch – a communal farmhouse within a tall defensive tower – and circular stone-walled houses which replaced the defensive
brochs later in the Iron Age. Higher still, a group of rectangular stone houses
remain from a Viking community which was here for over 200 years. On the
top of the mount is a sixteenth-century laird's house, which was built for Earls
Robert and Patrick Stewart. This was the basis of 'Jarlshof' in Sir Walter Scott's
novel *The Pirate*. Visitors' centre has displays on the Iron Age and the history of
the site.

■413■ NELSON'S MONUMENT
Calton Hill, Edinburgh
East end of Princes Street, then up Calton Hill
Open Apr–Sept: Mon 1–6, Tue–Sat 10– 6; Oct–Mar: Mon–Sat 10–3
Designed in 1807 and erected on Calton Hill, the monument dominates the east
end of Princes Street. Honouring Nelson's victory at the Battle of Trafalgar, it
was unveiled in 1816. The base is pentagonal in plan with corner bastions and
a battlemented top. The base is 456 feet (139 metres) above sea-level, and the
monument stands 106 feet (32 metres) high, giving excellent panoramic views
of Edinburgh when you climb the 170-step spiral staircase to the viewing platform at the top. The time-ball is lowered simultaneously with the one o'clock
gun fired from Edinburgh castle.

■414■ SCOTT MONUMENT ☎ 0131 529 4098
Princes Street, Edinburgh
Near the Mound, beside Princes Street Gardens
*Open Mar, Apr, May, Oct: Mon–Sun 10–6; June–Sept: Mon–Sat 9–8, Sun 10–6;
Nov–Feb: daily 10–4*
Ornate Gothic monument to the acclaimed Scottish writer Sir Walter Scott,
completed in 1846. The Scott Monument, at 200 feet (61 metres) dominates
Princes Street, and it is worth the climb to the top by way of the 287-step spiral

Fred's FAVOURITE

staircase for the views of the castle. The whole monument is richly ornamented with Gothic floriated panelling and carving. The marble statue of Scott, with his dog at his feet, is the work of Sir John Steel. A further sixty figures depict characters from Scott's novels and Scottish history.

■415■ WALLACE MONUMENT ☎ 01786 472140
St Ninians Road, Stirling FK8 2AD
Off A907
Open Jan–Feb, Nov–Dec: daily 11–4; Mar–May and Oct: daily 10–5; July and Aug: daily 9.30–6.30
Major landmark built in the Scottish baronial style to represent a medieval Scottish tower, rising from a courtyard, with a representation on the top of the Crown Royal of Scotland. The huge monument to medieval Scottish hero William Wallace is 220 feet (67 metres) high and 54 square feet (5 square metres) at its base. The walls are 16 to 18 feet (4.8 to 5.5 metres) at their thickest, tapering to 5 feet (1.5 metres) at their thinnest. It is estimated that over 30,000 tonnes of stone were used in its construction. The solid-bronze statue of Wallace on the outside of the building, sculpted by David Watson Stevenson, is about 30 feet (9 metres) from the ground and is itself 15 feet (4.5 metres) tall. Inside the building there are four rooms of about 25 square feet (2.3 square metres), with vaulted ceilings 20 to 30 feet (6 to 9 metres) high. The tower rooms are connected by a spiral staircase in the north-west corner, with 246 steps to the top. The parapet at the top of the tower gives magnificent views across the Forth Valley and towards the Ochill Hills.

▟▙ NORTHERN IRELAND   MAP 9

■416■ ARDBOE HIGH CROSS
Ardboe, Co. Tyrone
From Cookstown take B73 E for 9 miles
External viewing only
Standing on the shore of Loch Neagh, Ardboe High Cross is the best example of a high cross in Northern Ireland. The 18-foot (5.5-metre) cross dates from the tenth century and marks the site of an ancient monastery. The cross has twenty-two sculpted biblical panels. Old Testament scenes are displayed on the east side, starting with Adam and Eve at the bottom, while the west side depicts scenes from the New Testament.

■417■ SCRABO TOWER ☎ 028 9181 1491
Scrabo County Park, Newtownards, Co. Down
Signposted from Newtownards town centre
Open June–Sept: Sat–Thur 11–6.30
A tower built in memory of the third Marquis of Londonderry. The 122 steps lead up to the viewing platform to give spectacular views, at 135 feet (41 metres) of Strangford Loch and County Down. Part of the tower was lived in until 1970.

CHAPTER

6

TRANSPORT AND ENGINEERING

Close to where I lived in Bolton when I was a kid, there was a very splendid Victorian railway viaduct. It consisted of about five stone pillars, and as a kid they seemed to me to be made of the biggest stones in the world. Each one was about 5 feet (1.5 m) long and 2 feet (0.6 m) deep and 3 feet (0.9 m) wide, and you could see these beautiful dents in the middle of each one where the lifting dogs had gripped the stone when they lifted them up. I used to look at the thing and think about the beautiful symmetry of them, how nicely those stones fitted together. One day I found a date – 1847 – and it amazed me that they could make things like this so long ago. I know it's nothing in terms of real history, but it seemed to me a heck of a long time ago when I was little. You could actually get on this railway viaduct at one end and walk right across over a big valley, which seemed a million miles below when you were only six years old. When a train came over the top and you were up there on the viaduct, it all shook. It was magic, and those memories have never left me. The bridge is still there, but there's no railway track on it any longer and there are trees growing on the top. It's all so sad.

Since then I've always been fascinated by bridges and tunnels and by big construction and civil engineering projects. Thomas Telford was one of our greatest civil engineers. He built roads, bridges and canals, but one of his most dramatic engineering feats is the Pontcysyllte Aqueduct, which carries the Shropshire Union Canal high above the Dee Valley near Llangollen in North Wales. Work on the aqueduct, which is 1,007 feet (307 metres) long began in July 1795 and took ten years to complete. It is built of local sandstone and has nineteen arches, each with a span of 45 feet (13.7 metres). The waterway itself is carried over in a trough 11 feet 10 inches (3.6 metres) wide and 5 feet 3 inches (1.5 metres) deep constructed of cast-iron flanged plates

The Forth Bridge

bolted together – each casting dovetailing into the next with the joints sealed with lead and Welsh flannel.

The opening ceremony took place in November 1805 in the presence of 8,000 people, and six boats went over the aqueduct from north to south and back again. The canal is still open today, and you can take barge trips over the aqueduct. It's quite spectacular and, even for somebody like me with a head for heights, it can be a bit unnerving, because it feels as though the barge you are on is going to float right off the edge.

The aqueduct isn't the only great engineering feat of Telford's that you can see in North Wales. The historical suspension bridge next to the castle at Conwy was designed by Telford as part of the great highway between Chester and Holyhead. It was built simultaneously with the one over the Menai Strait, and both were opened for traffic in 1826. The first suspension bridge in Europe had been built over the River Tees in 1741. With a span of 70 feet (21 metres) it was small in comparison with one of 200 feet (61 metres) built in China in the twelfth century, but it was revolutionary because of its use of iron chains. The idea was taken up very quickly in many countries, but it was Thomas Telford, in collaboration with Captain Samuel Brown, who pushed forward the design and manufacture of wrought-iron chains which culminated in the building of the Menai Bridge and Conwy Bridge.

Bridges were needed at Conwy and over the Menai Strait to get traffic to Holyhead for the Irish ferries. It was this that led to the setting up of the Holyhead Road Commissioners in 1815 and, over the next fifteen years, with Telford as their engineer, they built a road from Shrewsbury to Holyhead which was regarded as a model of the most perfect road-making art that had ever been attempted in any country. In 1818 money was granted for Telford's suspension bridge over the Menai Strait. The construction of the bridge at Conwy, which was needed for traffic from Liverpool and Manchester which came via Chester, was sanctioned in 1821.

The first stone for the bridge was laid in April 1822, and by February 1825 the masonry was completed, as were the chamber anchorages for the suspension chains. The trickiest part of the building work was the fitting of the wrought-iron chains that had been made at workshops in Shrewsbury. Rather than being hauled up in one piece from a floating raft, as they had been at the Menai Bridge, the chains at Conwy were assembled *in situ*. Link upon link was joined together up on a rope bridge stretched between the towers.

Telford's suspension bridge and Robert Stevenson's tubular railway bridge at Conwy

With the chain successfully hanging, the construction of the suspension rods and road deck was comparatively straightforward and by 1 July 1826 Conwy Bridge was opened. Along with the Menai Bridge, it was a really great engineering achievement in its day.

The Menai Bridge became by far the largest to have been built up to that time and, as the nineteenth century progressed, bridge-building became more daring and dramatic. But it wasn't without mishaps. With a length of over 2 miles (3 kilometres) the Tay Bridge is the longest railway bridge in Britain, but it's its predecessor that has a place of notoriety in the history of British civil engineering. The 'Beautiful Railway Bridge of the Silver Tay' designed by the engineer Thomas Bouch was opened in 1878. But just a year later it collapsed in a storm just as a train was crossing it. The engine and all its carriages plummeted into the river below, and all seventy-five people on board lost their lives. It was one of the worst disasters in British railway history, and an enquiry concluded that it was caused by faults in the design, construction and maintenance of the bridge.

Prior to the collapse of the Tay Bridge, Bouch had submitted plans for the construction of the Forth Bridge, but the disaster and resulting loss of confidence in his plans put paid to any ideas he had for constructing the Forth Bridge. It is my opinion that the Tay Bridge disaster is the reason why the Forth Bridge is so grossly over-engineered. This great steel colossus, the like of which had never been seen before, rose above the waters of the Firth of Forth between 1883 and 1890. Fully 361 feet high (110 metres) from high water to the top of the main cantilever towers and 1 mile 1,050 yards (2.53 kilometres) in length, the great structure was the wonder of its age.

The need for the Forth Bridge was quite simple. The North British Railway Company, whose main line between Edinburgh and Dundee was cut by the Firths of Forth and Tay, was under pressure to bridge the gaps. Rail links across both of the estuaries had been seen as inevitable for a generation; the only things that were needed to make it happen were the technology and the materials. The technology was acquired painfully with the disaster on the Tay, and the material – steel – had become available in quantity thanks to Bessemer's recently developed process. Work started on the construction of the second Tay Bridge, and it was time to start a crossing of the Forth. By December 1882 all the factors came together, and a contract was placed with Tancred Arrol & Co., a consortium led by William Arrol of Glasgow. The engineers for the project were John Fowler and Benjamin Baker. The grand opening of this monumental piece of structural engineering was on 4 March 1890, when the Prince of Wales drove in the final, 6,500,000th rivet.

The cantilever system which is the main feature of the bridge consists of three double cantilevers known as the Queensferry, Inch Garvie and Fife cantilevers. The arms nearest the shore of the Queensferry and Fife cantilevers neither rest on nor are they fixed to the approach viaduct. I have recently climbed all over the Forth Bridge and it's amazing when you think how the great cantilevers aren't really mechanically connected at all. To allow for contraction and expansion, they are just linked up together like a chain. It is because of this, of course, that when you stand on the very top of it, 361 feet (110 metres) up in the sky, and a locomotive comes on to the bridge under the cantilevers, you can feel the whole thing rock. Quite a fantastic feeling and a credit to the men who built it.

When it was built, the Forth Bridge must have seemed like one of the great wonders of the world. I wonder what the Victorians would have made of the slim, graceful-looking suspension bridge that was built next to it in the 1960s. It was a time when Britain seemed to lead the world in the design and construction of suspension bridges. The biggest was the mighty bridge over the Humber, which was the longest suspension bridge in the world. It has only recently been overtaken by one in Denmark and one in Japan.

Approval for construction of the bridge was granted in 1959, although it was not until 1973 that the work finally began. Work on the construction proceeded for eight years, and during this time many thousands of tonnes of steel and concrete were used and upwards of a thousand workers and staff were employed at times of peak activity. The bridge provides dual carriageways for highway traffic, with a combined footpath and cycle track along each side of it. The anchorages are massive concrete structures each containing two chambers within which the main cables splay out into separate strands. Piers are reinforced concrete structures which support the towers. Each of the towers consists of two tapered vertical reinforced concrete legs braced together with four reinforced concrete horizontal beams. Each of the main cables is made up of almost 15,000 solid drawn wires, which for the purpose of erection and anchorage were divided into thirty-seven strands. The structure is suspended from the main cables by employing high-tensile steel wire strands, and the suspended structure consists of stiffened steel plates welded together to form a hollow box section. Its streamlined shape makes the bridge aerodynamically stable and greatly reduces wind loads on it.

When you look at the slenderness and the gracefulness of the Humber Bridge, it is quite fantastic to go down into the bowels of the earth at the end of it and see all those strands of wire that make up the cables that it is suspended from. They all fan out in this great underground chamber, which has got dehumidifiers in it to stop any rust developing on the ends of them. The amazing thing about it is that it moves about 14 feet (4.3 m) sideways in a gale, and goes back again. A very interesting piece of work.

In this last twenty years or so we've seen some very impressive engineering achievements. Two of the biggest projects have been the Channel Tunnel and the Thames Barrier. The great flood barrier across the Thames is one of the construction achievements of the twentieth century and a major advance in environmental control. The unique structure spans the Woolwich Reach and consists of ten separate movable gates, each one pivoting on and supported between concrete piers and abutments which house the operating machinery. When raised, the four main gates, each weighing 3,700 tonnes, stand as high as a five-storey building and as wide as the opening of Tower Bridge. Four thousand men and women all over Britain were engaged on the building of the barrier, and the work, which cost nearly £500 million, took eight years. The construction

The Thames Barrier

of the reinforced concrete piers 52 feet (16 metres) below the waterline was the first stage of the construction process. To do this, coffer dams, which are watertight boxes of interlocking steel plates, were first sunk into the bed of the river. The water was then pumped out and the piers were constructed.

The width of the river is divided by the piers to form four openings of 200 feet (61 metres) and two of 103 feet (31.5 metres) for shipping, along with four subsidiary non-navigational openings. To the north of the river, a huge dry dock was built in which the concrete sills were cast. After manufacture, the dock was flooded and tugs towed the sills into position between the piers. They were then sunk to the riverbed. The piers and the sills formed the supports and seating for the gates and platform bases for the operating machinery so they had to be accurately built and positioned. The work had to be carried out in difficult conditions in all kinds of weather.

The gates' design is both simple and flexible in operation. To operate the barrage and close the gates, reversible hydraulic rams, one pulling and one pushing, are used to move rocker beams connected to discs at each end. These rotate the gates into any one of four different positions. Each gate has two sets of operating machinery, one at each end, either of them powerful enough for rotation. During the first twelve years of operation, the barrier was closed twenty-nine times to protect London. Weather conditions are monitored twenty-four hours a day all year round, and in the control tower weather forecast and tide level information is received. A decision to close the barrier is taken by the duty controller, and action will be taken about one hour after low tide, five hours before an incoming surge tide could reach this point.

The Thames Barrier is a magnificent bit of engineering, and in the chief engineer's office I saw a back-of-a-fag-packet drawing of the original conception. The drawing was more like something that Brunel would have done, with beautiful towers to house the machinery on each of the piers rather than the present things, which remind me of the hood on a windmill clad in stainless-steel sheathing.

About a mile upstream from the Thames Barrier is one of Brunel's greatest achievements. Isambard Kingdom Brunel's father, Mark, took on the job of digging a tunnel under the River Thames. I think it was the first tunnel ever to be attempted under water. But when young Isambard was only at the tender age of twenty-one, his father disappeared off to Canada and left his son to carry on with the engineering work. He sank two great shafts, one on each side of the river, at Rotherhithe and Wapping and the grand plan was to have a spiral roadway going down the shafts to the bottom. At the base of each of the spiral roadways were the entrances to the tunnel itself.

At this time the Thames wasn't much more than a sewer, and where they were digging wasn't very far below the riverbed. During the building operation there were many occasions when the polluted Thames-water came flooding into the tunnel and, although there was no loss of life, the raw sewage that came flooding in had a very bad effect on the eyesight of the workers and on their health in general. One day, though, just as they seemed to be making good progress, the water suddenly came flooding in and washed them all out into the great chamber at the end. Brunel was in the tunnel at the time and, along with all the rest of the workers, was lucky to get away with his life. Everybody managed to get out, but the pumps couldn't get rid of the water, so Brunel bought a boat and sailed it out into the middle of the Thames. Then he plugged the hole in the tunnel roof with clay and puddling and started again. You have to hand it to him, when you think the guy was only twenty-one years old and was doing something that nobody else had ever attempted before. I wonder what he would have made of the Channel Tunnel. One thing's for sure: if he were around now he'd have been involved in building both it and the Thames Barrier.

PLACES TO VISIT

■**418**■ **ANVIL POINT LIGHTHOUSE** ☎ 01929 422146
Swanage, Dorset BH19 2JN
1 mile S of Swanage
Open early Apr–end Oct. Phone for details
Built of local stone and completed in 1881, Anvil Point Lighthouse was opened
by Neville Chamberlain's father. The light is positioned to give a waypoint for
vessels on passage along the English Channel coast. To the west it gives a clear
line from Portland Bill and to the east guides vessels away from the
Christchurch Ledge and leads them into the Solent. The light was originally lit
by a paraffin vapour burner. In 1960 the station was modernised and converted
from oil to mains electricity. The old fog signal, a five-minute cannon, was
replaced in 1981 by new automatic equipment and the fog signal discontinued.
In 1991 the lighthouse was automated and is now monitored and controlled
from the Trinity House Operational Control Centre at Harwich.

■**419**■ **BOX TUNNEL**
Box, Bath, Somerset
5 miles E of Bath, off A4 near village of Box

Brunel's Box Tunnel

Probably the most difficult single construction of Brunel's Great Western Railway. The tunnel, 1 mile, 1452 yards (2.94 kilometres) in length, is on a 1:100 gradient sloping down towards Bath, and in order to accommodate two of Brunel's broad-gauge tracks it had to be built 30 feet (9 metres) wide. The hard rock in the western section had to be excavated using gunpowder blasts, while the rest could be dug using pick and shovel. The tunnel is lined with brick, and the western entrance has a great classical portico built in Bath stone. At first, travellers were fearful of using the tunnel and many alighted the train before entering and took a horse and carriage over the hill. Legend has it that the sun shines through the tunnel at sunrise on Brunel's birthday.

■420■ BRISTOL TEMPLE MEADS STATION
Temple Gate, Temple Mead, Bristol BS1 6QA
Signposted in Bristol city centre
The station has two main sections: Brunel's original Great Western Railway station, which is now used as a car park, and the present station, built from 1865–78 and extended in the 1930s. The GWR train shed has a great wooden roof, supported by cast-iron arches and arcades. It is actually a cantilever structure, but Brunel disguised it to give the appearance of a great hammer-beam roof. The present station, dominated by the central tower, was built by Sir Matthew Digby Wyatt of variegated stone in the French Gothic style and is complete with pinnacles and battlements. At the time the tower was topped by a French pavilion turret, but this was taken down during the 1930s extensions. These were completed by P. E. Culverhouse and included extra platforms and red-brick office buildings.

■421■ LIZARD LIGHTHOUSE ☎ 01326 290431
Nr Helston, Cornwall TR12 7NT
Off A3083 at Lizard
Open early Apr–end Sept: 11–5. Phone for details
Completed in1751 by Thomas Fonnereau, Lizard Lighthouse consists of two octagonal towers with originally a cottage and now six houses built between them. The west tower is used for storage and the east tower houses the navigation light at a height of 190 feet (58 metres) above sea-level. Structural alterations made in 1812 left the station pretty much as it is today. The lantern was originally fired by coal and subsequently by oil, and was later superseded by a new lantern with an electric light. The lighthouse became automated during 1998.

■422■ PENDEEN LIGHTHOUSE ☎ 01736 788418
Penzance, Cornwall TR19 7ED
Off B3306 between St Ives and St Just at Pendeen
Open early Apr–end Oct. Phone for details
Designs for the building were prepared by Sir Thomas Matthews, the Trinity House engineer; construction was undertaken by Arthur Carkeek of Redruth and the lantern was supplied by Messrs Chance of Birmingham. The lighthouse was commissioned on 26 September 1900. Within the tower itself are two rooms, one over the other, and above them the lantern, which originally contained a five-wick Argand lamp. Oil was pumped to this from the room below. In 1926 the lamp was replaced by an electric one, and the old oil lamp is on display at the Trinity House National Lighthouse Centre in Penzance. The lighthouse is now monitored and controlled via a telemetry link from the Trinity House Operational Control Centre at Harwich.

■423■ ROYAL ALBERT BRIDGE
Saltash, Cornwall
Runs parallel with road bridge (A38) crossing River Tamar at Saltash
The only railway-carrying suspension bridge in the country. The bridge, at 2200 feet (670 metres) long, includes two great spans of 455 feet (138.6 metres) joined by a single deep-water pier in the middle of the river. This was constructed by sinking a wrought-iron caisson down to the bedrock within which the water could be removed using compressed air. The suspension chains are not anchored into the ground on either side of the bridge; instead, Brunel braced the chains against two wrought-iron cylinders that arch upwards in a parabolic curve in the opposite direction to the chains. This was to be the last of Brunel's great railway engineering feats. He was too ill to attend Prince Albert's opening ceremony in 1859 and was carried over the bridge lying on a wagon a few days later.

⛰ SOUTH-EAST   MAP 2

■424■ CHANNEL TUNNEL   ☎ 0990 353535
Folkestone, Kent
Signposted off M20

Fred's FAVOURITE

Open to fare-paying passengers only
The Eurotunnel transport system comprises three tunnels under the Channel, each approximately 31 miles (50 kilometres) long. The tunnel lies on average 130 feet (40 metres) below the seabed, although the path of the tunnel follows the soft strata and therefore undulates at varying depths. Two of the three tunnels are for railway traffic (shuttles and trains). Each rail tunnel has a single track, and has been designed so that it can be operated in either direction. Every 1,230 feet (375 metres), cross-passages connect the two rail tunnels to a central service tunnel, which provides access for safety and maintenance. The service tunnel, the only one of its kind in the world, is specially designed for adapted road vehicles (electric and diesel) used by the emergency services and maintenance workers. The service tunnel is kept at a higher air pressure than the rail tunnels, thus remaining free from smoke and fumes in the event of a fire in one of the rail tunnels, a safe haven in the event of evacuation. The tunnel operates round the clock, every day of the year, and approximately 360 shuttles and trains pass through every day.

■425■ CLAYTON TUNNEL
Nr Brighton, East Sussex
On London to Brighton line, 5 miles N of Brighton off A273 by village of Clayton
Built in 1841 for the London and Brighton Railway, the tunnel, 1 mile 499 yards (2.06 kilometres) long, is lined with five rings of brickwork and has eleven ventilation shafts. Its most notable feature is the portal at the northern end, which has two castellated turrets on either side of a cottage. This was probably inhabited by the person in charge of the gas originally used to light the tunnel.

■426■ MAIDENHEAD BRIDGE
Maidenhead, Berkshire
Crosses the River Thames at Maidenhead, S of road bridge
Fine arched bridge designed by Brunel for the Great Western Railway. Formed with two shallow elliptical arches each with a 122-foot (37-metre) span. The

'flat' design of the bridge was Brunel's solution to the problem that the bridge had to be high enough to allow for river navigation while low enough not to alter the gradient greatly of the railway line. The river piers have a broad cornice carrying the parapet, while there are four small semicircular arches at either end of the bridge. The work started in 1837 and was nearly completed when the centring was blown away in 1839. The bridge was widened in 1890 to accommodate four lines.

■427■ OUSE VIADUCT
Balcombe, West Sussex
On London–Brighton Line. Turn W off B2036 at Balcombe (unnamed road) towards Borde Hill Garden
One of the most impressive viaducts in Britain. Four ornate Italianate pavilions in Caen stone are at either side of the viaduct which crosses the Ouse Valley at a maximum height of 92 feet (28 metres). Built in 1840 for the London and Brighton railway, the thirty-seven brick arches each have a span of 30 feet (9 metres), and are crowned by a stone balustrade. The viaduct has recently undergone extensive restoration.

■428■ PADDINGTON STATION
Praed Street, Paddington, London W2 1HF
Signposted off A40(M)/A501 Marylebone Road
Terminus of the Great Western Railway, built between 1850 and 1854 to a design produced by a collaboration between Isambard Kingdom Brunel and Matthew Digby Wyatt. The magnificent three-bay arched roof has 189 decorative wrought-iron ribs, with a cast-iron column supporting every third rib. A fourth bay was added in 1916 in keeping with Brunel's originals, and the iron columns were replaced by steel stanchions. The station is unusual in that it has no principal exterior façade; instead, the head of the station is occupied by the Great Western Hotel, designed by P.C. Hardwick and opened in the same year as the station.

■429■ ST CATHERINE'S LIGHTHOUSE ☎ 01983 731417/730284
Niton Undercliff, Ventor, Isle of Wight PO38 2NF
At Niton Undercliff, 5 miles W of Ventor off A3055
Open early Apr–end Oct. Phone for details
The present tower was built in 1838 of ashlar stone with dressed quoins and was carried up from a base plinth as a three-tier octagon, diminishing by stages. The elevation of the light proved to be too high, as the lantern frequently became mist-capped, so in 1875 it was decided to lower the light 43 feet (13 metres) by taking 20 feet (6 metres) out of the uppermost section of the tower and about 23 feet (7 metres) out of the middle tier. This destroyed the beauty of the structure and made it seem dwarfed. At that time the fog signal house was situated near the end of the cliff, but owing to erosion and cliff settlements the building developed such serious cracks that in 1932 a new place was needed to house the fog signal. This was eventually mounted on a lower tower, which was built as a small replica of the main lighthouse. The result has been to give a well-proportioned step down between the two towers, which are now referred to as 'the Cow and the Calf'. The fog signal was discontinued in 1987, and the lighthouse became automated a decade later.

■430■ ST PANCRAS STATION

Euston Road, London NW1 2QP

Adjacent to King's Cross Station

Impressive terminus of the Midland Railway, opened in 1876. The magnificent train shed was designed by William Henry Barlow and has a 240-foot (73-metre) span roof which, at the time, was the largest in the world. The ribs spring direct from the floor and are tied to the platform floor, which is essentially at first-floor level. Underneath, the whole structure is supported by 690 cast-iron columns, and this ground-floor area was designed as a vast store for beer from Burton-on-Trent brought into London. The impressive frontage, designed as a hotel by Sir George Gilbert Scott, is a fine example of Gothic architecture, complete with spires, gables, turrets and a great clock tower.

■431■ THAMES BARRIER VISITORS' CENTRE ☎ 0208 854 1373

1 Unity Way, Woolwich, London SE18 5NJ

Car parking via A206 Woolwich Road

Open all year: Mon–Fri 10–5, Sat and Sun 10.30–5.30

One of the construction achievements of the twentieth century and a major advance in environmental control. The Thames Barrier was built to prevent the possibility of disastrous flooding in London. Basically, the rising gate barrier is a series of separate movable gates positioned end to end across the river. Each gate is pivoted and supported between concrete piers that house the operating machinery and control equipment. Closing the barrier when required seals part of the upper Thames from the sea. When not in use, the gates rest out of sight in curved recesses on concrete sills in the riverbed, allowing free passage of river traffic through the openings between the piers. If a dangerously high tidal surge threatens, the gates swing up through 90 degrees from their riverbed position, forming a continuous steel wall facing down river ready to stem the tide. The width of the barrier from bank to bank is about 1,706 feet (520 metres), with four main openings each having a clear span of 2,000 feet (61 metres).

■432■ TOWER BRIDGE ☎ 0207 378 1928

Tower Bridge Experience, Tower Bridge, London SE1 2UP

Tower Hill and London Bridge Underground

Open Apr–Oct: 10–6.30; Nov–Mar: 9.30–6 (last admission 1¼ hours before closing)

Fred's
FAVOURITE

Tower Bridge

One of London's best-known landmarks, the bridge, with its ornate towers 200 feet (61 metres) high, was built between 1886 and 1894. Two major piers had to be sunk into the riverbed to support the construction, and over 11,000 tonnes of steel provided the framework for the towers and walkways. The bridge was then clad in Cornish granite and Portland stone, both to protect the underlying steelwork and to give the bridge a more pleasing appearance. When it was built it was the largest and most sophisticated hydraulically operated bridge. Today, the hydraulic machinery is electronically operated, but the old steam engines that used to drive the machinery can still be seen.

🏛 EASTERN   MAP 3

■433■ CHAPPEL VIADUCT
Chappel, Essex
Above the village of Chappel, 9 miles NW of Colchester off A604
Longest viaduct in East Anglia at 1,136 feet (346 metres). Built in 1849, the 32 semicircular arches each have a span of 32 feet (9.7 metres). The viaduct cost over £30,000 and used in excess of seven million bricks that were made at a specially built brickworks nearby. The viaduct was designed to carry two tracks, but only one was laid as the expected increase in rail traffic in the area never materialized.

■434■ QUEEN ELIZABETH II BRIDGE
Dartford, Kent
Crosses River Thames at Dartford
Suspension bridge opened in 1991 that crosses the Thames at Dartford. The main span measures 1,476 feet (450 metres), with a viaduct 0.6 miles (1 kilometre) stretching on either side of the river section. Four 450-feet (37-metre) steel and concrete masts and fifty-six pairs of cables support the four-lane roadway.

🏛 CENTRAL   MAP 4

■435■ FOXTON LOCKS AND INCLINED PLANES
Foxton, Leicestershire
Part of Grand Union Canal. Off A6 between Leicester and Market Harborough at village of Foxton
Part of the extension of the Grand Union Canal to Braunston opened in 1814, Foxton Locks consist of two sets of five staircases with a short area in between to allow boats to cross. The locks raise the level of the canal by 75 feet (23 metres) to the summit. By 1900 the locks had fallen into disrepair and were causing delays for the canal traffic, so a boat lift was installed to bypass the locks. The lift, which was powered by a small steam engine, operated for ten years until the lack of canal traffic made it uneconomical to run. All that is left of the lift are the concrete foundations of the rails and the engine house.

■436■ WELLAND VALLEY VIADUCT
Harringworth, Northamptonshire
North of village of Harringworth. From A47 between Leicester and Peterborough, take turning for Seaton and Harringworth onto B672
The longest viaduct outside suburban London. Part of the Nottingham to Kettering line built by the Midland Railway to relieve the main Midland line to the south. The structure, 1,275 yards (1,166 metres) long, joins Northamptonshire with Rutland at a maximum height of 60 feet (18 metres) with a double line of track. The eighty-two semicircular red-brick arches cost £1,000 each when the viaduct was built in 1879. Each arch has a span of 40 feet (12 metres) and is made up of six courses with every sixth pier slightly wider than the others.

⛭ WALES   MAP 5

■437■ BRITANNIA BRIDGE
Near Bangor, Gwynedd
Connects Anglesey to mainland. Crosses Menai Strait as A5 to Holyhead
Robert Stephenson's tubular railway bridge was opened in 1850 to carry the
Chester to Holyhead railway across the Menai Strait. The bridge was made
up of two main spans of 460 feet (140 metres) with side spans of 230 feet
(70 metres) connected through three towers. The railway tracks ran through
two rectangular tubes consisting of wrought-iron rolled plates and angles hand-
riveted together. These were constructed on the shore and then floated into the
strait before being jacked up into place on towers. Four lions sculpted by John
Thomas sat at the entrance to each tube. In 1970 fire severely damaged the
bridge, and Stephenson's wrought-iron tubes had to be removed. They were
replaced with steel arched spans between the original towers. In 1980 a roadway
was added above the railtrack and the original lions still sit guarding each end
of the bridge.

■438■ CONWY SUSPENSION BRIDGE   ☎ 01492 573282
Conwy LL32 8LD
In centre of Conwy, adjacent to castle

Fred's FAVOURITE

Open late Mar–June and Sept–Oct: Wed–Mon 10–5;
July and Aug: daily 10–5
Historical suspension bridge designed by Thomas Telford as part of the great
highway between Chester and Holyhead. Along with his longer suspension
bridge over the Menai Strait (see entry 440), Conwy was revolutionary in its
use of wrought-iron chains to suspend bridges over greater expanses than
had ever previously been attempted. The span of the Conwy bridge is 327 feet
(99.6 metres) and its width 17 feet 6 inches (5.3 metres). The lower stonework
is rusticated in the Renaissance fashion but, above, the ashlar limestone
superstructure has a Gothic style. Clearly this is an attempt to harmonise
with the architecture of the castle, and of all Telford's 'Gothic' bridges this is
the most successful. The chain supports consist of pairs of solid-stone turrets
linked by a wall containing an arched opening 10 feet (3 metres) wide. The
turrets are battlemented, as is the machiolated top of the connecting wall.
The original chains survive and are arranged in two tiers of five links joined by
deeper plates.

■439■ ELECTRIC MOUNTAIN   ☎ 01286 870636
Llanberis, Gwynedd LL55 4UR
Off A4086, signposted in Llanberis
Open Apr–Sept: daily 9.30–5.30; Oct–Mar: Thurs–Sun 10.30–4.30
Power station in the heart of a mountain. Dinorwig ('Electric Mountain')
took over six years to build between 1976 and 1982. There are over 10 miles
(16 kilometres) of underground tunnels deep inside the mountain, and the construction of the power station required a total of a million tonnes of concrete,
200,000 tonnes of cement and 4,500 tonnes of steel. Six giant pump turbines
stand within an enormous machine hall, with massive 160-tonne ball valves
controlling the flow of water to the turbines.

■440■ MENAI BRIDGE
Near Bangor, Gwynedd
Connects Anglesey to mainland. Signposted from main A5 roundabout before
Britannia Bridge

Menai Bridge

Suspension bridge designed by Thomas Telford and completed in 1826, revolutionary because of its use of iron chains. Telford made such great advances in
the manufacture of wrought-iron chains that he was able to build a bridge that
was by far the longest suspension bridge in the world at the time. Built to
replace the ferry service across the Menai Strait, the main span of the bridge is
579 feet (176 metres) from tower to tower, while the overall length is 1,000
feet (305 metres). The roadway is now suspended by two sets of steel chains,
replacing Telford's original four wrought-iron sets, with the outer lengths of the
main chains pulled into a curve by suspension rods anchored into the masonry
arches. The towers are faced with Anglesey marble, and the roadway rests
100 feet (30 metres) above the strait. A steel deck was fitted to the bridge in
1839 when a hurricane destroyed the original timber deck. In 1940 two cantilevered footways were added on either side of the bridge and the deck was
replaced again to allow for the increased road traffic.

■441■ NASH POINT LIGHTHOUSE ☎ 01446 793471
Llantwit Major, Vale of Glamorgan CF6 1ZH
Off B4265 coast road betwen Barry and Bridgend
Open early Apr–late Oct. Phone for details
Designed in 1832 by James Walker to mark sandbanks in the Bristol Channel.
Two circular towers were built, each with massive walls and a stone gallery. The
eastern or high lighthouse is 121 feet (37 metres) high and the western or low
lighthouse 82 feet (25 metres) high. Nine hundred and ninety feet (302 metres)
apart, they provided leading lights to indicate safe passage past the sandbanks.
The high light was painted with black and white stripes and the low light was

white. In those days, both towers showed a fixed light, which was either red or white, depending on the direction from which a vessel approached. The red sector marked the Nash Sands. Early this century the low light was abandoned and the high light modernised and painted white. In place of the fixed light, a new first-order cataclioptric lens was installed, which gives a white and red group flashing.

■442■ PONTCYSYLLTE AQUEDUCT

Near Llangollen, Denbighshire
From Llangollen take A539 towards Wrexham. Aqueduct signposted off A539. For boat trips contact Welsh Canal Holiday Craft, Llangollen Wharf, Wharf Hill, Llangollen LL20 8TA. Tel 01691 690322
Dramatic aqueduct carrying the Shropshire Union Canal 120 feet (36.5 metres) above the River Dee. Built between 1795 and 1805 by Thomas Telford, and 1,007 feet (307 metres) long, Pontcysyllte Aqueduct is one of his most dramatic engineering feats. The towering aqueduct crosses the Dee Valley on eighteen piers of exceptionally fine construction. It is built of local sandstone, expertly cut and dressed by Telford's masons and bound together by mortar joints of unusual thinness. There are nineteen arches, each one 45 feet (13.7 metres) wide, and the waterway is carried over in a trough made of cast-iron flanged plates bolted together. The canal is still open today and, if you've got a good head for heights, there are barge trips across the aqueduct.

■443■ SOUTH STACK LIGHTHOUSE ☎ 01407 763207/760427

South Stack Island, Holyhead, Anglesey
On South Stack Rock, off Holyhead
Open early Apr–end Oct. Phone for details
Set on a rocky island just off the towering South Stack Cliffs and reached by a small bridge from the cliffs. The first light marked South Stack Rock in 1809. Erected at a cost of £12,000, it was designed by Daniel Alexander and originally fitted with Argand oil lamps and reflectors. Built from stone quarried on the site, it consisted of a traditional tower, tapered and painted white, with a gallery and lantern about 90 feet (27 metres) above the rock. The lighthouse is flanked by a long, low building, with a two-span pitched roof, and three smaller buildings. These were the engine room and dwellings. The station was electrified in 1938 and automated in 1984 and its keepers withdrawn. The light and the fog signal are now remotely controlled and monitored from the Trinity House Operational Control Centre at Harwich.

🏛 NORTH-WEST   MAP 6

■444■ BARTON SWING AQUEDUCT

Near Stretford, Manchester, Greater Manchester
Best viewed from adjacent Barton road bridge. Exit M60 junction 10, follow signs for Trafford Shopping Centre, then at roundabout follow signs for Eccles
Remarkable swing bridge carrying the Bridgewater Canal over the Manchester Ship Canal. The swing bridge was designed to allow ships to pass along the Ship Canal when open, and to allow barges on the Bridgewater Canal to cross the Ship Canal when closed. The Barton Swing Aqueduct consists of a 235-foot (71.6-metre) iron trough which is 18 feet (5.5 metres) wide and 7 feet

(2 metres) deep. It is supported by girders and it swings about its centre, which is on an island. When the bridge is to be opened, the ends of the trough are closed by gates with rubber seals.

■445■ BRIDGEWATER CANAL

Runs from Runcorn through centre of Manchester
Designed by James Brindley for the Duke of Bridgewater to carry coal from his collieries near Worsley to Manchester. From the canal basin at Worsley, Brindley designed a system of over 40 miles (64 kilometres) of underground canals that penetrated into the workings of the coal mines under Walkden and Farnworth. Work started in 1759 and 10½ miles (17 kilometres) cost over £50,000 to build. At Barton the canal crossed the River Irwell on Brindley's three-arched stone aqueduct. The canal opened in 1765, immediately cutting the cost of coal by half and soon earning the Duke of Bridgewater over £75,000 a year. During the eighteenth century the canal was linked to the Trent and Mersey Canal, the Rochdale Canal and the Leeds and Liverpool Canal, making it a vital link in the north-west transport system.

■446■ PEPSI MAX BIG ONE   ☎ 01253 341033

Blackpool Pleasure Beach, Ocean Boulevard, Blackpool, Lancashire FY4 1EZ
Signposted on all major routes into Blackpool
Open Mar: Sat and Sun 10–10; Easter–early Nov: daily: 10–10, subject to weather.
Phone for details

Pepsi Max Big One

The world's tallest and fastest rollercoaster. Opened in 1994 the steel structure reaches a height of 235 feet (72 metres), with the trains travelling up to 85 miles (137 kilometres) per hour. Two thousand six hundred tonnes of steel were used in the construction and a very high standard of corrosion protection was employed to resist the constant sandblasting effect of the westerly winds across the beach. The ride includes a 65-foot (20-metre) drop, the steepest in the rollercoaster world, and the rider experiences 3.5 positive G-force.

■447■ BERWICK-UPON-TWEED BRIDGES
Berwick-upon-Tweed, Northumberland
Follow signs for Berwick from A1
Three bridges cross the River Tweed close to the centre of Berwick. The fifteen-arch Jacobean stone bridge was a major engineering achievement for the time that it was built between 1611 and 1624. It carried the London to Edinburgh road across the Tweed until 1928 when, due to a big increase in the volume of traffic it had been designed for, a new four-span reinforced-concrete arch bridge was built next to it. The third bridge, the Royal Border, is a fine-looking railway viaduct, designed by Robert Stephenson and built between 1847 and 1850.

■448■ CAUSEY ARCH
Tanfield, Durham
Near Tanfield, off A6067 between Stanley and Whickham
The world's first railway bridge, built between 1725 and 1726 by Ralph Wood. It was designed to carry the horse-drawn wagons of the Tanfield Wagonway over Causey Burn. The semi-elliptical arch is 105 feet (32 metres) long and spans the burn at a height of 85 feet (26 metres). It is still one of the longest span masonry bridges in Britain.

■449■ FIVE RISE LOCKS
Bingley, West Yorkshire
Car park signposted in Bingley, then ½-mile walk along towpath, past Three Rise Locks

Five Rise Locks

Magnificent example of late-eighteenth-century canal engineering raises the water level of the Leeds and Liverpool Canal by means of a man-made staircase of locks built into the hillside. Opened in March 1774 and designed by John Longbottom of Halifax, Five Rise is part of a set of eight locks on this stretch of canal, with Three Rise Locks nearby. The five locks raise the level of the canal by just under 60 feet (18 metres) over a distance of 320 feet (97 metres). They were constructed by four local stonemasons.

Humber Bridge

■450■ HUMBER BRIDGE ☎ 01482 647161

Ferriby Road, Hessle, East Riding of Yorkshire HU13 0JG
Crosses Humber between Hessle and Barton-upon-Humber as A15

Huge but graceful bridge that elegantly and harmoniously combines engineering and aesthetics. The longest single-span suspension bridge in Britain without supporting columns, and from the time that it was opened in 1981 until very recently the longest in the world. The Humber Bridge has a main span of 1,543 yards (1,410 metres), and was opened for traffic in 1981. It provides dual carriageways for traffic, and there is a combined footpath and cycle track along each of its sides. The main towers of the bridge, which are made of reinforced concrete, are 533 feet (162 metres) high. Anchorages are massive concrete structures each containing two chambers within which the main cables splay out into separate strands. Each of the main cables is made up of almost 15,000 wires woven together into thirty-seven strands.

■451■ NEWCASTLE UPON TYNE'S BRIDGES

The bridges cross the Tyne in Newcastle city centre

Six bridges span the River Tyne in the centre of Newcastle. The oldest is the High Level Bridge, 155 feet (47 metres) high on two levels: the upper level for the railway with a roadway on the lower. It was designed by Robert Stephenson in 1849 and has six main spans supported by sandstone piers. The Swing Bridge, which was completed in 1876, was designed by Sir William Armstrong to replace an earlier fixed road bridge. It has a single swing section of 281 feet (86 metres) which creates two openings of 110 feet (34 metres). Hydraulically operated, the original steam pumps have been replaced by electric ones. No. 5 Bridge was completed in 1848 to carry the Newcastle to Berwick-upon-Tweed railway line over the road east of the Central Station. The cast-iron segmental bridge has a span of 60 feet (18 metres) and was widened in 1893. The best known of Newcastle's bridges and the one that symbolises the city is the Tyne Bridge, which was begun in 1925 and opened by King George V in 1928. It had the largest arch of any bridge in the world, but was soon surpassed by the Sydney Harbour Bridge.

■452■ RIBBLEHEAD VIADUCT

Part of Settle–Carlisle Line. Best viewed from B6255 NE of Ingleton,
North Yorkshire

Fred's
FAVOURITE

Spectacular twenty-four-arched railway viaduct on the Settle–Carlisle line. Ribblehead Viaduct is surrounded by the Three Peaks – Ingleborough, Whernside and Pen-y-ghent – in the heart of the Yorkshire Dales. The line was opened in 1875 by the Midland Railway, and it crosses some of the most difficult terrain faced by railway engineers. The 72 miles (116 kilometres) of line includes fifteen tunnels and twenty-three viaducts as well as the summit of Ais Gill at 1,169 feet (356 metres) above sea-level. The Ribblehead Viaduct is the longest and highest along the line with a span of 440 feet (134 metres) and a maximum height of 165 feet (50 metres). It has twenty-four arches of 45-feet (14-metre) span in four groups of six. Other impressive features along this stretch include Arten Gill and Dent Head viaducts and the Blea Moor tunnel, which is 500 feet (152 metres) underground and 1 mile 869 yards (2.4 kilometres) long.

■453■ SOUTER LIGHTHOUSE ☎ 0191 529 3161

Coast Road, Whitburn, Tyne & Wear SR6 7NH
Coast road 2 miles S of South Shields
Open Apr–Oct: Sat–Thur and Good Fri 11–5 (last admission 4.30)

Souter Lighthouse overlooks the cliffs of Marsden Bay, high above the rocks and currents of the Whitburn Steel which have wrecked dozens of ships. The lighthouse, 75 feet (23 metres) high, started operating in 1871 and at the time was the most advanced in the world. The lighthouse has a bioptic light, in its original condition, and was the first reliable electrically powered lighthouse light. Explore the lighthouse starting in the engine room, which is still in working order, and learn about how lighthouses work, see the cramped living quarters and climb the seventy-five steps to the top to enjoy the views of the coastline.

■454■ TIMOTHY HACKWORTH VICTORIAN AND RAILWAY MUSEUM ☎ 01388 777999

Shildon, Durham DL4 1PQ
Museum signposted in Shildon
Open Easter–late Oct: Wed–Sun and Bank Hols 10–5. Group bookings at other times

Engine sheds and workshops of the Stockton and Darlington Railway. Soho Cottage was the home and workplace, from 1831 to 1850, of Timothy Hackworth, superintendent engineer to the Stockton and Darlington Railway. The cottage is now the Timothy Hackworth Victorian and Railway Museum, part of it furnished as it would have been when Hackworth and his family lived there and part of it devoted to the story of his involvement with the Stockton and Darlington Railway. Next to the house is the engine shed where he had his locomotive works. Other early railway structures include stables and coal drops.

■455■ UNION SUSPENSION BRIDGE

Near Berwick-upon-Tweed, Northumberland
Crosses River Tweed 5 miles W of Berwick

Fred's
FAVOURITE

Links England to Scotland across the River Tweed. Completed in 1820, it is the earliest surviving road suspension bridge in Britain and has a main span of 361 feet (110 metres). The roadway is suspended by 12 wrought iron chains, with a total length of 600 feet (183 metres). The unique feature of the bridge is that it has only one stone tower, at 60 feet (18 metres), which is on the north bank; on the south bank the cables are anchored directly into the rock face.

York Station

■456■ YORK STATION
Station Road, York
Signposted in York
Completed in 1877 to replace the original station of 1841 that became impracti-
cal to work with the increasing amount of rail traffic. From the exterior the
station is not unduly impressive, but it is the magnificent curved iron train shed
roof that is regarded as one of the finest pieces of railway architecture. The roof
has four main spans of varying height and width, the widest being 81 feet
(25 metres) and the tallest 48 feet (15 metres) high. The ribs are five-centred
arches, with every third one supported by cast-iron Corinthian columns with
open-work spandrels. The intermediate two ribs rest on the arcade girders but
project below these to meet the ribs of the next span.

🏛 SCOTLAND	MAP 8

■457■ CALEDONIAN CANAL
Highland
*Fine views all along the Great Glen from A82. For information about sailing on
Caledonian Canal contact British Waterways on 01463 233140*
Links 45 miles (73 kilometres) of lochs to create a route between the east and
west coasts of Scotland. The canal exits the North Sea at Inverness via the
Moray Firth, and the Atlantic Ocean at Corpach near Fort William. It has a
series of twenty-eight locks running through 22 miles (35 kilometres) of the
spectacular scenery of the Great Glen. Built by Thomas Telford and William
Jessop, construction began in 1803 and was completed in 1822. Unusually
the project was funded entirely by the government, whereas earlier, similar
engineering projects had been supported by entrepreneurs.

■458■ FORTH BRIDGE
South Queensferry, West Lothian
Part of East Coast Line, crossing Forth between South and North Queensferry. Forth Road Bridge (A90) runs parallel. Also good views from the shore at South and North Queensferry and at Dalmeny Station (South Queensferry) and North Queensferry Station
Masterpiece of Victorian civil engineering, which was regarded as one of the wonders of its age. Designed by Sir John Fowler and Sir Benjamin Baker, the massive tubular-steel structure is 361 feet (110 metres) above the waters of the Firth of Forth. Built in the 1880s, the main feature of the bridge is its cantilever system, which is made up of three double cantilevers. These are each supported on four huge circular masonry piers. The bridge is 1 mile 1,005 yards (2.53 kilometres) long from shore to shore, and the internal viaduct, which carries two railway tracks, is formed by two lattice girders 16 feet (4.9 metres) centre to centre with cross-girders about every 11 feet (3.3 metres). In an average year only ninety to a hundred days are available for painting exposed areas because of wind.

■459■ KINNAIRD HEAD LIGHTHOUSE   ☎ 01346 511022
Fraserburgh, Aberdeenshire
On promontory in Fraserburgh (A92)
Open all year. Phone for details
Sixteenth-century castle converted into a lighthouse in 1787 to make it one of Scotland's oldest. The four-storey rectangular keep has a parapet with open rounds at the corners and machiolations in the centre of each parapet. The lighthouse was the first put in service by the Commissioners of the Northern Lighthouses and is still in working order, but it has now been replaced by a small, unmanned light nearby.

■460■ NAIRN VIADUCT
Near Inverness, Highland
E of Inverness, off B9006
At 600 feet (183 metres) Nairn Viaduct is the longest masonry viaduct in Scotland. It was built in 1898 for the Highland Railway line linking Aviemore and Inverness. It has twenty-eight red-sandstone arches, each with a span of 50 feet (15 metres) along with one arch of 100 feet (30 metres) spanning the river. It was designed by Murdoch Paterson and is 130 feet (40 metres) above ground level at its maximum height. It is near Culloden Moor, the battlefield that saw the end of the Jacobite uprising.

■461■ TAY BRIDGE
Part of East Coast Line. Crosses Firth of Tay between Dundee and Newport-on-Tay. Parallel with Tay Road Bridge (A92). Good views from B946 (south shore) and A85 (north shore)
Longest railway bridge in Britain, at 2 miles 50 yards (3.26 kilometres). The present Tay Bridge was the second one to be built over the River Tay. The first, designed by Sir Thomas Bouch and opened in 1878, collapsed in a gale, killing seventy-five people on board a train. The present bridge was completed in 1887 and used many of the girders from the earlier bridge. There are seventy-four spans, of which thirteen are over the central channel, with twenty-four on the north shore and thirty-seven on the south. The bridge is supported by eighty-six piers, the foundations of which were sunk using the same technique Brunel pioneered on the Royal Albert Bridge (see entry, West Country). Iron cylinders were sunk into the river, and the water pumped out. The soft riverbed was then excavated until the cylinder reached the firm bedrock.

GLOSSARY

Arrow slit Narrow rectangular opening in a castle's battlements from which archers would fire their arrows
Ashlar Square block of stone

Bailey Open court of a castle, also known as the 'ward'
Balusters Vertical pillar of a balustrade
Barbican Defensive fortifications around the gatehouse
Bastion Protection from the outer fortifications of a castle that allows the garrison to see and defend the ground before the ramparts

Caponier Covered passage within a ditch of a fort
Casemated wing A bomb–proof wing of a castle's fortifications, providing emplacement for the artillery
Corbel A bracket or support made of stone or brick
Curtain wall Outer wall of a castle

Drawbridge Wooden bridge, normally spanning a moat, which can be raised to close off a gateway

Embrasure Recess for a window or door
Enceinte wall Main enclosure of a fortress

Garderobe Medieval name for lavatories

Hammerbeam Beam projecting horizontally from the top of a wall

Keep The main inner tower of a castle

Linenfold Panel decorated with the representation of a piece of linen laid out in vertical folds
Loggia A room open on one or more sides
Lunette Semi–circular opening over a door

Machicolation Openings between supporting corbels for directing missiles below
Motte Large earthen mound
Mullion Vertical post dividing a window
Murder hole Opening in a castle's fortification from which stones and missiles could be thrown at attackers

Parapet Wall or screen on top of a rampart to protect garrison and artillery from enemy's observation and fire
Parterre Garden laid out with turf of flower beds, with a design cut into by paths
Pilaster Column projecting from wall
Pinnacle A turret–like crown to the top of a spire, parapet or buttress

Quadrangle Rectangular courtyard enclosed by buildings on all sides
Quoins Dressed stones at the corners of buildings

Revetment wall Wall that supports the weight of each earth or water
Rococo Style of decoration typified by lightness in colour and weight

Spandrels Triangular space above the haunch of an arch
Stucco Type of slow–setting plaster

Wattle and daub Plaster made from horse hair and manure

Yett A gate or door

INDEX

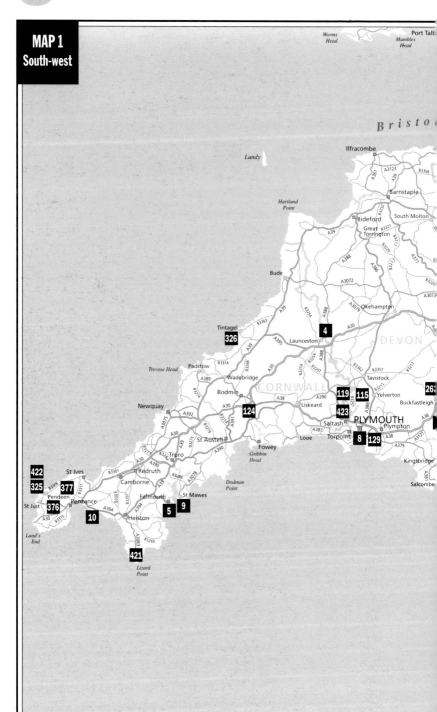

MAP 1
South-west

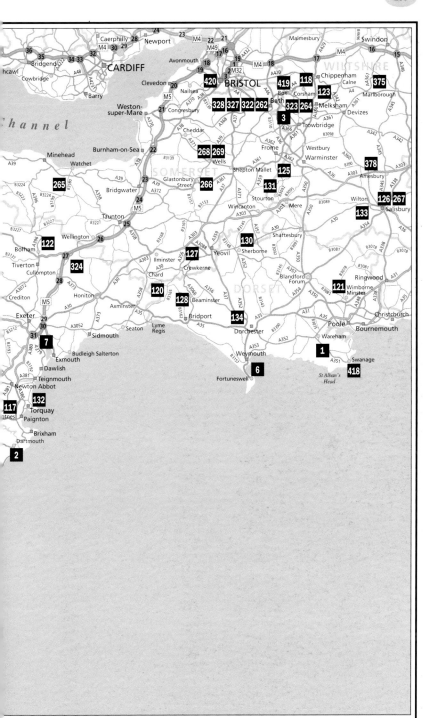

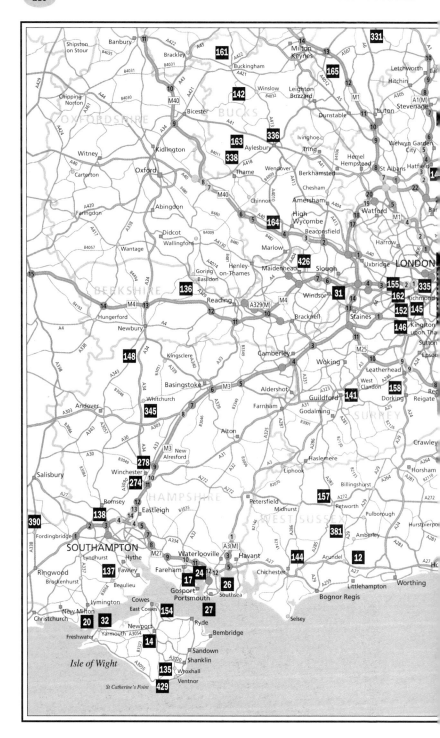

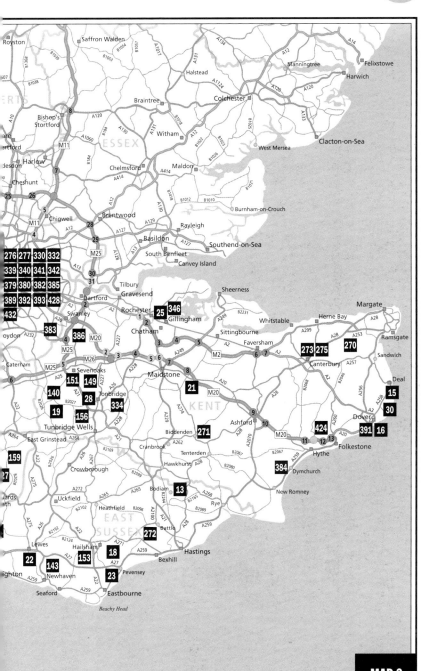

**MAP 2
South-east**

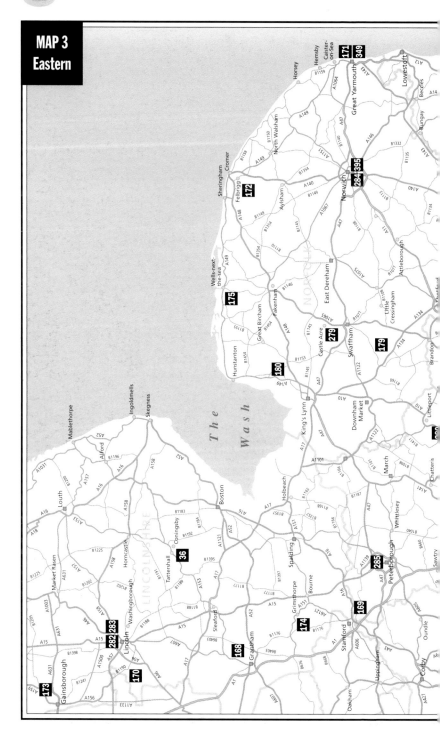

**MAP 3
Eastern**

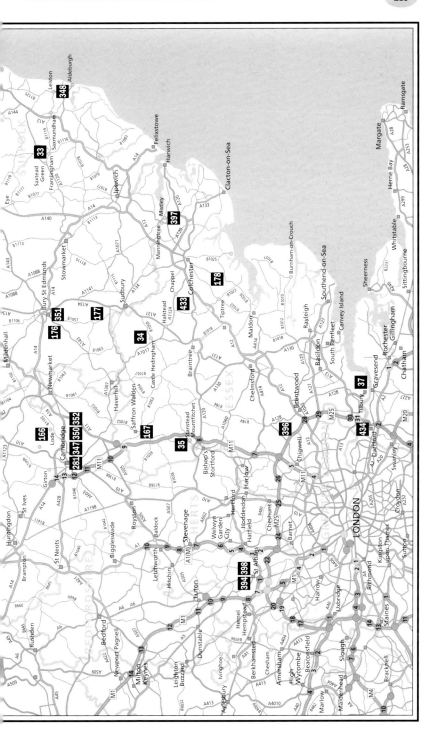

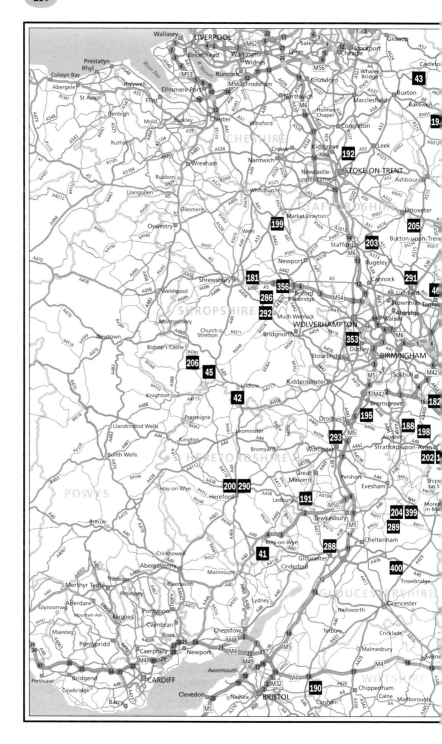

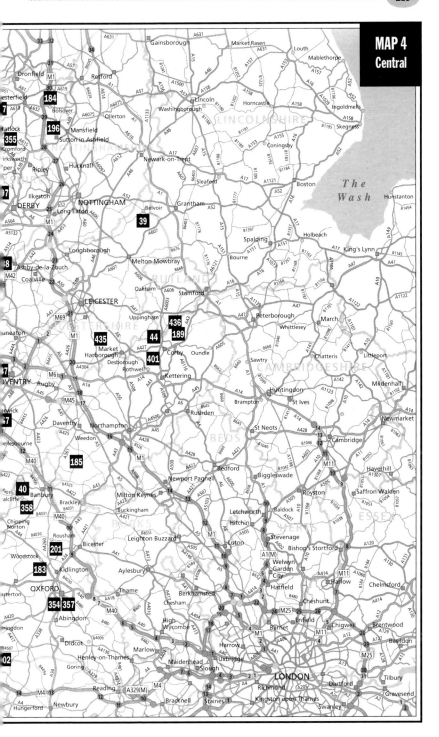

MAP 4
Central

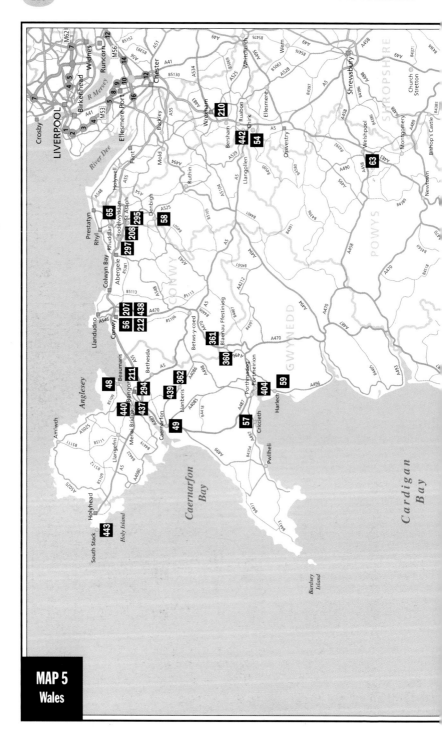

MAP 5
Wales

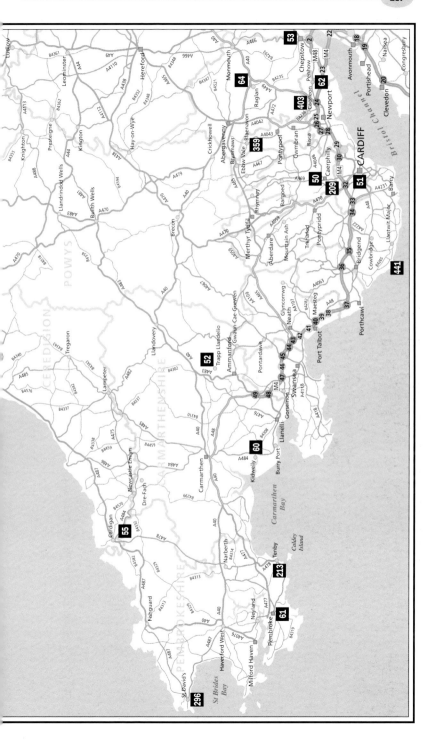

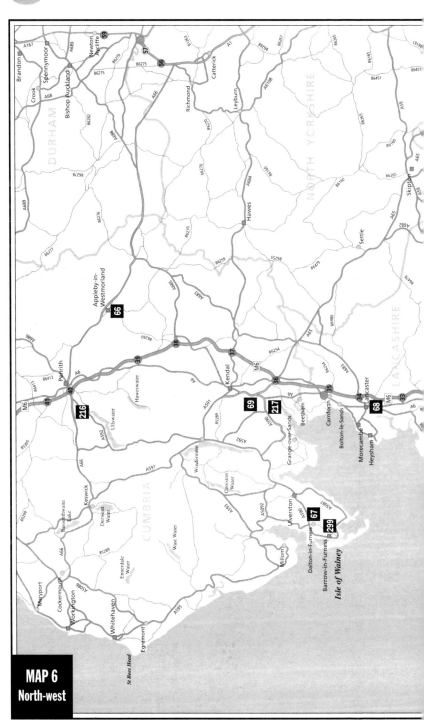

MAP 6
North-west

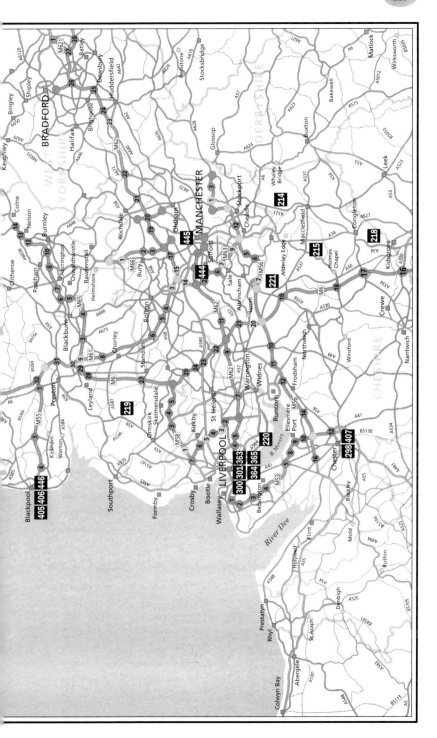

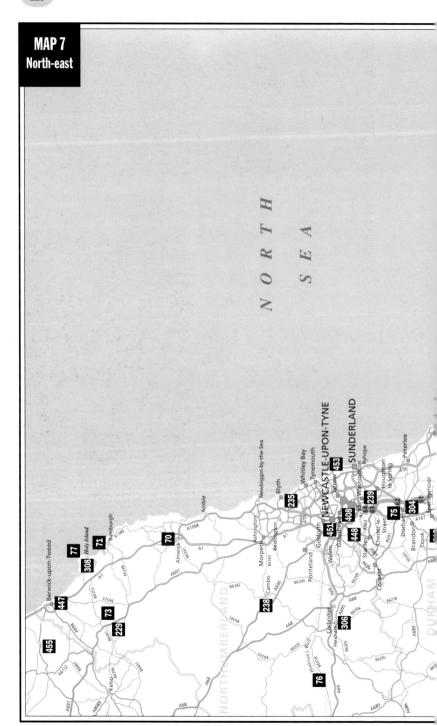

**MAP 7
North-east**

NORTH SEA

Berwick-upon-Tweed
Holy Island
Bamburgh
Alnwick
Amble
Newbiggin-by-the-Sea
Blyth
Whitley Bay
Tynemouth
NEWCASTLE-UPON-TYNE
SUNDERLAND
Ryhope
Houghton le Spring
Peterlee
Easington
Ashington
Morpeth
Bedlington
Gosforth
Jarrow
Gateshead
Washington
Chester-le-Street
Stanley
Consett
Durham
Brandon
Crook
Ponteland
Wylam
Cambo
Corbridge
Hexham
Hadrian's Wall
Kelso

NORTHUMBERLAND
DURHAM

77 71 70 235 453 451 408 239 304
308 447 73 229 455 238 306 76 448 75 62

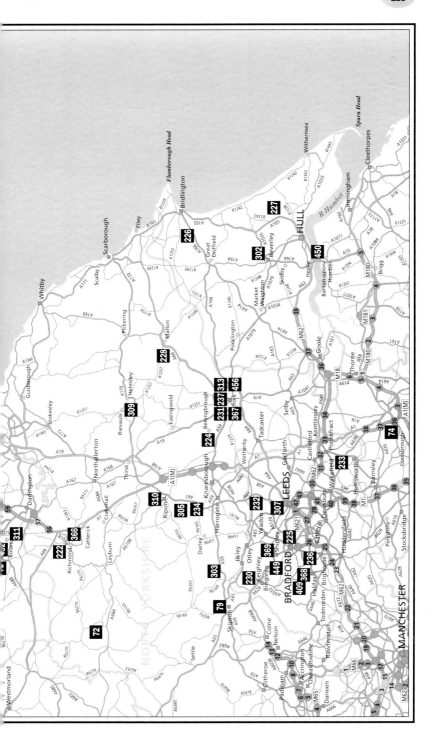

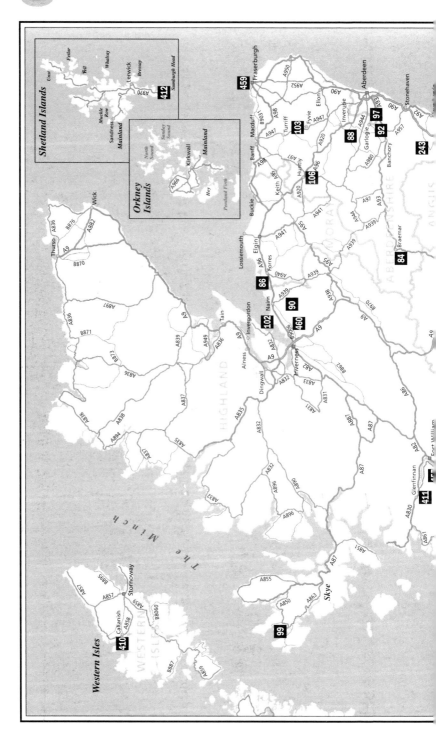

Shetland Islands

Unst
Fetlar
Yell
Whalsay
Lerwick
Bressay
Sumburgh Head
A970
412

Orkney Islands

North Sound
Sandwick Sound
Kirkwall
Mainland
Hoy
A966
Pentland Firth
459

Fraserburgh
A990
A952
Aberdeen
Stonehaven
A90
A92
97
Macduff
B9031
Ellon
Inverurie
A93
A944
Gartcosh
92
A957
Turriff
Fyvie
A947
A920
A980
Banchory
88
103
Banff
A98
A97
A93
A984
243
Huntly
A96
A920
A97
A939
Braemar
106
Keith
A95
A941
A944
84
Buckie
A95
A939
Lossiemouth
A941
A939
A95
A939
A939
Elgin
A96
A940
A9
A939
A95
A9
A938
86
Forres
Nairn
A939
90
Invergordon
102
460
A9
Inverness
A862
A96
Alness
A9
A9
A87
Dingwall
A832
A833
A831
A87
Tain
A836
A949
A832
A831
A887
A87
A9
A839
A836
A835
A832
Glenfinnan
Fort William
411
A830
A861

Thurso
A836
B876
A882
Wick
A9
B870
A897
A836
B871
A838
A836
B873
A837
A835
A838
A894
A837
A832
A896
A890
A998
A855
A850
A863
Skye
A851
99

The Minch

Western Isles

Stornoway
A859
A857
A858
B895
Callanish
A857
410
A858
WESTERN ISLES
B8060
B887
A859

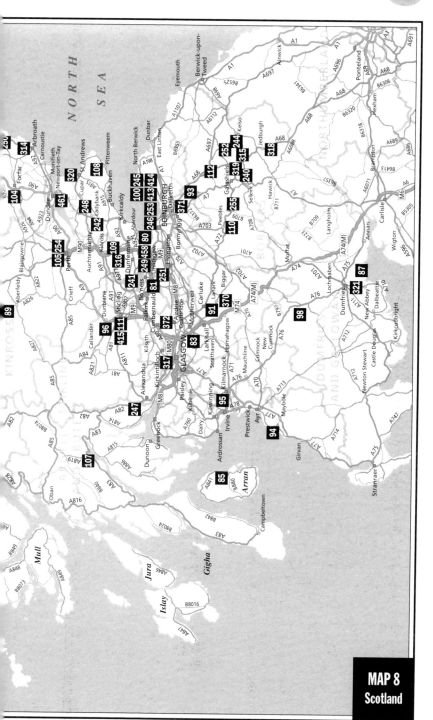

MAP 8
Scotland

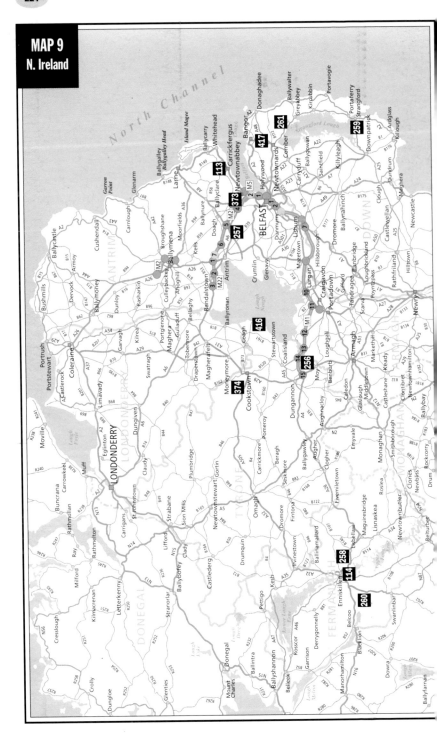

MAP 9
N. Ireland